Increasing Productivity in the United States
A Political, Social, and Economic Policy Approach

by

Harold E. Arnett

Professor of Accounting
The University of Michigan

and

Neill R. Schmeichel

Executive Vice-President, Finance
National Tel Data Corp.

A study carried out on behalf of the
National Association of Accountants
Montvale, New Jersey

Published by

National Association of Accountants
10 Paragon Drive,
P.O. Box 433,
Montvale, N.J. 07645
Norma Frankel, Editor
Mandel & Wagreich, Inc., Cover

Foreword

In most discussions, the productivity problem is viewed within a narrow context of specific business operations, companies, or industries. More general approaches still tend to focus on certain specified causal factors. The resulting recommendations are often fragmentary, and the attempts to do something about the problem—be it decline or stagnation in the level of productivity—have usually been piecemeal.

In their study the researchers tried to take a comprehensive look at the productivity problem. In their search for basic causes, they make a critical distinction between the "natural" barriers, which are inherent to the conduct of business, and the "artificial" barriers, which some may prefer to call "environmental." It is this environment, which breeds and nurtures the artificial barriers, that is identified by the authors in all the major areas studied as playing a major role in declining productivity.

In the first place, the researchers maintain, we are not following some of the fundamental tenets of representative democracy, especially in regard to economic matters. This is the basic cause of the productivity decline—a basic conclusion of this study. We have already paid a heavy price, culminating in the 1979–82 recession, but many of the underlying conditions still persist. Unless a substantial effort is made to overcome them, it is likely that the unfortunate experience will be repeated. The authors also offer a multiple set of recommendations.

Guidance in the preparation of this research report was kindly and generously provided by the Project Committee:

Robert U. Boehman (Chair)
Jasper Rubber Products
Jasper, Indiana

Geraldine F. Dominiak
Texas Christian University
Fort Worth, Texas

Thomas J. O'Reilly
Coopers & Lybrand
Cleveland, Ohio

James W. Truitt
Martin Industries, Inc.
Florence, Alabama

The report reflects the views of the researchers and not necessarily those of the Association, the Committee on Research, or the Project Committee.

Stephen Landekich
Director of Research
National Association of Accountants

Preface

This project has been one of the most interesting and challenging in our careers. Not only did it provide us with the opportunity for taking a broad perspective in considering the issue of productivity changes and prospects in the United States, but it also allowed us to express many personal biases, which we readily admit. We concede that our backgrounds and environments have instilled in us a strong belief in individual freedom and a free market economy. We began the project committed to the idea that significant productivity increases can be achieved over the long run and with them an increasing standard of living, only through dedication to a free market economy. And this, in turn, will come about only if individual freedom is promoted and supported at all levels and in all aspects of society.

In terms of our library and empirical research, we made every effort to be as objective and unbiased as possible in our selection of writings to be reviewed and of the firms from which to obtain empirical data, in the characteristics we studied, and in the analyses and interpretations of the data. And we stood ready to change our attitudes and beliefs, if the evidence supported such a change. It did not. If anything, our general beliefs were strengthened by the evidence, although a number of specific conclusions emanating from those general beliefs altered in their order of importance.

Our approach, as discussed in Chapter 1, was broad in scope. Any single aspect of our study could be a major research project in its own right. We studied, researched, derived conclusions, and made recommendations at the policy level. That was the intent from the start, and, in the final analysis, the monograph will be successful if it causes the readers to broaden their perspectives and to consider the interrelationships and interdependencies of the major factors that impact on productivity at that level. Beyond that, we would be delighted if the conclusions and recommendations convinced politicians, labor leaders, and businessmen that their long-range best interests, those of the groups they serve, and those of society at large will best be served by following the ideals suggested.

We wish to thank the National Association of Accountants for its generous financial support, and most particularly the Research Committee and its subcommittee assigned the task of reading and commenting on the drafts. Their assistance has been invaluable.

We are indebted to Stephen Landekich, director of research at NAA, who offered support and encouragement while in no way attempting to influence the development of the research or its conclusions. We also appreciate his careful reading of the manuscript and numerous thoughtful criticisms, suggestions, and recommendations. We thank him for his efforts and patience throughout the project.

We would also like to acknowledge the assistance of William Sasso, a Ph.D. student in computer and information systems at the University of Michigan. His contribution was substantial, particularly in connection with the computer work.

The study could not have been brought to completion without these people and others. We are indebted to them, and we do not imply that they necessarily agree with the recommendations and suggestions contained in the study. Responsibility for the conclusions, as well as any errors in logic and judgment, must be borne by us alone.

Harold E. Arnett
Neill R. Schmeichel

Table of Contents

Chapter   Page

1. Synopsis
General Overview   1
Specific Approaches to a Solution   3
Conclusions and Broad Recommendations   7

2. Productivity: Facts and Myths
General Overview   11
Alleged Causes of the Productivity Problem   13
Inflation and Interest Costs   16
Regulation   22
Taxes   27
Capital Formation   29
Research, Development, and Innovation   31
Workers and Supervisors   32
Management   33
Energy   35
Federal Procurement   36
International Trade   36
Product Liability   37
Health and Accident Insurance   37
Summary and Conclusions   37

3. Productivity in Small Businesses: An Empirical Analysis
General Observations   43
Sources of Empirical Data   46
Profile of Firms in the Questionnaire Survey   47
Profile of Firms Interviewed   49
Demographics of Firms in the Survey   53
Degree of Competition   53
Degree of Unionization   56
Size of Responding Firms   57
Changes in Productivity   64

Detrimental Impacts on Productivity of Certain Major
Factors   68
    Effects of Unions   68
    Inflation and Small Businesses   78
    Impact of High Interest Rates on Small Businesses   84
    Impact of Government Regulations   96
    Taxes and Small Businesses   103
Summary and Conclusions   114

**4. Applying a Basic Philosophy: The Key to
Maximizing Productivity**
General Overview   119
Placing the Problem in Perspective   121
Reasons for Lack of Progress   122
    Complexity   122
    Measurement Problems   126
    Lack of Agreement Among Economists   129
    Time Lapse in Representative Democracies   131
    The Essential Reason for Failure   132
A Brief Historical Review   132
Productivity Is a Political Issue   138
The Basic Tenets of Representative Democracy   139
Summary and Conclusions   145

5. Essentials in the Philosophical Foundation
Overview of Conceptual Foundation   153
The Basics of the Philosophy   156
    Individual Freedom   156
        A Long-Range View Is Needed   157
        The Word "Fair" Must Be Reevaluated   157
        The Consumer Is King   158
        Special-Interest Groups   159
        Egalitarianism—Unthinkable and Unworkable   163
    Resources are Scarce and Wants are Insatiable   165
    Summary to This Point   170
    A More Demanding and Better Balanced Education   173
General Economic Solutions at the Macro Level   176
    Labor Unions and Management   176
    Supply-Side Versus Demand-Side Economics   183
Summary and Conclusions   189

**6. Applying the Philosophical Foundation to
Solving Macro Problems**
Overview of Small Businesses   195
Inflation, Capital Formation, and Interest Costs   197

Contents

        High Long-Term Interest Rates   198
        Government Safety Nets—Not the Answer   199
        Small Businesses and High Interest Rates   200
      Regulations   202
        Changing Basic Attitudes and Approaches   202
        No Special Consideration for Small Businesses   204
      Taxes   205
        Basic Criteria for a Good Tax System   205
        Phasing Out Business Taxation   206
        Taxation of People   207
        Increase Taxes to Reduce the Deficit?   208
      Capital Formation and Retention—Small Businesses   209
        Proposals for Small Businesses   210
        Conclusions Regarding Proposals for Small Businesses   211
        Venture Capitalists on the Increase   212
        Government Involvement   214
        Elimination of Estate Taxation   215
      Research, Development, and Innovation   215
        Consortia of Companies   215
        Encouraging Small Research and Development Firms   216
      Workers and Supervisors   217
        Reasons for Difficulties   217
        Freedom of the Individual   218
      Management   219
        The SBA   220
        Entrepreneurial Education   220
        Information Dissemination   220
        Free Market Economy   221
      Energy   221
      Actions by the Federal Government   222
      Cumulative Effects   223
      Summary and Conclusions   223
        General   223
        Small Business in Particular   224
        An Overview of the Monograph to This Point   225

7. **Some Thoughts About the Future**
      General Overview   229
      Labor   230
        Minimum Wage Law   231
        High Average Cost of Labor   232
      Social Security   235
      Research, Development, Innovation, and Capital
        Formation   241
      Inflation, Interest Rates, and Government Expenditures   243

Taxes   246
Regulations   248
Special-Interest Groups   248
Workers and Supervisors   248
A Wrap-Up   249

Figures

Figure 3-1   Business Failures   44

Figure 3-2   Michigan Sample: Distribution by Industry   50

Figure 3-3   Colorado Sample: Distribution by Industry   51

Figure 3-4   Texas Sample: Distribution by Industry   52

Figure 3-5   Competition as Perceived by Small Businesses   54

Figure 3-6   Competition as Perceived by Small Businesses: Comparison by State   55

Figure 3-7   Unionization of Small Businesses   58

Figure 3-8   Unionization of Small Businesses: Comparison by State   59

Figure 3-9   Sample Distribution by Total Assets and Gross Sales   60

Figure 3-10   Changes in Gross Sales   61

Figure 3-11   Sample Distribution by Total Debt   62

Figure 3-12   Sample Distribution by Total Assets: Comparison by State   65

Figure 3-13   Change in Productivity for Small Businesses, 1979 Through Mid-1982   66

Figure 3-14   Change in Productivity: Comparison by State   67

Figure 3-15   Effect of Unionization on Productivity   69

Figure 3-16   Specific Detrimental Effects of Unions on Small Businesses   72

Figure 3-17   Specific Detrimental Effects of Unions: Comparison by State   73

Figure 3-18   Specific Detrimental Effects of Unions: Comparison by Industry   75

Figure 3-19   Effect of Inflation on Small Businesses   79

Figure 3-20   Impact of Inflation: Comparison by State   80

Figure 3-21   Detrimental Effects of Inflation on Small
              Businesses   81

Figure 3-22   Specific Detrimental Effects of Inflation:
              Comparison by State   82

Figure 3-23   Effect of High Interest Rates on Small
              Businesses   85

Figure 3-24   Effect of Higher Interest Costs on Small
              Businesses   87

Figure 3-25   Effect of Increased Uncertainty on Small
              Businesses   88

Figure 3-26   Impact of High Interest Rates: Comparison
              by State   89

Figure 3-27   Specific Detrimental Effects of High Interest
              Rates on Small Businesses   91

Figure 3-28   Second-Order Effects of High Interest Rates
              on Small Businesses   92

Figure 3-29   Beneficial Effects of High Interest Rates on
              Small Businesses   95

Figure 3-30   Effect of Government Regulations on Small
              Businesses   97

Figure 3-31   Relative Importance of Federal, State, and
              Local Regulations on Small Businesses   98

Figure 3-32   Effects of Specific Regulations on Small
              Businesses   100

Figure 3-33   Effects of Unnecessary Requirements on
              Small Businesses   101

Figure 3-34   Detrimental Effects of Unnecessary
              Requirements: Comparison by Industry   102

Figure 3-35   Specific Detrimental Effects of Regulation:
              Comparison by Industry   104

Figure 3-36   Detrimental Effects of Regulation:
              Comparison by State   105

Figure 3-37   Effect of Taxes on Small Businesses   106

Figure 3-38   Specific Detrimental Effects of Taxation on
              Small Businesses   107

Figure 3-39   Specific Detrimental Effects of Taxation:
              Comparison by State   109

Figure 3-40   Detrimental Effects of Specific Taxes on Small Businesses   110

Figure 3-41   Detrimental Effects of Specific Taxes: Comparison by State   111

Figure 3-42   Specific Detrimental Effects of Taxation: Comparison by Industry   113

Figure 4-1   National Income from Manufacturing and Services   134

Tables

Table 2-1   Annual Change in Manufacturing Productivity
for 1960–1979, %   12

Table 2-2   International Comparisons of Real GNP
Growth, %   13

Table 2-3   Cost of Regulation, in Billions of Dollars   23

Table 3-1   Employed Wage and Salary Workers in Labor
Organizations, by Industry   57

Table 3-2   Productivity Changes Related to Degree of
Unionization   70

Table 5-1   Proposed Reduction in Federal Deficit   190

Table 7-1   Annual Rates of Change in Leading Economic
Indexes   230

Chapter 1

Synopsis

General Overview

Many causes for declining productivity have been cited, including governmental regulations, a confiscatory taxation system, and various insurance costs, such as unemployment compensation. Although each of these has been the subject of writings and speeches, to our knowledge *very little research has been done to determine how these causes interrelate* or whether they impact impartially on different segments of the business sector. More importantly, we feel *no attempt has been made to develop a coordinated, integrated policy statement recommending a workable plan to overcome these problems and increase productivity.* Such a plan is needed. . . . And independent actions without coordination could work at cross-purposes. *We want to make one point clear. Our objective is not to concentrate on the question of "fairness" between small and large businesses,* although some consideration must be given to this issue. . . . We will concentrate on the problems and needs of small businesses primarily because we feel the factors impacting on their productivity will be easier to establish and document. . . . Many of our suggestions and recommendations for increasing productivity will benefit large businesses as well. . . . *So, as we see it, this is really not a question of small versus large or one type of industry versus another. Our goal is increased productivity and we will utilize small business data as a stepping-stone to reach that objective.* (emphasis added)

The quotation above was taken from the research proposal we submitted to the National Association of Accountants. We need to explain and clarify those statements to ensure that the reader understands exactly what our objectives were and what approaches we took to reach them.

Our overriding goal or objective was to make recommendations and suggestions that, if adopted and followed, would reverse the trend of declining productivity in the United States *in toto.* It is possible, holding other things constant, that implementation of our recommendations might decrease productivity in any given firm or, in fact, in a given industry group. Our concern, then, was with productivity at the macro level; our specific objective was to develop a coordinated, integrated policy statement to overcome productivity problems created at that level. All other objectives were secondary to this basic objective, and the development of our research methodology was directed at obtaining and analyzing data to reach that basic objective.

It became clear early in the research that we needed first to develop a basic philosophy to serve not only as a springboard to give direction to the approach we should take, but also as a foundation to which our conclusions and recommendations must attach—a foundation from which they had to follow if they were to be logical and consistent. Certainly the reader can challenge whether or not our conclusions and recommendations do flow logically from the basic premises of the philosophy; if they do, however, it must follow that the reader who disagrees with them disagrees in some manner with the basic philosophy.

At the macro level, one could hypothesize that most of the major problems we face in the United States regarding productivity stem from one of three basic causes:

1. We do not have a basic societal philosophy.
2. If we do, it is not one that follows logically from our heritage and traditions.
3. If we do, and it is consistent with our heritage and traditions, we are either not developing policies and procedures consistent with it or we are not following those policies and procedures.

Testing hypothesis 1 or 2 is far beyond the scope of this writing. We accept the basic societal philosophy in the United States to be democracy, from which a basic concern for the preservation of individual rights stems. This philosophy is consistent with our heritage and traditions. Thus the basic hypothesis of the study is that we are either not developing policies and procedures consistent with our philosophy or we are not following them.

Admittedly this study deals extensively with the opinions and perceptions of those we surveyed and interviewed. We did not test the validity of these opinions and perceptions through analysis of data relating to these people's firms; we did not test the correctness or incorrectness of their assertions. Nevertheless, they must be dealt with, whether correct or incorrect. Without necessarily determining their accuracy, however, we do hope to clarify and bring understanding to them. Some readers undoubtedly would prefer more of the data in this writing to be based on hard facts. But what would hard facts consist of, in a study like this one, dealing as it does with societal relationships? Moreover, advances in social relationships come mainly from compromises of feelings and attitudes, not from hard facts one person or group has to support its position. But our approach was not entirely anecdotal. We relied heavily on empirical data, as indicated in the next section, and we attempted to be as objective and independent as possible in our analyses of those data and in the conclusions we drew from them.

Specific Approaches to a Solution

Three approaches were taken toward testing the basic hypothesis. First, certain conceptual problems needed to be solved by creative thinking, selection, and synthesis. Second, there were logical problems to be solved by deductive methods where solutions were implicit in the premises. Third, there were empirical problems for which inductive reasoning based on observations of phenomena aided in verification or rejection of questions of fact. These three approaches, as they relate to productivity, are not mutually exclusive. Conceptual solutions need to be substantiated or eliminated on the basis of observations of real-world phenomena. Such real-world observations help to solve conceptual questions. Thus, even though our approach to the project consisted of the following four distinct phases, these phases did overlap.

The first phase was primarily a literature search. It was basically conceptual in that we concentrated on identifying what others perceive to be the causes of decreased productivity. In the writing of this phase (Chapter 2) we tried not to interject our feelings and biases or to weight some arguments disproportionately. When we quoted or paraphrased closely, we used footnotes. The remainder of the chapter is in our words, but the ideas on which they are based belong to others. Those discussions are designed to clarify the ideas of others as objectively as possible, not to reflect our opinions or conclusions about those ideas. Our goal in this phase was to gather significant amounts of background data to set the stage and to act as a foundation for our interviews and questionnaire development.

In the second phase (Chapter 3) our goal was to accumulate enough empirical evidence to test the perceptions described in Chapter 2 and, perhaps more importantly, to analyze and explain differences. Occasionally a real problem turned up that had not been identified in Chapter 2. Perceptions of problems or causes did not always prove accurate. Also, problems often proved to be more or less critical than they had been perceived to be. These are the types of things we searched for, making use of questionnaires and interviews as described in Chapter 3.

We used data on small businesses because we felt that the factors impacting adversely on their productivity would be easier to establish and document. Such findings would then be used to draw inferences about the impacts of certain factors on businesses on the average and in total, and about what needed to be done, mainly at the macro level, to reverse the trend of decreasing productivity. Such findings were not intended to be used to determine fairness between large and small businesses. In fact, although not explicitly stated in our research proposal, the implication was clear that we believe too much effort, often unsuccessful, has been exerted in attempting to show that certain policy decisions have been biased in favor of large versus small businesses, or any given group versus another, when that was not the essential question to be resolved in the first place.

Take regulations, for example. The basic, essential question is whether the degree of regulatory control exerted over us as citizens of a democratic country represents an ideal state. The answer, in turn, revolves around the importance of individual rights versus the so-called public good. To a significant degree, it takes care of the question of fairness with regard not only to small versus large businesses, but also to any group versus any other group. In any case, we must approach, or at least work toward, the ideal state first, a state that has nothing to do directly with small versus large per se but, rather, deals with conditions and factors outside such considerations.

Looked at in a different light, we were concerned with distinguishing artificial barriers to success from natural barriers. Defining artificial barriers is difficult but necessary:

> If the success of a firm depended solely on the honesty, intelligence, innovativeness, aggressiveness, perseverance, hard work, personality, and competence of those who run the firm, the only barriers to success would be "natural," i.e., the absence to some degree of any of these characteristics relative to those with whom they compete. In such a situation each individual could exercise his capabilities to the fullest, with maximum benefits thereby accruing to them as well as to all members of society. Any rule, regulation, law, or circumstance preventing this ideal state is an "artificial" barrier; ideally, all such barriers should be eliminated.

Obviously, complex societies must have rules and regulations in order
to cause individuals to act in what are perceived to be acceptable ways.
Our point is that such rules and regulations should promote the attainment of the ideal stated above as much as possible. At the very
least, they should not thwart attainment of the ideal any more than
is necessary.[1]

In all the major areas we studied, we found artificial barriers—
which have been major causes for declining productivity. We discovered some artificial barriers for small businesses that did not
exist for large businesses or for one type of small business and not
another type, and we discuss some of those in the report. In the main,
however, these were few and far between. Keep in mind, however,
that our primary goal was not to make such determinations. For
example, interest rates are high because of certain fiscal policies of
government, among other factors. Such policies are the artificial
barrier. If removed, if the ideal state were reached, and interest rates
fell, any differences in interest rates for one firm, large or small,
rather than another, would be caused by what we are terming natural barriers, such as the differences in financial and economic risks
between firms.

Certainly we did not compare empirical data from large firms
with those from small firms to arrive at that conclusion. We did
compare data from firms of various sizes within our "small" classification, from firms in different types of industries, from firms in
different types of economic environments, and from firms in different
phases of the manufacturing and distribution processes. Some were
financially sound; others were not. Some entered the era of high
interest rates in a highly liquid position; others did not. We found
varying interest rates because of these and other factors. Because
higher interest on investments followed higher interest costs on bor-
rowings, those in a highly liquid position were pleased with the
higher interest rates, while those in a borrowing position were not.

The point is that even in an ideal state there would be variations
in interest costs between firms, but those differences would not be
caused by artificial barriers. They would exist because of differences
in the economic and financial risks attached to the firm and the
functions it performs as perceived by those lending funds. These are
what we term natural barriers, and government should make no
attempt to remove them. They are inherent in the particular business
undertaking or are created by those who manage the business, and
are part of a natural competitive environment.

Our objective, then, was to ascertain the major problems and needs of small business firms in general, to analyze them by major subclassifications of firms in the small business area, and then to use these data to prepare the way for attack and solution at a broad policy level.

In the third phase (Chapters 4, 5, and 6), using the data accumulated and analyzed in the first and second phases, we identify the major causes for productivity declines at the macro level and establish a basic philosophy, and policies based on that philosophy, designed to turn the situation around; and we make it clear why timely, continuous, and substantive efforts must be made.

We do not claim to have discovered unique problems. All of those we discuss have existed for a number of years. Those both within the business area and outside it know them well. But their consequences are understood differently and to different degrees and, certainly, recommendations for their solution have varied considerably. To a significant degree, these variations result because problems generally have been considered piecemeal and solutions have been sought on that basis. When this piecemeal approach is followed, potential adverse impacts in other areas—which might exceed any benefits of an immediate solution to a particular problem—are overlooked or ignored. We considered them jointly—at least the most significant ones—in the broad context of major political, economic, and social factors, in order to observe their interrelationships and interdependencies.

Thus, the individual, major items of concern also had to be approached from a broad perspective. Each of these—interest rates, taxes, regulations, and the others—could by itself be the subject of a monograph or more. And many of them individually deserve additional intensive study and analysis. Such study was neither intended nor possible in a writing such as this. We were concerned with developing a consistent, integrated approach at the policy level. Other research will have to determine implementation guidelines— the rules of the game. Ours was a standard-setting objective that we hope can and will be used by others to develop more specific conclusions and recommendations concerning the items we studied.

The fourth phase (Chapter 7) projects our findings into the future to determine the consequences of doing nothing and the potential effects if our recommendations are implemented. Also, reluctantly, we stated our conclusions about what is likely to happen—reluctantly, because our analyses do not leave much room for optimism.

Conclusions and Broad Recommendations

Problems related to productivity are not unique to any given social order. Such problems exist in democratic, socialistic, and totalitarian countries. Many of the specific problems related to keeping productivity at a high level are the same, while others are not, but because of the nature of the varying political systems the approaches to solving the problems vary considerably.

Decreasing productivity in the United States has come about because we do not have a free market economy and have not had one for many years. Or, at the very least, the dictates of the free market economy have been consistently, and devastatingly, eroded or eliminated during the past five decades, the ultimate consequence of which has been a severe decrease in productivity.

Does this mean that socialistic and totalitarian forms of government preclude high levels of productivity? Statistics and history indicate that this is not the case in the short run, but just as assuredly that it *is* the case over the long run. Very simply, when small numbers of individuals make decisions regarding the production and distribution of goods and services over significant periods of time, productivity will not be as high as it would be in a free market economy in which basically the consumer makes such decisions. And we believe the larger and more complex a society becomes, the truer this is. Over the long run, the highest possible standard of living for individuals in total and on the average will result only if the dictates of a free market economy are followed.

A free market economy is only possible in pure democracies or representative democracies; moreover, it is a necessary ingredient in democracies. This is so because all rights, whether they are political, economic, religious, or sociological, are so interrelated and interdependent in a pure or representative democracy that either they all coexist or the form of government changes. A substantial reduction in economic rights is a move toward socialism. Thus a socialistic society can have religious rights with few, if any, economic rights. But pure democracies or representative democracies cannot. And it is virtually axiomatic that a reduction in some rights, whatever they may be, inevitably leads to a reduction of other rights. This is why all rights must be considered equal in importance. It is when they are placed in some hierarchical order of importance that some of them are reduced or eliminated.

Over the years we have sacrificed a great deal of our free market economy on the altar of short-run expediency, and have allowed the evolution of a political and economic system antithetical to an economic philosophy that would be consistent with our basic representative democracy. This, in larger part, has resulted in a serious decline in productivity growth. To turn the situation around, consequently, we must embrace the philosophy of a free market economy and alter the system to support such a philosophy.

Many specific recommendations are presented in Chapters 5 and 6. It is our belief that their implementation, along with the implementation of the following broad recommendations on which they are based, will accomplish that objective and maximize productivity in the United States:

• We must adopt a long-range outlook, which means we must be willing to accept the short-run political, economic, and sociological consequences of representative democracies. Otherwise, the system won't work. It must be flexible enough to adjust to the disequilibriums that certainly must arise in complex societies. This is only possible when the costs, hurts, and responsibilities of representative democracies are accepted. If it is not flexible, the benefits cannot be realized. A representative democracy is not Utopia, and any substantial attempts to try to make it so will destroy it. Remove all risks and responsibilities and no rights will remain.

• We must accept the consequences of the free enterprise system as being fair. In an ideal state, those who work to satisfy consumers are rewarded according to their abilities and contributions. Those who do not are removed from the marketplace. Individuals must be willing to accept the dictates of such a system; otherwise, the system cannot survive. The question, then, is simple: is it better that consumers, en masse, make such determinations, or that one or a few individuals do so? We maintain that in a representative democracy it must be the consumers.

• We must resist the move toward *egalitarianism*. All individuals are not equal in all respects. From an economic viewpoint, certainly, to hold that all individuals are equal in terms of their rights to share wealth, regardless of their abilities and capabilities in generating that wealth, flies in the face of the nature of man and reduces the incentive for individuals to maximize their output. Productivity increases, and hence the standard of living, can be maximized only when individuals contribute according to their abilities. Basically, they are encouraged to do this when they share according to their contributions. Certainly those who are truly needy should be provided help. What we recommend does not deny this.

• Where necessary, the social, business, and political systems need to be altered to ensure that the basic philosophy of a representative democracy is being supported and, certainly, that it is not being circumvented. For example, the bureaucracy—at the federal level in particular—has become so vast and complex that it has nearly taken on an independent existence of its own. As a consequence, rules and regulations have proliferated, often to the detriment of individual rights. Complex societies must have rules and regulations to cause individuals to act in what are perceived to be acceptable ways, of course. Basically, however, the determination of what these rules and regulations are to be is a function of the citizens (or their elected representatives acting on their behalf), not of the bureaucrats. Our point is that such rules and regulations should promote the attainment of democratic objectives as much as possible. At the very least, they should not thwart attainment of the ideal any more than is necessary. Much more oversight is needed regarding the activities of the various bureaus in Washington. People do react to stimuli built into a system, and those stimuli can alter or develop a philosophy when they ought to be vehicles for carrying out the philosophy. Laws and regulations, from an economic viewpoint, generally should be limited to those necessary to promote and preserve a free market economy.

• A better balanced education for all is needed. At best, the economic education of the general populace is incomplete; at worst, it has been biased and unbalanced. Education, in a representative democracy, requires alternative points of view to be presented objectively and in an unbiased fashion, so that the learner can make reasonable, rational decisions. Without such an education, it is easy for the electorate to be misinformed and misled.

• Although labor unions, one of the strongest special interest groups, could be helpful in making a free market economy work efficiently and effectively, as they are presently constituted and run, most of their actions are antithetical to a free market economy. A change in attitude is necessary, a belief and acceptance that the long-range interests of labor are best served by a free market economy. Specific actions and policies will follow from this. The activities of labor unions must be constrained when they interfere with others' rights.

• Government expenditures must be reduced and the deficit must be eliminated over some reasonable period of time. Otherwise, artificially high interest rates are likely to continue and inflation may increase substantially as we progress through the recovery period.

• At a minimum, the activities of other special interest groups antithetical to a free market economy must be constrained substantially. Ideally, these groups should go out of existence. They are an artificial barrier to the functioning of a free market economy. Each group is trying to control, to dictate, the distribution of wealth without serious consideration of the impact on other groups or on the economy in general.

• Management must give more than lip service to the free enterprise system: it must live it in developing and carrying out the policies of its firms. If the potential benefits of a free market economy are to be sought, the commensurate risks and responsibilities must be accepted. It is inconsistent with the system, and destructive of it, to support it when things go well and then run to the government for help when problems arise.

• Politicians have become one of the strongest special interest groups, many of them placing their interests above those of the constituents they serve. They must reevaluate their roles and display those leadership characteristics the electorate has a right to expect. This means they must set aside petty political squabbling, act in a manner above reproach, and work together, regardless of political party, to aid in seeing to it that the tenets of a representative democracy, including a free market economy, are supported and promoted.

Notes

[1]Harold E. Arnett and Paul Danos, *CPA Firm Viability—A Study of Major Environmental Factors Affecting Firms of Various Sizes and Characteristics* (Ann Arbor, Mich.: The Paton Accounting Center and Division of Research, Graduate School of Business Administration, University of Michigan, 1979), p. 2.

Chapter 2

Productivity: Facts and Myths

General Overview

The slowing of productivity gains in the United States is reaching crisis proportions, according to a report released in April [1983] by the Committee on Economic Development. A reversal of this trend is vital to maintaining the U.S. position in the world economy . . . and will require major changes in federal government policies and American business practices.

. . . It's a long-term trend that has been with us for the better part of two decades. . . . Japan, the U.K., and the major European economies had slowdowns, but productivity growth is still twice ours in Europe, and roughly three times ours in Japan.[1]

Productivity is measured variously as output per person employed, output per hour paid, output per hour worked, or output per total factor input, including labor, capital, and purchased materials and services. No matter which published statistics one considers or which measures are used, it is certain that productivity has declined precipitously during the past 35 years. The annual growth of productivity (on an output per labor-hour basis) averaged about 3.3% per year during the period 1947–1966, dropped to an average of 2.1% per year in the 1966–1973 period,[2] and fell further to an average of 1.2% during 1973–1977.[3] The average continued to decline, reaching a *negative* growth rate of -0.4% by the end of 1980. Although the first quarter of 1981 reflected a significant turnabout that caused some economists to predict a 1 to 2% growth rate for 1981,[4] this figure was not reached. During 1982, according to the U.S. Department of Commerce, production in U.S. factories and mines fell 8.2%, while the real gross national product (GNP) dropped 1.8%, the sharpest decline since 1946.[5] From the position of preeminence held by the United States—it had the highest rate of productivity growth in the world during the 1950s and early 1960s—this country fell to twelfth among the top Western industrial nations between 1966 and 1976. By 1976, for example, the rate of growth of U.S. productivity was less than one third that of Japan.[6]

The United States probably still enjoys the highest average standard of living in the world, in the opinion of most experts on the subject. Nevertheless, statistics on U.S. productivity indicate two important things: (1) Our standard of living will decrease if the trend is not reversed, or at least will not rise as rapidly as it has in the past. (2) Other nations of the Western world are overtaking us. "Primarily because of our productivity slowdown, the United States no longer enjoys the highest per capita Gross National Product in the world."[7]

> Compounding the problem of a trailing productivity growth rate is the fact that the U.S. leadership in absolute productivity is now threatened. In 1960 . . . Japan's absolute productivity was less than a third of ours. Today [1983], their absolute productivity has almost surpassed our own.[8]

The United States is not the only country plagued by productivity problems, of course. However, even though the productivity growth rates of other major industrial nations (Japan, West Germany, France, the United Kingdom, and Italy) also fell off during the 1973–1979 period, in most cases they were still significantly above ours.[9] The data in Table 2-1[10] clearly support this assertion. As reflected, the percentage of decline in the United States was greatest of all countries listed except the United Kingdom and substantially greater for all other countries except Canada.

In terms of changes in real gross national product, the United States didn't fare much better, as shown in Table 2-2.[11] As can be seen, between 1960 and 1973, only the United Kingdom and Eastern Europe had real GNP growth rates lower than that of the United

Table 2–1
Annual Change in Manufacturing Productivity for
1960–1979, %

Country	1960–1973	1973–1979	Decline, %
United States	3.1	1.4	54.8
Canada	4.6	2.2	52.2
Japan	10.3	6.9	33.0
West Germany	5.5	5.3	3.6
United Kingdom	4.0	0.5	87.5
8 European countries	5.8	4.0	31.0
10 foreign countries	6.5	4.8	26.2

Source: Joint Committee of the Congress, "1981 Mid-Year Review of the Economy," Washington, D.C.: U.S. Government Printing Office, 1981.

Table 2–2
International Comparisons of Real GNP Growth, %

Country or Area	1960–1973	1973–1980	Decline, %
United States	4.2	2.4	1.8
Canada	5.4	2.6	2.8
Japan	10.5	4.2	6.3
France	5.7	2.9	2.8
West Germany	4.8	2.3	2.5
Italy	5.2	2.8	3.4
United Kingdom	3.2	0.9	2.3
USSR	5.0	2.9	2.1
Eastern Europe	4.1	3.3	0.8

States. Between 1973 and 1980, the U.S. GNP growth surpassed that of West Germany and stayed higher than that of the United Kingdom, but remained lower than those of the other countries listed.

Interpreting such statistics is something like looking at a glass half-filled with a favorite beverage and taking either the optimistic view that the glass is half full or the pessimistic view that the glass is half empty. On the optimistic side, the United States started from a strong position in 1960, with a considerably higher standard of living than that of the other countries listed, and the 1.8% decline in its real GNP growth rate between 1973 and 1980 was less than those of all the other countries listed except those of eastern Europe. Relatively, then, we have not suffered as much as most countries in terms of drop-off. On the pessimistic side, our growth rate between 1960 and 1980 was less than those of most other countries listed, and it is therefore a cause for concern.

Alleged Causes of the Productivity Problem

The word "alleged" in the heading was deliberately chosen. Although much has been written and said about productivity, relatively little empirical evidence has been accumulated and analyzed. Consequently, up to now the causes cited mainly have been a result of each researcher's point of view, and the solutions given mainly have been assertions. Of course, perceptions and assertions are important; and if they are based on the observations of large numbers of writers and speakers, they can provide a general direction for solutions. But what is needed is evidence—a data base—that will support or reject these perceptions and assertions. We will attempt to present such evidence in Chapter 3. In this chapter, however, we will present only the perceptions and assertions of others, as a basis for understanding the empirical data assembled later and for placing the productivity issue in perspective.

Consider the following eight opinions about the causes of productivity declines:

1. The productivity problem comes from government measures and it can be solved by eliminating the obstacles that government has placed in the path of productivity improvement. The major government measures responsible for the slowdown in productivity are: high marginal tax rates, . . . inflation, . . . excessive governmental regulations, [and] . . . the wide uncertainty about future governmental policies with respect to inflation, taxation, and regulation. . . .[12]

2. The American business sector must take the initiative by making workers more effective on the front line—the work station—the place where productivity begins.[13]

3. Our actual drop in productivity is temporary. It is a worldwide problem, and is the result of two factors: the current recession and the increase in real OPEC oil prices.[14]

4. In generation after generation, our system of democratic capitalism has given its workers more tools to work with. . . . Our capital stock no longer keeps pace with the growth of our labor force. Since 1969, on average, each new worker has had to make do with fewer, not more, capital resources. This capital shortage has been a key factor in declining productivity growth.[15]

5. Today's productivity crisis does not stem from a shortage of resources. It's basically a social problem. Many people are simply not willing to make the sacrifices necessary for economic growth.

Right now, we have a group of people—largely upper middle class, worldwide—who are becoming increasingly hostile to productivity.[16]

6. Much has been said about the work ethic and worker attitudes as contributory factors [to lagging productivity]. That attitude is shaped in large measure by employers and employer representatives and, as it is reflected by the relationship on the plant level, is generally adversary in nature. It is not designed by management to be other than adversary. It is a boss–worker relationship that carries with it a certain hostility in which workers are not always overly concerned about the boss's best interests. That relationship reflects itself in productivity.[17]

7. Tax disincentives, the decline of the work ethic, problems with government regulation, obsolete plant and equipment, insufficient R&D, and poor labor relations all have little to do with industry's faltering productivity. Management ineffectiveness is by far the single greatest cause of declining productivity in the United States. Most companies' efforts to improve productivity are misdirected and uncoordinated.[18]

8. Dwindling competitiveness and productivity in U.S. business often are blamed on management flaws stemming from graduate-level business education. But [some] contend many submanagement workers also fail to measure up, and that their low quality is linked directly to the kind of education provided by the nation's primary and secondary schools.[19]

These statements were made by economists, businessmen, bankers, union officials, directors of research institutions, and professors. We could present any number of other views, but these are sufficient to make some generalizations. Some place blame almost entirely on the federal government, while others assert that government has little to do with productivity declines. Some writers feel that there is one significant cause, while others feel there are a number of individually less significant causes. Some feel salvation will come primarily at the macro level, while others believe the problems exist primarily at the firm or plant level and that solutions must first be found at that level. Some feel the problems are basically social because their roots lie in people's value systems. Some blame management for productivity declines, while others blame a deterioration in the work ethic. Others place the blame primarily on the educational system. Yet other writers feel the causes are basically external to the United States—for example, the energy crisis.

All of these people are knowledgeable and influential in their professions, and they are undoubtedly sincere in their beliefs. Nevertheless, they cannot all be correct in their perceptions. If solutions are to be found, if an acceptable policy statement is to be developed, all such perceptions will have to be addressed and supported or refuted—and an acceptable compromise position will have to be found.

Certainly the political, economic, and philosophical beliefs of individuals influence their thinking about the causes for the declines in productivity, as reflected in the following statements by Campbell

R. McConnell, professor of economics at the College of Business Administration, the University of Nebraska-Lincoln.

> The neo-Marxists' [radical economists'] point is that labor's increasing desire to achieve worker control has been frustrated by the bureaucratization and segmentation of work processes and that this frustration has intensified the deterioration of worker morale and productivity.[20]
>
> Free market, or libertarian, economists contend that the private sector has been subjected to increasing intervention and control by the public sector. Although they believe there are legitimate economic reasons for some government interferences in the market economy, . . . in practice government activities and policies are frequently misguided, overextended, and inappropriate to the problems they are intended to resolve.
>
> . . . According to the libertarians, the productivity slowdown is rooted in deviations from the traditional institutional and ideological characteristics of that system.[21]
>
> . . . the neo-classical economists [the mainstream] explain the rate of productivity growth largely in terms of changes in the stock of real capital relative to labor, changes in the composition and allocation of the labor force, improvements in human resources, and technological progress.[22]

Thus, whether they realize it or not, people's perceptions regarding the productivity slowdown reflect their beliefs about the type of social and political system that should exist, as well as their economic beliefs. This observation will be even more important later when we come to consider the recommended solutions.

But first, let's consider the major *specific* perceptions about why productivity has declined. The following alleged causes of productivity declines are not discussed in any particular order of importance; in fact, there is substantial disagreement about their relative importance. In addition, these causes frequently *overlap,* although they must be listed separately for the sake of organization.

Inflation and Interest Costs

Inflation impacts on most sectors of the economy, but it appears to have a more devastating impact on small businesses than on large ones. Keep in mind that inflation not only affects prices and the pricing mechanism but also the allocation of goods and services. It does not affect all individuals and businesses uniformly. For instance, if the inflation rate is 10% and one individual receives an annual increase in wages or salary of, say, 15%, his real purchasing power has increased 5%. (This assumes that he is consuming the same "mix" of goods and services as that included in the general price index that reflects the inflation rate [or at least another combination of goods and services that balances out to the same rate].) His command over goods and services *in general* has improved. Why?

A perfect index to reflect inflation would use the weighted average change in the specific prices of all the goods and services in the universe being considered (say, the United States) after adjusting for quality and technological changes, new products and services added, and old products and services no longer provided. In practice, it is impossible to construct such an index, so a surrogate measure is used. The consumer price index (CPI), for example, is a surrogate based on the *weighted average* change in the specific prices of a *representative* sample (or mix) of goods and services consumed by *representative* families in *representative* locations throughout the United States. Such an index *presumably* is a reasonable estimation of the weighted average change in the prices of all the goods and services in the economy. Whether it *is* a reasonably good estimation is open to question—and it often is questioned—but we are not going to pursue the discussion of such measurement problems.

The critical point is this: even if the index *does* measure inflation perfectly, the prices of some goods and services do decrease (especially high-technology items, such as pocket calculators), some remain constant, and others increase—and some increase or decrease more or less than others. If any firm or individual consumes goods and services whose average prices are higher or lower than the CPI, that individual or firm will be either better or worse off than the "average" reflected by the consumer price index.

Second, some firms, whose products and services are bought almost regardless of their price, are able to pass on input price increases to their customers. Some wage earners receive raises greater than the inflation rate. Since the GNP is a total given amount for any particular year, this means that such firms and individuals get a larger slice of the GNP for that year. Their slice is offset by the smaller piece received by firms and individuals who are unable to raise their prices or wages as much as the inflation rate. (This assumes that the individual's or firm's consumption pattern is the same as the average measured by the CPI, as we just discussed.) Thus, inflation does create a new allocation of scarce goods and services.

We must be careful, then, as we try to determine and interpret the impact that inflation may have on productivity. Some of the price changes may be due to changing supply and demand factors related to a particular good or service, rather than to the factors causing inflation. For example, suppose that the only price changes in the economy during the year were for peas and carrots: the price of peas increased 10% while the price of carrots decreased 10%, and both have equal weight in the market. Holding everything else constant, the CPI at the end of the year would be the same as at the beginning. There would be no inflation because people buy equal amounts of peas and carrots, and the 10% decrease in the price of one exactly offsets the increase in the price of the other. Specific prices have changed, of course, but those price changes were caused by factors not related to inflation. From a *general* price level viewpoint, on the average everyone is as well off at the end as at the beginning of the year. Those who consume neither peas nor carrots are not affected in any way. Those who like carrots and eat more of them than of peas are better off; those who prefer peas and continue to eat more of them are worse off. But neither group is better or worse off because of *inflation*. Their change in fortunes is due to other factors.

Thus, to discuss inflation and its impact on productivity at the macro level is certainly appropriate in that the economy is being considered en masse. But as discussions are brought down to the level of the sector, and particularly to firm and plant levels, care must be exercised because the patterns of consumption of goods and services at these levels and the weights given to them may not be the same as those used for developing the CPI or any other general price index that reflects what is happening to the economy en masse. Changing prices at these levels may be caused by factors other than, or in addition to, those causing inflation. Another point here, therefore, is that recommendations to control inflation at the macro level very likely will affect different sectors of the economy and specific firms and plants in different ways, and thereby affect productivity differently.

The new Federal Reserve Policy [tight money policy] must be viewed as a plus from the point of view of international considerations, but poses considerable risks for the domestic U.S. economy generally and small business particularly. In terms of strengthening the dollar and halting the panic buying of precious metals and other commodities, the policy has already proved successful. However, there are negative factors to be considered. There is potential harm—particularly to small business—from a full-blown credit crunch. The new policy intensifies weaknesses in the U.S. economy and leads to much higher unemployment.[23]

As the following quotation indicates, some feel that not only inflation, but also the so-called illusory profits resulting from using past-cost statements, is creating serious problems concerning capital formation and maintenance, with consequent adverse effects on productivity.

But the optimism will be misplaced. Inflation renders much of the so-called profit . . . nonexistent. Because past costs are much lower than current costs, the traditional historical cost assumption used by accountants creates the illusion of prosperity—particularly for capital-intensive companies with older assets.

For example, the Commerce Department estimates that profits reported in 1979 were overstated by approximately 50% due to inflation. In individual cases distortions can be even more extreme; after eliminating the effects of price increases, Southern New England Telephone's 1979 income from continuing operations was a full 92.4% less than the traditional profit number.

But it is the illusory profits that seem to have the greatest impact on the general public, legislators, and policymakers. In the words of [then] SEC Chairman Harold Williams, this situation "leads . . . to [misguided] demands . . . to moderate these profits." Most important, since taxes are also based on the illusory figures, retained profits are already inadequate to maintain existing productive capability in certain industries.

As the 1979 annual report of the Dillingham Corporation points out: "Under present laws the effective tax rate has risen to confiscatory levels, resulting in after-tax earnings that are insufficient to replace assets, provide a positive return to shareowners and generate the cash required for growth. As the new methods of inflation accounting indicate . . . our 1979 effective tax rate rises from 46% in the conventional statement to . . . 89% using the current cost method." And the imposition of new taxes (like that on windfall oil profits) worsens the capital formation crisis and could threaten the very survival of essential business sectors.[24]

Third, interest rates tend to increase when inflation is high. Whether interest rates increase partially because of inflation or whether inflation is caused partially by high interest rates is a hotly debated issue we will not try to settle. Once in motion, however, each is partially the cause and partially the effect of the other. It becomes a vicious spiral. In brief, the interest rate does two things:

1. Even without inflation, the interest rate fluctuates in response to such factors as the supply and demand for dollars in the market.

2. Because the dollars paid back are cheaper (will buy fewer goods and services on the average) than the dollars borrowed during inflation, interest rates fluctuate to adjust, however roughly, for anticipated inflationary factors.

Whether inflation increases interest rates or vice versa is not of primary concern to us as stated; the fact that interest rates have increased substantially and affect firms and individuals in different ways is. Small businesses frequently have a higher debt-to-equity ratio than large businesses, because they finance a larger proportion of their operations with debt.[25] Also, small businesses often have a higher percentage of short-term debts.

With high inflation and interest rates, expenses (wages, materials, interest) increase, sales drop off, and many small businesses become less liquid as the cash flows from operations decrease. Often it is not possible for small businesses to pass the increased costs along to their consumers, either because this would make them less competitive with larger businesses or because they have many competitors of approximately the same size in their geographical area, which makes the price of their goods and services more elastic. Because small businesses frequently have higher debt-to-equity ratios, interest costs rise faster for them than for larger companies: they are a greater financial risk, so the incremental cost of borrowing is higher. The greater cost of money plus the reduced cash flows often make it difficult to turn over or refinance their short-term debt. The more the interest rates and inflation rise, the greater this competitive disadvantage becomes.

In any case, certainly there is a cause-and-effect relationship between inflation and interest rates and what the Federal Reserve does to bring these under control. Often an action can work favorably on one aspect while compounding difficulties with the other. For example, prior to 1979—during the 1960s and 1970s—federal deficits were financed in the main through an increase in the money supply. This action creates demand–pull inflation (too many dollars chasing too few goods), but tends to keep interest rates low. In 1979, the Federal Reserve tightened the money supply, forcing the federal government into the financial markets to compete with private industry for funds. This action tends to reduce inflation but increases interest rates and makes them more variable.

Of course, the cash flow crunch causes a reduction in outlays for research and development, new machinery and equipment, and the expansion or building of new facilities. All of these in turn decrease the creation of new jobs and increase unemployment, thereby decreasing productivity.

The housing industry, which contains a significant number of small businesses, is a good example of the impacts of inflation and high interest rates.

> According to figures from the home builders association, the median price of a home in 1974 was $36,000. Today [early 1980], it is $63,000 and will escalate to $100,000 by 1984. That represents an increase of 73 percent. Meanwhile income will go up by only 48 percent over the same period.[26]

During 1980, real income for the median family dropped about 5%; the drop continued through 1981 and 1982. Even though the picture improved during the first half of 1983, no substantial improvement is predicted for the immediate future. Thus, the estimated 48% increase in income between 1974 and 1984 might well turn out to have been optimistic. In many specific areas, and on the average throughout the United States, the cost of housing has increased faster than the general inflation rate, because of the decreasing supply of land and large increases in the costs of materials and labor. These factors alone would have caused difficulty for the housing industry.

Add the high interest rates, and the situation worsens considerably. At a 14% mortgage rate for a 30-year mortgage, a buyer pays approximately *four* times more for a home than its cash price (excluding tax considerations), and about *three* times more than its net price after taxes, assuming a 30% incremental tax rate. The president of a construction firm comments:

> A ripple effect runs outward from the construction industry. . . . What affects us now will soon touch many other segments. It starts with the layoff of construction workers due to building cutbacks, then it moves out to the lumber and building materials industry and then out toward the appliance manufacturers. . . . It even hurts the lawyers who handle real estate matters.[27]

These factors compound the problems of business in general, and small businesses in particular. For example, small businesses must plow back a good portion of their internally generated funds in order to operate and grow. Inflation generates a demand for higher wages, with attendant increases in social security and unemployment taxes. Material and supply prices, among others, go up. If these costs cannot be passed on to the consumer, cash flows go down, reducing the funds available for building up the business.

Regulation

It was probably during the Great Depression of the 1930s that regulations began mushrooming, growing to almost unbelievable numbers, at least through 1979.

> The *Federal Register,* in which federal government regulations are published, offers a good benchmark. In 1969 it had 20,500 pages; then it grew at a rate of 15% per year to 45,400 pages in 1974 and to 61,300 pages in 1978. In 1979 the pace of regulation escalated 25%, typified by 77,500 pages in the *Federal Register.* Then we saw a change! As our awareness increased that regulation wasn't working, the rate of increase in regulation declined, resulting in a *Federal Register* of only 23,000 pages in 1980—roughly the 1969 level. While this is still substantial, it represents a laudable start on reducing the relative impact of regulation in our economy.[28]

There is no doubt that government regulation has had a substantial impact on businesses, small businesses in particular. No one knows for certain the exact extent of this impact. (The Small Business Administration [SBA] is developing a data-base system for collecting information to indicate the cost and benefits of such regulation.) However, the amount has been estimated on a number of occasions.

> The SBA's office of advocacy has completed a project in which more than 800 small business owners kept a diary of how much time they spent filling out government forms and the costs of complying with reporting requirements. . . .
>
> The study reveals that the average compliance cost to a small business is $1,270, but the cost for individual companies ranged from $400 to $72,000 per year.
>
> Assuming that there are about ten million small businesses, the annual burden can be set at about $12.7 billion. . . . Since about 74 percent of the reporting requirements are federal, it is possible to conclude that the federal reporting burden on small business is just slightly under $10 billion per year, and the combined state and local burden is close to $3 billion.[29]

Table 2–3
Cost of Regulation, in Billions of Dollars

	1976	Extrapolation		
	(Study year)	1977	1978	1979
Administrative costs	$ 3.6	$ 3.7	$ 4.5	$ 4.8
Compliance costs	62.9	75.4	92.2	97.9
Total	$66.5	$79.1	$96.7	$102.7

In total, regulatory costs are even more startling, as reflected in Table 2-3.[30] Only direct costs are included; i.e., government outlays plus the direct costs to industry of fulfilling the regulations. Richard A. Warne, commenting on these and other data, says:

> But that's only the direct cost. What about the further cost to the consumer—the loss of productivity, the loss of smaller companies, the barriers to entry, the costs of delay of new products, the absence of addition of new products that cannot be economically justified under regulatory rules, and the loss to society of the gains in productivity that could come from new processes that cannot be introduced? Moreover, there are the further impacts on the economy of the loss of new capital formation, innovation, scientific progress and research and development.[31]

That costs go far beyond just the direct costs to the companies involved, and extend to taxpayers, consumers, and laborers, also is emphasized by Murray Weidenbaum:

> The costs arising from government regulation are basic: (1) the cost to the taxpayer for supporting a galaxy of government regulations, (2) the cost to the consumer in the form of higher prices to cover the added expense of producing goods and services under government regulation, (3) the cost to the worker in the form of jobs eliminated by government regulation, (4) the cost to the economy resulting from the loss of smaller enterprises which cannot afford to meet the onerous burden of government regulations, and (5) the cost to society as a whole as a result of a reduced flow of new and better products and a less rapid rise in the standard of living.[32]

Regulations have become so excessive and costly that some individual companies have gone so far as to devote considerable space in their annual reports to the topic. For example, in its annual report for the period ending December 31, 1978, Dow Chemical Company devoted five pages to the adverse effects of excessive, costly regulations, citing many specific examples. We won't repeat all of those here, but portions of the president's letter to the stockholders summarize some of the impacts well.

> . . . unlike the rules that govern sports, the rules imposed on business sometimes get so confusing and costly that they get in the way of accomplishing what they are designed to do. That's why I've been spending a great deal of time in recent years speaking out against excessive, wasteful and needless government regulations. They're not just unfair to Dow, but also the public—the fans, if you will. . . .
>
> . . . Would you believe that in 1977, the last year studied, the bill [for regulatory costs] came to $268 million? That's equivalent to seven cents on every U.S. sales dollar, money that our customers and the consumer ultimately must pay!
>
> The study also showed that 48 percent of the total, or $129 million, was either clearly excessive, needless, wasteful or questionable according to good business and scientific practice.
>
> Regulations represent our fastest growing costs—up 44 percent over the previous year. If that isn't inflationary, nothing is.
>
> Make no mistake about it—we want adequate, fair rules to protect everyone involved. We need safe products, safe working conditions, a clean environment and a chance for everybody to play the game to win. I'm not talking about compromising any of our goals or standards. I am talking about rules that are unfair.[33]

Other direct and indirect costs, which can be estimated with reasonable reliability, are involved. The direct costs include the time required of the owner and/or employees to fill out the forms and the legal and accounting expertise that often must be acquired in order to do the job as required. "The Office of Management and Budget estimates that individuals and businesses spend 787 million man hours per year complying with federal reporting requirements."[34] Nevertheless, the indirect costs may well exceed the direct ones. Indirect cost is made up mainly of the opportunity cost (the profit forgone) of using money to comply with regulations rather than for more profitable purposes, such as replacement of aging plant and equipment, research and development, initiation of new projects, and expansion of the business.

In a broad sense, regulation of business is both private and public. Private regulation includes such organizations as the Financial Accounting Standards Board (FASB), which sets the accounting standards and principles to be followed by companies, trade associations, and professional organizations to which businessmen belong. Public regulators include local, state, and federal government units and all the agencies through which they work, such as the Securities Exchange Commission (SEC), the Occupational Safety and Health Administration (OSHA), and the Environmental Protection Agency (EPA).

> It is paradoxical. One of the purposes of regulation is to curb excess, yet the cumulative bulk of today's regulations is itself excessive. Some 90 regulatory agencies now issue approximately 7,000 rules per year. Government has reached the point where it is stifling business, frustrating the public and undermining its own credibility.[35]

Most people feel that government has some role to play in the regulation of business, as it has in other areas, but one question is frequently heard: Has government gone too far in the regulation of businesses? Even if regulations were costless in terms of dollars, there are psychological and emotional costs—the loss in individual freedom and the frustration of having to take time away from managing a business efficiently to fill out countless forms and deal with government regulations. Although these costs are indirect and hard to measure, they must be considered.

Most of what we have discussed to this point applies to all businesses, regardless of size. Small businessmen feel that they bear an unfair share of the burden of government regulation—some estimates are as high as 60% of total regulatory costs—mainly because of what might be called the "fixed cost syndrome." Although large businesses often must provide more complex information than small businesses to comply with regulations, a certain amount of basic information must be provided by all businesses, regardless of size. There is a basic fixed cost of providing the information, regardless of the size of the firm. However, larger firms can spread the cost over larger numbers of units produced and sold, or people served, making the average cost per unit lower than for smaller businesses. This creates what owners and managers of small businesses perceive to be an arbitrary competitive disadvantage.

Others have indicated that "the regulatory burden is similar to an excise tax with a rate that declines as the firm gets larger."[36] They feel that the cost is inequitable because businesses receive differential treatment on the basis of size, with the smaller businesses paying a higher percentage of their income for government regulations than large ones do. Also, labor-intensive firms pay a higher percentage of the cost than capital-intensive industries. This, too, they feel is unfair in that small businesses, on the average, tend to be more labor-intensive than large firms.

Benefits also are difficult to measure, of course. Many feel intuitively that the costs of regulations generally exceed their benefits, and there are any number of specific examples to prove them right. A case in point: one man started a fish farm to domesticate abalone. "Some 42 federal, state, and local governmental agencies regulate his business; he estimates it takes at least 50 percent, and probably closer to 70 percent, of his time to deal with the government."[37] It is arguable whether regulations benefit society as a whole enough to outweigh the direct and indirect costs to individual firms such as this one.

Even assuming social benefits do exist, those benefits are frequently "paid for" more than once because agencies do not coordinate their activities and exchange information. Many times businesses must provide the same information to two or more agencies, often in somewhat different format, and the requirements are often inconsistent and unnecessarily complex. As an example, as a result of having *one* foreign shareholder, one small business was required to submit a 90-page form that had to be filled out by following 15 pages of difficult instructions.

Many of the same points can be made regarding regulations in the private sector, although both the extent of regulation and the costs are less than in the public sector. Generally accepted accounting principles, promulgated by the FASB and its predecessors, must be followed by all audited companies, regardless of size, unless they are explicitly excluded. Some feel that many of the complex principles, rules, and standards do not make much sense and are not very useful for small company audits—and they are costly to implement, as well. Although the FASB has made exceptions for earnings per share requirements, little else has been done to this point.

However, the FASB has a research project under way to study the application of different accounting principles to private companies and to publicly held companies (little GAAP versus big GAAP). Also, the American Institute of Certified Public Accountants has divided into two sections, one concerned with private companies and one concerned with SEC practices—one of several ways it recognizes the differences in the size and nature of various businesses and in the CPAs who serve them.

Taxes

All businesses indicate that taxes of all kinds are an ever-increasing burden. Taxes remove funds that could be used for other purposes, such as capital investment or research and development. Certainly governments need taxes to finance their legitimate functions. Again, the basic question is whether the benefits derived from some government expenditures exceed those that could be derived if the funds were left in the hands of individuals and firms to spend or invest. The mood in the country today reflects a desire by the citizens to cut both government expenditures and taxes. In some cases, this stems from the feeling that government is doing things the citizenry does not want. In other cases, people want government to perform certain functions, but not to the present extent.

As inflation pushes people and businesses into higher tax brackets (so-called bracket creep), their incentive to increase their earnings by working harder is decreased.[38] Often the greater income, even before tax increases, is not enough to offset inflation, which reduces the *real* income of the individual or business. The funds many businesses, particularly small businesses, can retain for growth are not sufficient as these businesses depend more heavily on internally generated funds for expansion purposes.

High marginal tax rates also encourage people to evade taxes. These rates have caused an expansion of what has come to be called the "underground economy," which is made up of two groups. The first group commits illegal acts and fails to report the resulting taxable income. High marginal tax rates do not have a direct impact on the size of this group. It is involved in the illegal act—prostitution, illegal gambling, drug-traffic—primarily to obtain the high revenues involved, not to evade the taxes per se. The second group is involved in legal acts, but conducts its transactions and activities in a covert fashion in order to cover its tracks. For example, its members might do part-time painting on the weekends, collecting cash for the service and providing no receipts to the customer. They pay no taxes on this work, and their tax evasion is hard to uncover. These types of activities are on the rise and are encouraged by high marginal tax rates. "In 1981, the loss in federal income tax revenues from such activities was estimated at $88 billion dollars, and is growing by about 10-15 percent per year."[39]

One could take a purist view, that people should not do these things, regardless of the size of the marginal tax rates. It's true; they shouldn't. We assume in this book that people are basically "good," but that the system must be such as to encourage and support the basic natural instincts to be good. The system itself can overcome or thwart such attitudes. When the marginal tax rates rise to a level significant numbers of people feel is unfair and unjust, some people will seek to counterbalance it. Not only do such activities result in large losses of tax revenue; more importantly, they help destroy loyalty and respect for the government, which could have a destabilizing effect. It has been reported that ". . . 30 percent of Italy's GNP is subterranean and [there may be] a connection between that phenomenon and the country's chronic political instability."[40]

Finally, as we mentioned earlier, many taxes, rules, and regulations work at cross-purposes. For example, the minimum wage has risen so high that businesses, particularly small businesses, do not hire people, such as high school and college students and unskilled workers, they otherwise might. These groups therefore suffer from higher unemployment; at the same time, the government is developing programs and spending large sums of money to employ them gainfully.

A number of people we interviewed indicated that social security and state and federal unemployment compensation taxes have risen so high that they have been forced to lay off employees, again adding to unemployment and reducing productivity. These taxes, as well as the increased minimum wage, they said, affect the generally labor-intensive small businesses even more than larger ones.

Some feel that our national policies are protecting workers too much and that they encourage unemployment by reducing the incentive to work. In addition to unemployment compensation per se, supplementary unemployment compensation funds have been established at some firms, food stamps are available to many, and the Trade Adjustment Assistance Program (amounting in 1982 to about $4.8 billion per year and to $7.1 billion in 1983) provides additional benefits for those laid off as a result of foreign competition. It is not uncommon for some workers to receive 80 to 95% as much when they are unemployed as they do when working. This being true, an unemployed person might question the value of working 40 hours a week just to get 5 to 20% more money than he or she can get without working. That person may find little incentive to look for another job until the benefits decrease or end. In other words, the marginal utility of the additional income may appear to be less than the marginal cost of earning it. When that is so, productivity suffers.

> Some 21 states have borrowed money from the Federal Government
> to meet unemployment benefit demands. Michigan has borrowed $2.2
> billion with Illinois, Ohio, and Pennsylvania not far behind. In total
> $10.7 billion has been borrowed by the 21 states, all of it non-interest-
> bearing debt, except $2.8 billion carries a 10% interest rate (prior to
> April 1, 1982, the loans were interest-free). For Michigan, the debt
> translates into $505 for each member of the labor force. Considering
> that the present collection from employers is seven-tenths of 1 percent
> on the first $6,000 of wages (about $42 for each worker), this amounts
> to approximately the equivalent of 12 years' collections.[41]

Michigan is considering allocating the $2.2 billion between em-
ployers and employees in some fashion and collecting it from them.
In any case, unemployment compensation has contributed to driving
some states to near-bankruptcy. No matter what the method of recovery, marginal rates of taxes on individuals and businesses must
increase, depleting funds that could have been reinvested in businesses and utilized by individuals for increased saving and consumption. Benefits have nearly doubled since the recession of 1975–
1976, indicating, again, that state legislatures have not lived up to
their responsibilities to keep states solvent.

Finally, we might mention two other taxes small businessmen
find burdensome. (We discuss these in some detail in Chapter 6.)
The capital gains tax discourages business owners from switching
into another line of business because the tax paid on the sale of the
first business reduces the capital available to invest in another. The
federal estate tax makes it more difficult for small businesses to
continue after the death of the owner. At the very least, estate taxes
reduce the capital available for continuing the business; at worst,
the business must be sold to obtain the money needed to pay the
taxes.

Capital Formation

A general decrease in capital investment is one of the basic causes
for the decline in productivity.

> . . . the United States did become a seriously underinvesting economy
> during the 1970s, by any kind of measure. Whether you're looking at
> the amount of physical investment newly being put in place per person
> being added to the labor force, whether you're looking at the stock of
> capital, the net stock of capital as best this kind of thing can be meas-

ured per person in the labor force—any of these data would indicate that the U.S. economy during the last decade fell very seriously behind.[42]

There are two main reasons small businesses frequently are heavily leveraged (have high debt-to-equity ratios). First, traditionally it has been difficult for small businesses to raise equity capital even if they wished to do so. Second, most small business owners do not wish to dilute their ownership interest—and their authority and control—by selling ownership shares.

Even in the best of times, a typical small business has a limited supply of capital, both to start with and to use for operating and expanding the business. Many small businesses begin on loans obtained from family members and friends as they lack the collateral and successful operating history needed to get bank loans. High interest rates and inflation have made the situation even more difficult; for example, it is hard to obtain the refinancing of loans necessary to keep the business operating. "In 1969, 550 firms with assets of less than $5 million raised an aggregate of $1.5 billion in the equity market. In 1974–1977, only 80 similar companies were able to raise a total of $415 million."[43] Somewhat different statistics on the same subject are supplied by others.

> In 1975, the ability of small business to raise equity capital was at a low ebb. One way of raising capital is through stock issues but it was getting increasingly difficult for small companies to use this route. In 1975 only three small companies (with a net worth of less than $5 million) were able to raise capital by selling stock to the public, compared to 698 such companies which went public in 1969. There was no question that capital was truly drying up for the small business community and there was no single, simple remedy.[44]

Another reason small businesses face a decrease in investment funds is that there are more and more institutional investors and fewer individual investors.

> In the early 1960s, only about 25 percent of all common stocks were owned by institutional investors; it is predicted that by 1985 that figure will reach 50 percent. [Since] institutional investors are risking others' money and are constrained by legal requirements and restrictions, they are less likely to invest in small business; individual investors are more inclined to take risks with their own money.[45]

Because of their inability to raise capital, many businesses are operating with antiquated buildings, machinery, and equipment. Thus they are less productive and at a competitive disadvantage with more modern U.S. firms, as well as with foreign competitors such as those in Japan and West Germany.

Although small businesses have special problems, many people feel that inflation and the tax laws are the real reasons capital formation is so difficult. Inflation and high taxes encourage consumption and discourage investment, and both are made even worse by excessive government expenditures. Sometimes tax programs and monetary policies work at cross-purposes. The government spends tax money to reduce unemployment and then adopts monetary policies to reduce the resulting inflation; the result is tight money and high interest rates.

Assuming the business does get started, the next problem is obtaining enough capital to continue operating. Many small businesses are family affairs, passed along from parents to children. Sometimes the children choose other occupations or professions and the business must be sold. Often one or more employees may be highly qualified to take over the business, but cannot do so because they lack either the capital to buy it outright or enough collateral to get a loan. The value of the business is often a significant portion, or even all, of the owner's retirement funds; consequently, it would be extremely risky for the owner to accept payment from an employee buyer over a number of years at an appropriate interest rate unless the loan were guaranteed. As a consequence, the owners frequently liquidate or sell out to other, and usually larger, businesses.

Research, Development, and Innovation

The decrease in expenditures on research and development by businesses also has affected productivity growth adversely.

> . . . the number of patent applications per quantum of economic activity . . . has been declining now for about twenty years. Now, of course, one such patent of the magnitude that spawned the semiconductor industry, for example, will make up for a lot of others that are less important. Nonetheless, . . . if we have been generating technology more slowly and because of sluggish investment introducing it into the economy more slowly, then our economic processes inevitably are reflecting aging technology.[46]

Small businesses have historically been characterized by a high degree of research, development, and innovation, resulting in the creation of new and useful products and services. Such accomplishments also are on the wane.

> According to the Office of Management and Budget, small businesses employing fewer than 1,000 people accounted for roughly half of the nation's innovations between 1953 and 1973. That figure is four times greater per research-and-development dollar than for larger firms.

> Still, the National Science Foundation says, "private research and development dropped by 13 percent between 1968 and 1978."[47]

One reason often cited is "the hostility of governmental policies toward innovation."[48] The cost, both in terms of dollars and time, to get through the regulatory process and to obtain patent protection causes people to discard creative ideas. In addition, tax policies and rules discourage the use of capital in highly risky ventures.

It is alleged that the government is unwilling to take chances on small businesses with good ideas, and small businesses are becoming less and less willing to take chances on the government. Federal funds are available for research and development. However, present patent law holds that inventions resulting from the use of federal funds belong to the public. There are not likely to be many takers under such a policy because entrepreneurs and inventors are unable to reap the benefits of their innovations unless they hold exclusive rights to the products they develop.

Things do look brighter for small businesses. On July 22, 1982, the President signed into law the Small Business Innovation Development Act, which will allow greater participation of small businesses in federal research and development. "This Act requires that all federal agencies with a budget of $100 million or more establish Small Business Innovation Research programs and earmark a percentage of their total R&D budget for small business. . . . The Small Business Administration estimates that when this Act is fully implemented in 1987, small firms will receive between $275 million and $450 million a year in R&D work from major federal agencies."[49]

Workers and Supervisors

Some feel strongly that the work ethic has deteriorated badly in the last 20 years or so, and that this is a major explanation for productivity decreases. It is estimated by some that workers spend as little as 50% of their time on the job actually working. Those making this argument point to slow-down rules in labor contracts, increased paid vacation and sick days, decreasing quality of output, increased unemployment compensation, and the general attitude of workers. More broadly, they perceive lower worker productivity to be a result of the national state of mind. The problem lies in the value system of the people, and hard, productive work does not have a very high priority in that value system. Doing as little as possible for as much reward as possible seems to be the goal.

Others feel that the initiative or the value system of workers is not at fault: they feel that workers have not changed in any basic way during the past 20 years, but that the reward system has changed and workers are merely reacting to those changes. A number of examples are cited frequently: Marginal tax rates on workers are too high and reduce the incentive to work hard. Unemployment compensation is too high and removes the incentive of workers to look for work when they become unemployed, at least until the benefits run out. Or, workers are encouraged to work only long enough to qualify for benefits and then stop—and workers also will take advantage of whatever sick days and vacation days are allowed.

Yet others believe the problem lies primarily with inadequate supervision on the job. Workers are not as productive as they might be because of rework, idle time waiting for parts, and the defective condition of machines and tools. Good supervisors would detect and correct these problems quickly and thereby increase worker productivity.

Others attribute the decrease in worker productivity to management attitudes and practices. They believe management often creates an adversary relationship with the workers by maintaining a boss–worker atmosphere rather than allowing the workers to participate in the decision-making process. This attitude, they feel, is most common where management resists the collective bargaining process. Workers are aware of the firm's problems and could be helpful in finding solutions for them if allowed to do so. But they aren't, it is alleged.

Management

To some, one of the major reasons for business failures is poor management: a lack of sound, basic management skills in operating businesses efficiently and effectively, resulting in low productivity.

> . . . [A panel of top business executives] blame[s] management for being
> too concerned with short-term results, too casual about lagging pro-
> ductivity, too hostile to organized labor and too willing to leave the
> making of key decisions to one man. . . . A few agree . . . that much
> of American management today is "too fat and lazy" to keep up with
> hard-driving foreign producers. . . . The Japanese, West Germany and
> Switzerland have taught us the need to address long-term results.[50]

Others feel businessmen often do not have enough entrepreneurial
education and skills to be successful, for a number of reasons. First,
students at the primary and particularly at the high school levels
may learn too little—or nothing at all—about business, the free enterprise system, and the role of profits and productivity in business
success.

> Ideally, teaching entrepreneurship should begin at the secondary
> school level, where interested students could learn basic business
> principles and the skills of management, marketing, accounting and
> capital acquisition. Later, in colleges and graduate programs, these
> skills could be focused and sharpened.

> Such an educational process would accomplish a number of objectives.
> First, it would provide necessary, but hard to obtain, skills on how to
> run a business successfully, and thereby increase the entrepreneur's
> probability of success. Second, it would demonstrate that an entre-
> preneur has been exposed to the intricacies of managing an owner-
> operated business. Finally, it would serve to interest young people in
> entrepreneurship.[51]

Of course, neither the hope nor the objective is to turn all high
school graduates into competent businessmen. That would be impossible. But one of the basic objectives of public education through
the high school level is to provide those entering the "real" world
with an adequate understanding of that world and adequate basic
skills to become effective members of society. Many of them will
work for business firms, all of them will deal with businesses, and
all of them will be making decisions at the polls and elsewhere that
will affect business. Some will go on to college. But they will all need
a basic knowledge of the business environment to help them make
rational decisions.

Second, although a few colleges and universities have excellent
courses related to the operation of small businesses, on the whole
they place too little emphasis on small businesses at this level. Although they don't do it deliberately, many business schools use programs and approaches to business education that cause their students

to think of careers only in large organizations. The students do not learn enough about the differences between small and large business to make rational choices based on their desires, interests, goals, and objectives in life. Not only do fewer college graduates enter small business, but some students embark on the wrong career before they realize they have a choice; they then have to switch in midstream, causing trauma both to themselves and to their employer.

Third, although there are a few outstanding continuing education programs directed to the needs of small businessmen, there are not enough to make them easily accessible to the many small businessmen spread around the country.

Energy

Small businesses make up the majority of firms drilling for new oil in this country. Some estimates say they are responsible for drilling as much as 80% of new oil wells. Small firms also conduct most of the marketing and distribution of heating oil and gasoline. But they are having problems.

> As dependable sources of energy become more scarce and prices rise, the survival of these small businesses in the energy sector of the economy becomes more problematic. It is becoming increasingly difficult for these small firms to obtain fuel or obtain it at competitive prices. Credit is tight, and smaller fuel oil dealers cannot obtain sufficient capital.[52]

Through 1981, small businesses were often forced to purchase energy supplies on the "spot" market, rather than at competitively bid prices. Such supplies are more expensive and less dependable. Thus small businesses that deal in oil products were having difficulties because of the scarcity and increasing prices of oil. Although the situation improved in 1982 and through early 1983, prices are again on the rise and are expected to continue rising at least through 1990.

The other side of the coin concerns the users of oil and oil products. Some writers ascribe the sharp productivity declines in 1973 and 1974 to the significant increases in OPEC oil prices at that time, and some feel the continuing high prices and changeable patterns of scarcity through 1981 (depending on the production schedules of OPEC countries) had a negative impact on productivity. Dollars used to acquire energy are taken away from other uses in businesses (capital investment, expansion, research and development, and so on). And more dollars are spent in searching for alternate energy sources, with the same consequences.

The following items may be classified under "miscellaneous," but they are not insignificant; it's just that they require only a short discussion to indicate how each reduces productivity, particularly in small businesses. Whether or not these items affect productivity at the macro level is another question.

Federal Procurement

"Statistics reveal that although small business accounts for nearly 50 percent of the Gross National Product, it receives only about 25 percent of the almost $100 billion spent in federal government procurement."[53] Although a number of acts of Congress have attempted to increase the small businesses' share of federal purchases, none has been very effective. There are two basic problems. One, many federal projects, such as large weapons procurements, are so huge and complex that small businesses are precluded simply because they do not have the capacity to handle these projects. Two, and tied closely to one, many large manufacturers do not subdivide contracts into smaller pieces that could be handled by small businesses.

International Trade

Many small businesses are reluctant to become involved in international trade, and some people feel this is a principal cause of the international trade problems of the United States. As a matter of fact, only 200 firms account for more than 85% of all U.S. export sales.[54]

Small businesses often lack the funds to develop international markets. In addition, they often are not aware of international trade possibilities; even when they are, their personnel lack the necessary expertise to handle the maze of details involved in customs documents, shipping, and marketing in foreign countries. Finally, small businesses are less prepared than large businesses to assume the risks of currency fluctuations.

The remaining two items relate to the cost structures of small businesses. In a word, the large and ever-increasing amounts expended on these items remove funds that might otherwise be used to increase productivity.

Product Liability

Product liability litigation has increased significantly during the past 10 to 15 years. Not only have the costs to defend such suits been increasing, but also courts have been very liberal in the dollar awards to plaintiffs. As a result, insurance premiums have risen dramatically. Many small businesses find it difficult to renew policies or to replace canceled coverage. Others find the premiums so high that they drop their coverage and "self-insure." This increases their risks significantly and, of course, could drive them into bankruptcy in the event of a legal action.

Hardest hit are companies with sales of less than $75 million. In some instances, their premiums have jumped from less than 1 percent of sales to 15 percent and more—jeopardizing their entire profit. These escalating product liability claims affect customers as well as manufacturers. Whereas a few may benefit, the average consumer is encountering higher prices and, in some cases, may find products unavailable.[55]

Health and Accident Insurance

Many small businesses pay 50% or more of the premiums for health and accident insurance policies covering their employees. Premiums have soared over the past decade or so, placing a great deal of financial pressure on small businesses.

Summary and Conclusions

If there is one general observation that can be made about business generally, and small business in particular, it is that businesses are in a continual process of evolution, for the simple reason that the social, political, and economic environments in which they operate are changing continually. The realm of activities in which business engages has become larger and more complex, which, in turn, has affected the relations between business, government, and individuals.

In general, the impacts of these environmental changes on businesses have been relatively gradual and have hardly been noticed by those outside the business area. At times, however, the pace of change has quickened, becoming nearly revolutionary in its impact, particularly on small businesses. The changes of the last decade, such as the rapid increases in inflation and interest rates, have been particularly dramatic. But change started many years before. The introduction of federal income taxation in 1913, the phenomenal growth of government that began in the 1930s, the rapid growth in the numbers and size of business firms after World War II, and the unparalleled interest that U.S. congressional committees have exhibited in businesses are all examples of such changes (discussed in more detail in Chapter 4).

Productivity certainly has declined substantially during the last 35 years, particularly the last 15. A great variety of alleged causes have been given for the decreasing productivity growth of business in general and small business in particular in the United States. Although some of the causes are listed again and again as being important, a great deal of disagreement exists as to which are of greatest importance; apparently there is no order of priority that would find general acceptance. Without agreement as to causes, of course, it is difficult to arrive at any generally accepted approaches to a solution.

Our basic objective is to develop a policy statement that, if implemented, will aid businesses generally, and small business in particular, in increasing their productivity. In order to do this we need empirical data to provide a basis for deciding which of the alleged causes and solutions for the productivity problem to accept and which to reject. This will be our goal in Chapter 3.

> One reason why small business participation in economic policy decisionmaking has not been greater is the lack of data to prove the small business case. Currently economic indicators are not broken down by business size (employee number), sales or asset level. Without the data, it is difficult to analyze the performance of the small business sector, or compare it to the performance of the entire economy. The solution to this problem lies in the creation of a small business economic data base.[56]

The Small Business Administration has started to develop such a data base, but it will be some time before the project is completed. In Chapter 3, we will develop a data base sufficient for our purposes here.

In considering the data, we also will have to give some consideration to the impact that recommended solutions will have on various sectors within the small business category. Construction firms, light manufacturing firms, financial institutions, and any number of types of service organizations, among others, fall within the "small business" classification. In a word, the firms making up small businesses are not homogeneous. Therefore, it may be that solutions at the macro level will not affect them all similarly. In addition, different solutions may be necessary for firms falling into different sectors, or at the least they may require different weighting. Or perhaps not. In accumulating and interpreting the empirical data, we will give some consideration to the different sectors to determine whether different solutions are necessary.

Last, as is often true when dealing at the policy level, one needs to be concerned as much with what is possible as with what is ideal. Whatever solution is finally found will have to be politically acceptable. Agreement and support must be obtained from state and federal politicians, and the type of solutions they find acceptable will depend in large measure on the mood of the electorate and various special interest groups.

But although we will discuss political feasibility at various places in this report, our basic concern is to develop an ideal state, that is, to determine what is necessary to maximize productivity increases in the United States. Anything less that can be attained, though not ideal, will be a step in the right direction.

Notes

[1]Peat, Marwick, Mitchell & Co., *Executive Newsletter,* Vol. 9, No. 5 (May 9, 1983), p. 1.

[2]Council of Economic Advisers, *Economic Report of the President: Transmitted to the Congress January 1977* (Washington, D.C.: U.S. Government Printing Office, 1977), p. 45.

[3]Campbell R. McConnell, "Why Is U.S. Productivity Slowing Down?" *Harvard Business Review,* Vol. 57, No. 2 (March–April 1979), p. 36.

[4]"Productivity Grew at 4% Rate in First Quarter," *The Wall Street Journal,* May 28, 1981, p. 4.

[5]"Economy's Worst Slide since 1946," *The Ann Arbor News,* January 19, 1983, p. Al.

[6]Alan Waldman, "Executive Report: The Apostle of Productivity (C. Jackson Grayson)," *Mainliner* (May 1980), p. 111.

[7]McConnell, p. 36.

[8]Peat, Marwick, p. 1.

[9]Council of Economic Advisers, *Economic Report of the President: Transmitted to the Congress January 1980* (Washington, D.C.: U.S. Government Printing Office, 1980), p. 85.

[10]Joint Committee of the Congress of the United States, "The 1981 Mid-Year Report: Productivity Report," July 23, 1981, 97th Congress, 1st Session.

[11]Edward M. Gramlich, "Some Misconceptions about the U.S. Productivity Slowdown," *Dividend*, Vol. 12, No. 3 (Spring 1981), p. 2.

[12]David Gilman, Interview with Milton Friedman, *World*, Vol. 15, No. 1 (Winter 1981), p. 21.

[13]David Gilman, Interview with Robert B. Kurtz, *World*, Vol. 15, No. 1 (Winter 1981), p. 22.

[14]David Gilman, Interview with Paul Samuelson, *World*, Vo. 15, No. 1 (Winter 1981), p. 23.

[15]David Gilman, Interview with Gordon T. Wallis, *World*, Vol. 15, No. 1 (Winter 1981), p. 24.

[16]David Gilman, Interview with Herman Kahn, *World*, Vol. 15, No. 1 (Winter 1981), p. 26.

[17]David Gilman, Interview with Lloyd McBride, *World*, Vol. 15, No. 1 (Winter 1981), p. 28.

[18]Arnold S. Judson, "The Awkward Truth about Productivity," *Harvard Business Review*, (September-October 1982), p. 93.

[19]"Lack of Self-Discipline Blamed for Dwindling Employee Productivity," *The Ann Arbor News*, August 26, 1982, p. D4.

[20]McConnell, p. 42.

[21]*Ibid.*, p. 48.

[22]*Ibid.*, p. 37.

[23]*Discussion and Comments on the Major Issues Facing Small Business*, A Report of the Select Committee on Small Business, U.S. Senate, to the delegates of the White House Conference on Small Business, 96th Congress, 1st Session, December 4, 1979 (Washington, D.C.: U.S. Government Printing Office, 1979), p. 28.

[24]Lawrence Revsine, "Let's Stop Eating Our Seed Corn," *Harvard Business Review* (January–February 1981), pp. 128–129.

[25]Roberta Graham, "Small Business: Beset, Bothered, and Beleaguered," *Nation's Business*, Vol. 68, No. 2 (February 1980), p. 23.

[26]*Ibid.*

[27]*Ibid.*

[28]Richard A. Warne, "A Controller Looks at Regulation," *Management Accounting* (June 1982), p. 15.

[29]Graham, pp. 25–26.

[30]Murray Weidenbaum, *The Future of Business Regulation* (New York: American Management Associations, 1979), p. 23.

[31] Warne, p. 18.

[32]Weidenbaum, p. 6.

[33]Dow Chemical Company, *Annual Report*, December 31, 1978, p. 1.

[34]*Discussion and Comments on the Major Issues Facing Small Business*, p. 48.

[35]*Ibid.*, p. 46.

[36]Graham, p. 25, quoting Robert E. Berney, chief economist, Small Business Administration.

[37]*Ibid.*, p. 24.

[38]Gilman, Interview with Milton Friedman, p. 21.

[39]"Underground—Many Evade Taxes in America's Flourishing Informal Economy," *The Ann Arbor News*, November 19, 1982, p. A3.

[40]*Ibid.*

[41]"Michigan Not Alone in Struggle to Repay Unemployment Debt," *The Ann Arbor News*, January 12, 1983, p. F1.

[42]Paul W. McCracken, "Reindustrialization of America," *Tax Foundation's Tax Review*, Vol. 42, No. 1 (January 1981), p. 2.

[43]Graham, p. 28.

[44]*Discussion and Comments on the Major Issues Facing Small Business*, p. 4.

[45]*Ibid.*

[46]McCracken, p. 2.

[47]Graham, p. 30.

[48]*Ibid.*

[49]"Small Business Act Will Help the Economy," *The Ann Arbor News*, October 15, 1982, p. 8A.

[50]"What's Wrong with Management?" *Dun's Business Month* (April 1982), p. 48.

[51]*Discussion and Comments on the Major Issues Facing Small Business*, pp. 15–16.

[52]*Ibid.*, p. 17.

[53]*Ibid.*, p. 24.

[54]*Ibid.*, p. 36.

[55]"Coping with the Product Liability Crisis," *Compressed Air Magazine* (November 1977), p. 35.

[56]*Discussion and Comments on the Major Issues Facing Small Business*, p. 12.

Chapter 3

Productivity in Small Businesses: An Empirical Analysis

How is "small" to be defined?

"Small," of course, is a relative concept that depends on the criteria by which it is being judged. For example, a firm with 700 employees is large to a firm with 50 employees and small to a firm with 6,000 employees, if the number of employees is the criterion used to make the judgment. A capital-intensive firm with 50 employees might have total sales of $100 million, while a labor-intensive firm with 700 employees might have total sales of $25 million. If total sales is the criterion used to judge smallness, the 700-employee firm might be considered smaller than the 50-employee firm. Because our reason for concentrating on small businesses is that we feel the factors impacting on their productivity will be easier to establish and document, any firm large enough or complex enough to make this difficult or impossible is "large." We felt the best data for our purposes would be obtained from firms with fewer than 500 employees. Most of these firms produce only one product, probably in one location. In a word, their operations are likely to be simple enough to allow us to trace and observe more reliably the impacts of the causes for productivity declines. Thus we used firms with fewer than 500 employees for accumulating data.

General Observations

Without question, small businesses have suffered during the recession of the past few years. Bankruptcies are at the highest point since the 1930s,[1] rising from 11,742 in 1980 to 31,334 in 1983, a whopping 266.9% increase, as reflected in Figure 3-1, and most of them have been small businesses,[2] as we have defined that term. Although a substantial part of this increase in bankruptcies is attributable to a softening in the law, which reduces the financial consequences and personal stigma attached to bankruptcy,[3] most are

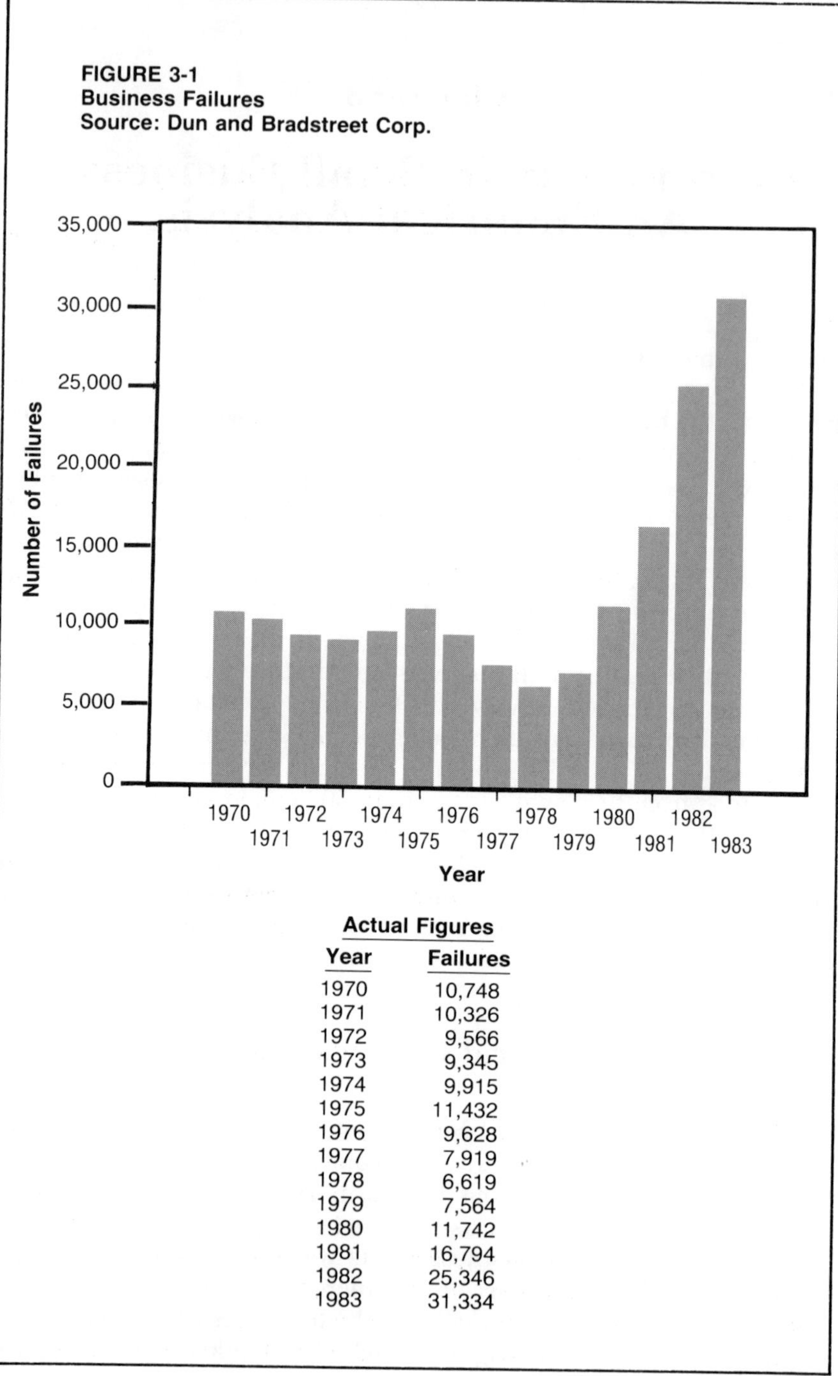

Actual Figures

Year	Failures
1970	10,748
1971	10,326
1972	9,566
1973	9,345
1974	9,915
1975	11,432
1976	9,628
1977	7,919
1978	6,619
1979	7,564
1980	11,742
1981	16,794
1982	25,346
1983	31,334

the result of poor economic conditions, high interest rates,[4] and reactions to those conditions.

In addition to the loss of jobs and reduction in competition brought about by bankruptcies, they reduce credit available to new businesses and to those that have not failed, by tying it up in companies that are not well managed. In other words, bankruptcies result in an inefficient allocation of resources. Many of those filing for bankruptcy could pay a substantial amount of their debt. When they don't, their debts are passed on to other borrowers in the form of higher costs of borrowing and/or decreased credit availability.

> . . . the major effect of bankruptcies is to lower asset values, increase borrowing costs, discourage the banks from lending because their costs of money rise and finally, to depress capital spending. . . . the wave of bankruptcies . . . is intensifying the recession and retarding the recovery. . . .[5]

On the other hand,

> In each business cycle, free-market economists argue, failure guarantees the continuing revitalizing of capitalism because only the fit survive. Long-term secular development—the progress of technology, for example—also requires that some businesses fail, a process economist Joseph Schumpeter labeled creative destruction. . . . It is what capitalism consists in and what every capitalist concern has got to live in.

> Not only are inefficiently managed resources passed on to more efficient managers through failure, . . . but even the shadow of failure falling across an enterprise promotes efficiency.

> Bankruptcy may be healthy even for the victim. . . . If a company reorganizes successfully, it can emerge in better shape than when it went in. This is possible . . . when unproductive assets are sold off and liabilities are restructured.

> . . . one company's bankruptcy can "benefit an industry." For example, Braniff's failure will help raise profits for the remaining airlines. . . . Because the airlines had overexpanded after deregulation, rate wars hurt profitability across-the-board. When Braniff withdrew from the market, excess capacity was reduced, the discounting of fares subsided and load factors on the surviving airlines improved.

> For the economy as a whole, overdevelopment of entire industries must be pruned by failures to keep the economy healthy, the free-market theorists say.[6]

And even though large numbers of businesses are failing, "new

businesses are coming into existence in record numbers, nearly double the pace of even seven years ago. . . . Many of these were created
by persons laid off in other industries who decided to start their own
businesses."[7]

> In any case, the overall general reaction to the recession by managers
> and owners of small businesses has been to reduce employment, reduce
> capital investment, reduce borrowing and spending, reduce previous
> borrowings, and reduce inventories; in a word, to cut operations to
> the bone in order to weather the storm until economic conditions im-
> prove. The game is not just maximizing profitability, but also surviv-
> ing. One advisor to the National Federation of Independent Businesses
> indicated that of the 1,700 [small businesses] that they are in close
> contact with, at least 1,300 verge on bankruptcy[8] [a whopping 77%].

Sources of Empirical Data

In order to obtain empirical data to determine the causes for this
severe situation, we conducted interviews and solicited data through
a questionnaire.

We should emphasize that we present descriptive statistics sum-
marizing our data. Inferential statistical methods are intended for
the testing of hypotheses, which is time-consuming and fairly complex. Most importantly, the use of inferential statistics presupposes
the existence of hypotheses concerning the phenomena under study.
Such techniques could be applied to portions of our data. One could
take, say, one portion of respondents out of the manufacturing classification and, through rigorous statistical analyses, determine
whether its responses differ significantly from those of the manufacturing classification overall. This in itself could be a lengthy research project.

We don't deny that such research would be useful for certain purposes; in fact, we indicated in Chapter 1 that we thought such research should be undertaken. However, such approaches were not
necessary for our purpose—to develop enough valid data to suggest
the general effects of certain factors on productivity in order to draw
conclusions, make recommendations at the policy level, and provide
direction for future research. Descriptive statistics are appropriate
for that purpose. The following statement by a statistician clearly
expresses our approach:

The processes of criminal justice are clearly divided between the search for the evidence—in Anglo-Saxon lands the responsibility of the police and other investigative forces—and the evaluation of the evidence strength—a matter for juries and judges. *In data analysis a similar distinction is helpful. Exploratory data analysis is detective in character. Confirmatory data analysis is judicial or quasi-judicial in character. Only exploratory data analysis will be our subject here.*

Unless the detective finds the clues, judge or jury has nothing to consider. Unless exploratory data analysis uncovers indications, usually quantitative ones, there is likely to be nothing for confirmatory data analysis to consider.

Exploratory data analysis can never be the whole story, but nothing else can serve as the foundation stone—as the first step.[9] [Emphasis added]

Profile of Firms in the Questionnaire Survey

Keep in mind that there are millions of small businesses located throughout the United States. Because of such large numbers of firms, their almost unlimited types and varieties of activities, and cost considerations, which limited the number of questionnaires that could be mailed and analyzed, we concluded that some initial stratification of our sample was necessary. Without such stratification, the number of returns in each category was likely to be too small to be useful.

Although at the time of the survey (late 1981), the U.S. economy in general was in a depressed state, there were areas in the United States in which the economy was booming and others somewhere in between these extremes. Because we were attempting to accumulate data on the impacts certain factors were having on productivity, we felt the data would be more meaningful and useful if we surveyed firms in areas in these different economic settings. Any number of states would have fulfilled these requirements. We selected Michigan (depressed state), Texas (relatively well-off economically at the time of the survey), and Colorado (somewhere in between), because we were familiar with the economies of these states and felt they would fulfill our requirements. (We selected states rather than areas, such as the so-called SunBelt, because states are politically contained areas—that is, many laws and regulations are constrained by state boundaries.) It is important to keep in mind that the survey period was late 1981; by the first quarter of 1983, the situation had begun to reverse.

Lower energy prices and interest rates are fueling a recovery in the automobile and housing industries, but creating a deepening recession in energy and capital goods production.

While industrial and timber regions are beginning to show some signs of recovery, the oil-producing states are on a downward slide that could last several more years.

The two-tier economy that was so apparent during the recession, in which Michigan (autos) suffered while Texas (energy) prospered, has a flip side—Texas goes down as Michigan rebounds.

Despite the industrial recovery, however, it is unlikely that Midwestern states will regain the employment and production levels of the late 1970s.[10]

Working from listings of firms such as Chamber of Commerce membership directories, we selected a sample of 936 firms that we considered representative. We then divided these into seven major categories: construction, manufacturing, wholesale, transportation, retail, financial, and service firms.

Because our basic objective was to develop conclusions and make recommendations to improve productivity, we felt we would get a clearer picture of the causes for declines in productivity if we concentrated on firms in the depressed state. Consequently, we sent two thirds of the questionnaires to firms in Michigan, and approximately half of the remaining one third each to firms in Texas and Colorado.

Having made these decisions, we sent a total of 936 questionnaires to a sample of the stratified firms. Of the total, 156 (17%) went to firms in Texas, 150 (16%) to firms in Colorado, and 630 (67%) to firms in Michigan. We received 203 responses (22%) that were usable for some or all of our analyses. In some cases respondents didn't answer all the questions, or responses to specific questions on a given questionnaire were not usable for a variety of reasons. For example, most firms are not unionized. Therefore, the number responding to questions concerning unions was below the 203 total. Some did not fill in an answer related to an industry, and we therefore could not use it for our industry charts. Therefore, in some instances our statistics are based on fewer than 203 responses.

Of the 203 usable responses received, 65.5% came from Michigan, 19.7% from Texas, and 14.8% from Colorado, so the proportion of responses by state stayed fairly close to the percentage of total questionnaires sent to each. Of these responses, 13.4% came from firms in the construction industry, 40.9% from manufacturing firms, 2.6% from transportation companies, 12.9% from wholesale firms, 14.4%

from retail businesses, 6.4% from financial institutions, and 9.4% from service firms. However, as Figures 3-2 to 3-4 indicate, the industry breakdown was not uniform by state.

Manufacturing is well represented in all three states, but construction is disproportionately higher in Colorado than in Michigan and Texas, retail is highest in Michigan, and wholesale is highest in Texas.

In addition to general demographic data concerning the firms surveyed, the major factors about which to accumulate data were determined on the basis of the findings from our literature search discussed in Chapter 2. These broad factors included unionization, inflation, interest rates, government regulations, and taxes. Each of these was subdivided into a number of specific effects. For example, the impact of unionization was broken down into fringe benefit demands, wage demands, work rules, seniority systems, and time spent on union matters.

As can be seen, there are an almost unlimited number of combinations and permutations possible using these data. We analyzed the data to determine total impact by major factor. For regulations, for example, we determined the effect of all government regulations on all small businesses. We also determined the total impact for firms of each state. In addition, we determined the total specific impacts for each major factor. Again for regulations, we determined the impact on all firms of duplicate requirements, inconsistent requirements, form length, requirement complexity, and unnecessary requirements. We then determined the impact by type of business. Here, for example, we determined the total impact of each specific detrimental effect of regulations, such as duplicate requirements and form length, on construction, manufacturing, wholesale, retail, financial, and service firms.

We attempted few analyses beyond this point—for example, to determine specific impacts of a major factor by industry classification for each state—either because the numbers of responses were too small to support meaningful analysis or because the sheer magnitude of the analysis that would be required was too great.

Profile of Firms Interviewed

We interviewed owners or managers of 23 small businesses in the Houston, Texas, and Detroit, Michigan, areas. Each interview lasted between one and two hours. The firms varied in size from 40 to 275

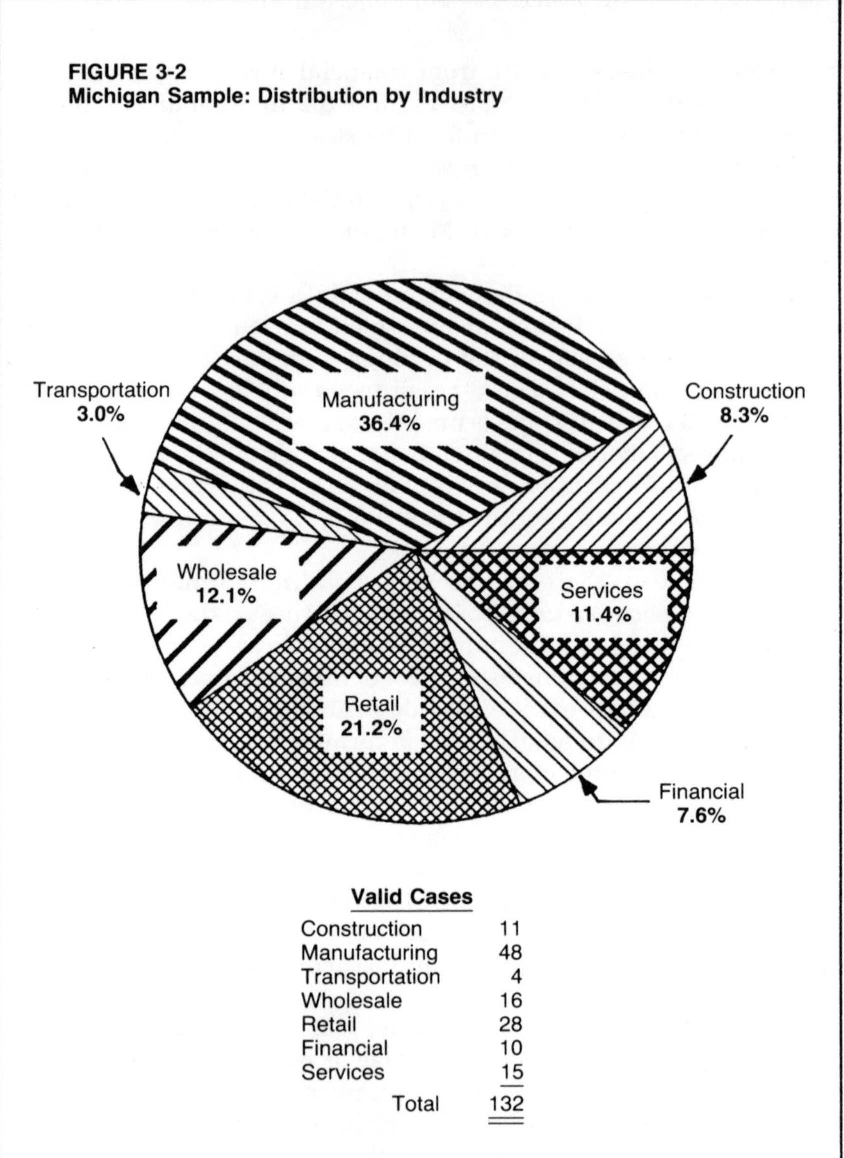

Valid Cases

Construction	11
Manufacturing	48
Transportation	4
Wholesale	16
Retail	28
Financial	10
Services	15
Total	132

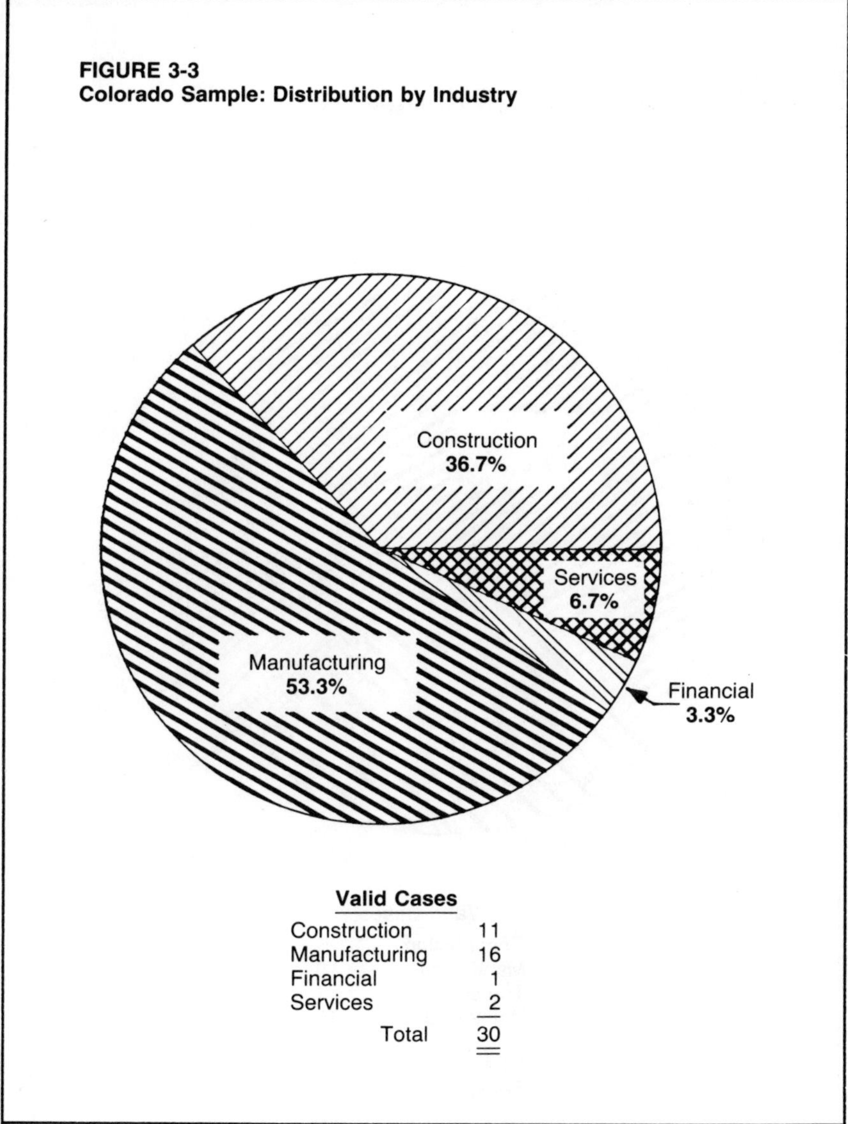

FIGURE 3-3
Colorado Sample: Distribution by Industry

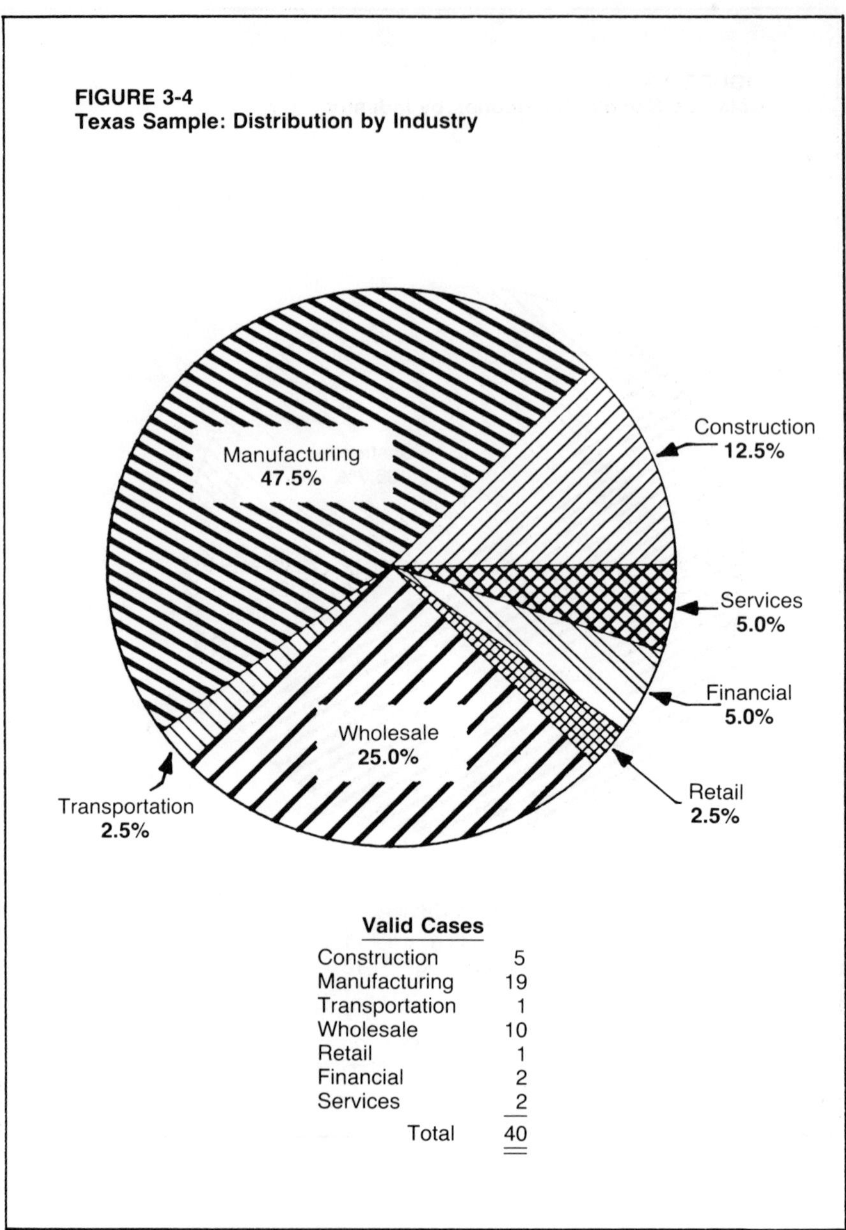

Valid Cases	
Construction	5
Manufacturing	19
Transportation	1
Wholesale	10
Retail	1
Financial	2
Services	2
Total	40

employees; about half of the firms had between 125 and 250 employees. None of the firms in Houston was unionized; eight of fifteen we interviewed in Detroit were unionized.

In Houston, we selected eight firms to cover a variety of activities and industry groupings. One firm was basically an assembler of various types of rotating equipment, such as pumps and separators; another manufactured sheet metal products, such as electrical cabinets; one manufactured pressure control equipment and parts related to oil drilling; another fabricated and distributed heavy pumps and compressors for the petroleum industry; one basically was engaged in producing telephone equipment cabinets; another sold audio and video equipment at both the retail and wholesale levels; another manufactured high-temperature, high-control valves; and one sold tires. One of the firms was 100% dependent on the oil industry; two others depended substantially on the fortunes of the petroleum industry.

We interviewed 15 owners or managers of small businesses in the Detroit metropolitan area. Again, our selection of firms was designed to cover a variety of activities and industries. One firm mainly sold electrical supplies to automotive shops and tested electrical systems to be used in automobiles; another leased, sold, and serviced copiers; one manufacturerd high-precision balls and roller bearings for jet engines; one supplied and installed equipment, such as seats in assembly halls and classrooms for schools; one primarily was engaged in nondestructive testing of parts used in various types of machinery and equipment for industrial and government use; another was a manufacturer and distributor of envelopes. Four firms were tied closely to the automotive industry; three depended heavily on the airline and space industries.

Demographics of Firms in the Survey

Degree of Competition

Generally, small businesses are highly competitive in their industry. Figure 3-5 presents the results to the question: "How would you describe the competition your firm faces in its industry?" Almost two thirds of those responding felt competition was severe, and 95% felt it was moderate or severe.

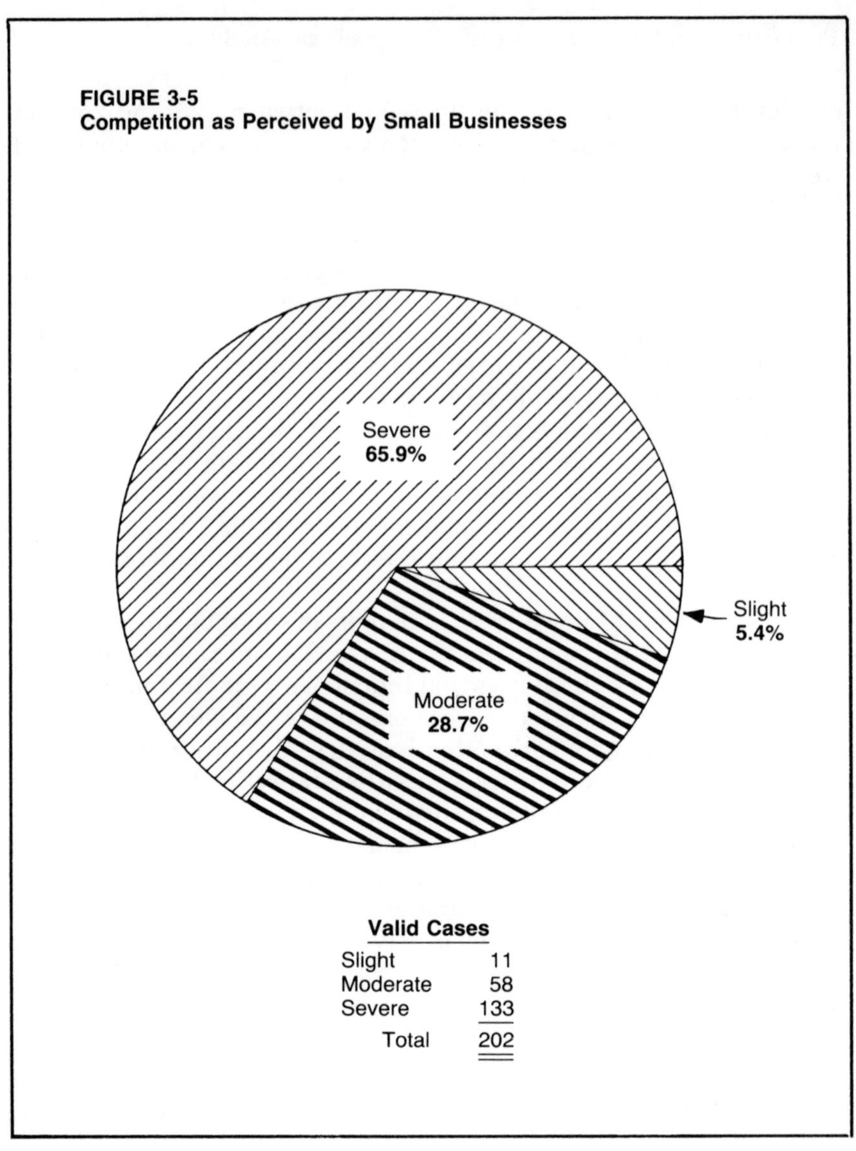

FIGURE 3-5
Competition as Perceived by Small Businesses
Severe
65.9%
Slight
5.4%
Moderate
28.7%
Valid Cases
Slight   11
Moderate   58
Severe   133
Total   202

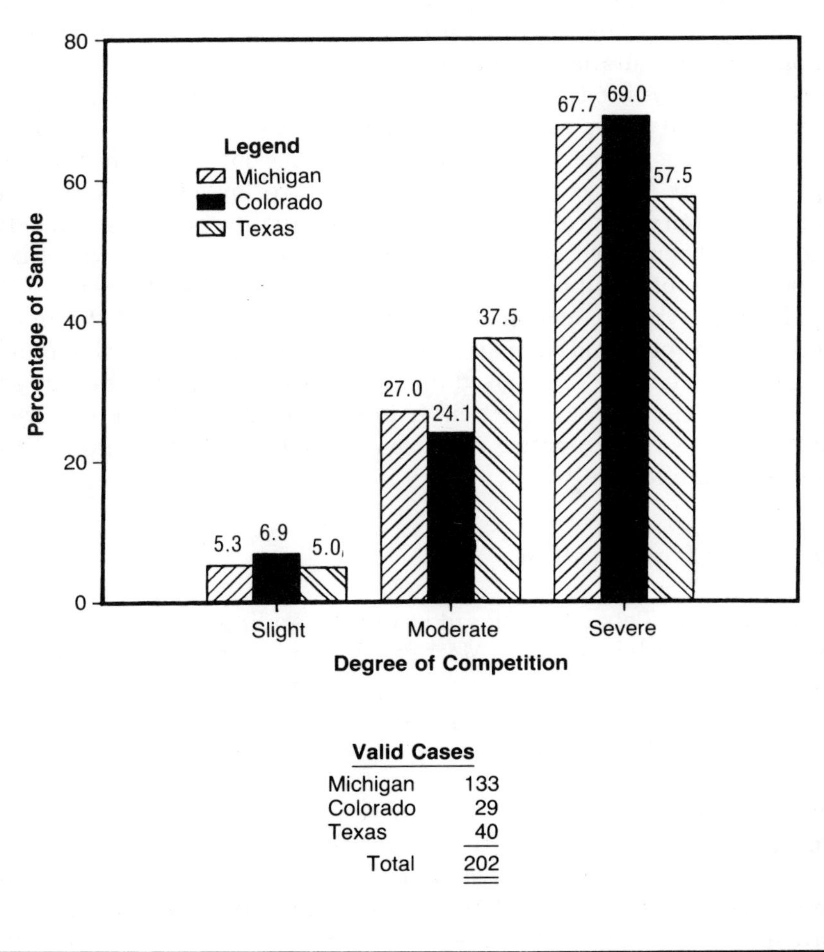

FIGURE 3-6
Competition as Perceived by Small Businesses: Comparison by State

Figure 3-6 (p. 55) indicates that the specific results on perceived competition by states were not substantially different from the general results. Also, as Texas was disproportionately high in wholesale firms, Colorado in construction firms, and Michigan in retail businesses, competition in all industry segments appears high.

These results were not unexpected. Many small businesses fit into the classical definition of pure, if not perfect, competition. Often there are many competitors within a relatively small geographical area supplying very similar—even identical—products and services. Historically, entry into the area of activity has been easy, although this is not the case under current conditions. Most firms have reasonable knowledge about the market they serve. Price cutting is often widespread under such conditions, and firms are forced to operate on relatively narrow profit margins. "Price cutting is widespread. It has never been more pervasive in the history of the . . . survey. Sixteen percent of small businesses reported lower selling prices. . . ."[11]

However, these conclusions are not universal. Some of the most successful owners and managers we interviewed are those who found or developed a niche and moved into it. They determined or developed a market demand for a particular product or service and acquired or developed the expertise necessary to satisfy that demand efficiently and effectively.

Degree of Unionization

The data in Table 3-1 will aid in understanding our statistics and analyses regarding unions. Most small firms are not unionized. In answer to the question, "Is your firm unionized?" we obtained the results shown in Figure 3-7. By state, there are some important differences, as Figure 3-8 reflects. Because of Michigan's reputation as a big labor state, we expected it to be more heavily unionized than the chart reflects. We probably found less unionization than expected because such a large percentage of the firms included in the survey are in the retail industry, which Table 3-1 shows is not unionized to the same degree as construction and manufacturing. Given this, Michigan firms are still somewhat more unionized than those in Colorado; the difference would have been greater except for the higher proportion of manufacturing and construction firms in the Colorado survey than in Michigan—industries much more unionized than retail, wholesale, service, and financial industries, as reflected in Table 3-1. Michigan also is unionized to a much greater degree

Table 3–1
Employed Wage and Salary Workers
in Labor Organizations, by Industry

Industry		Workers Unionized, %
Retail		9.8
Wholesale		11.4
Manufacturing		32.3
Construction		31.6
Service		18.9
Financial		1.6
Transportation	Railroads	81.8
	Other Transportation	42.1

Source: Bureau of Labor Statistics, *Earnings and Other Characteristics of Organized Workers,* Bulletin 2105 (May 1980), pp. 59–60.

than Texas. Texas is substantially unionized only in the trades— carpentry, plumbing, electrical.

Size of Responding Firms

Figure 3-9 presents data regarding the size of the responding firms. To the question "During the past three years, have the firm's gross sales increased, stayed the same, or decreased?" 61.5% indicated that gross sales had increased, 10.0% that they had stayed the same, and 28.5% that they had decreased. For those firms that reported that gross sales had changed, Figure 3-10 shows the percentage of those changes.

Although at first glance the increases in gross sales look impressive, keep in mind that inflation was running at 10 to 14% during most of the period from mid-1979 through mid-1982. Therefore, in order for a firm to maintain a constant level of gross sales in terms of dollars of constant purchasing power, gross sales would have had to increase by approximately 35% in nominal dollars. On that basis, only 26 out of 143 firms showing increases, or 18.2%, showed *real* increases in gross sales during the period. And, perhaps more important, *real* decreases were much more substantial than is indicated by nominal dollar figures. On average, therefore, small businesses have not been able to increase selling prices enough to offset the decrease in the purchasing power of the dollar; selling prices have not kept up with inflation.

Figure 3-11 reflects the total debt of responding firms as of the date of the latest balance sheet. Although we did not ask for point

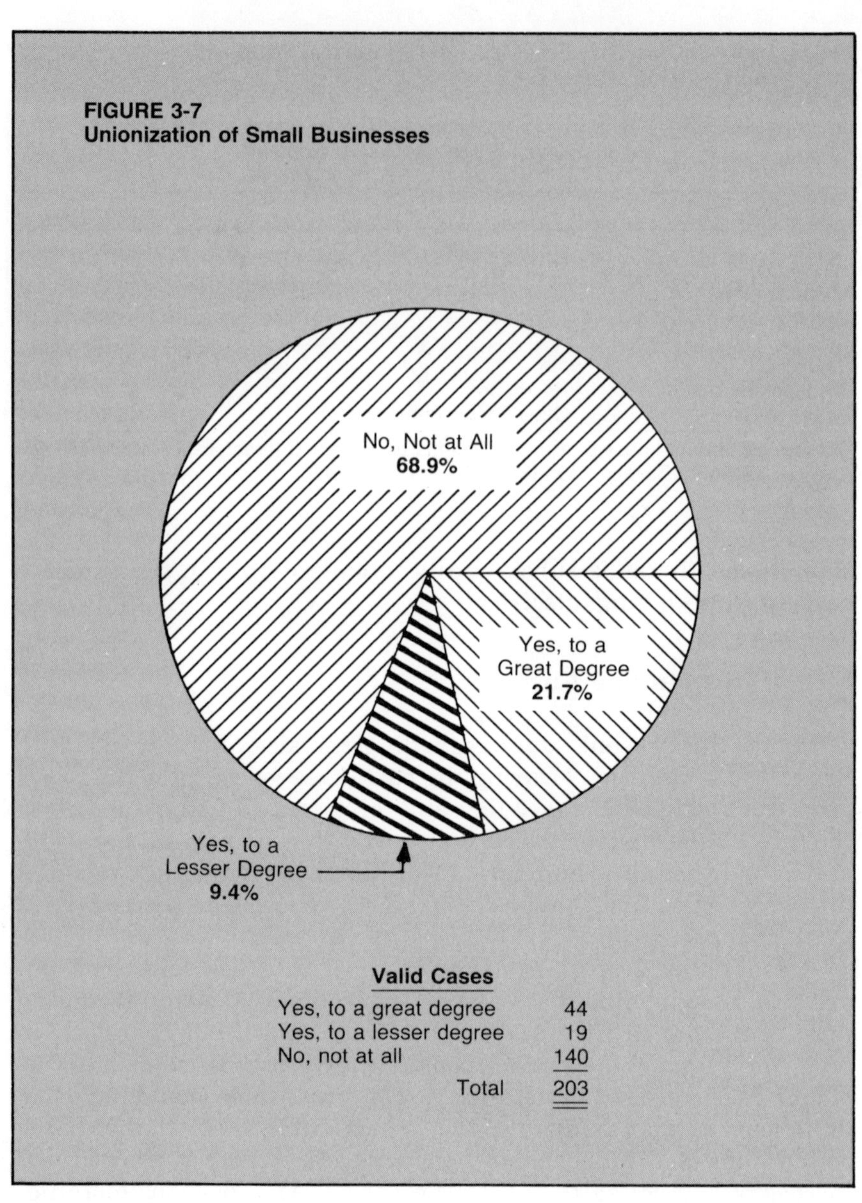

FIGURE 3-7
Unionization of Small Businesses
No, Not at All
68.9%
Yes, to a
Great Degree
21.7%
Yes, to a
Lesser Degree
9.4%
Valid Cases
Yes, to a great degree 44
Yes, to a lesser degree 19
No, not at all 140
Total 203

FIGURE 3-8
Unionization of Small Businesses: Comparison by State

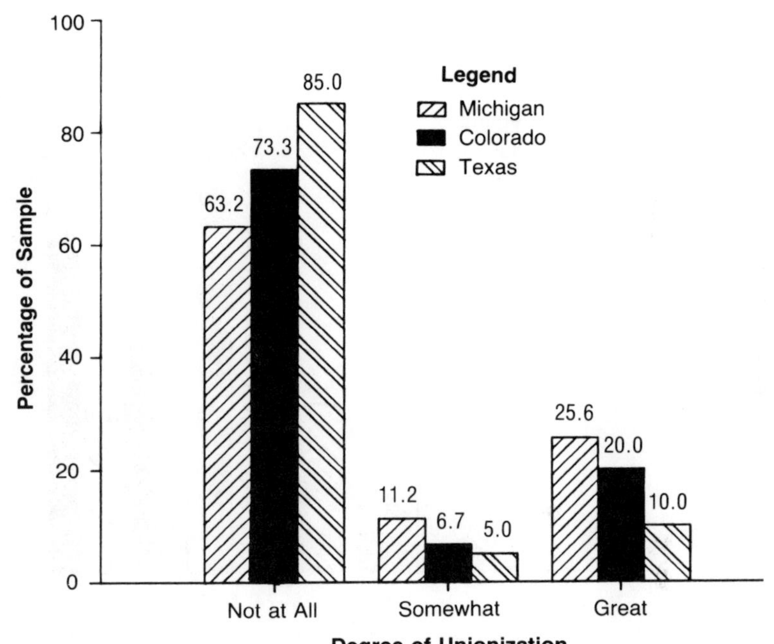

100
80
60
40
20
0
Percentage of Sample
Legend
Michigan
Colorado
Texas
85.0
73.3
63.2
11.2
6.7
5.0
25.6
20.0
10.0
Not at All
Somewhat
Great
Degree of Unionization
Valid Cases
Michigan   133
Colorado   30
Texas   40
Total   203

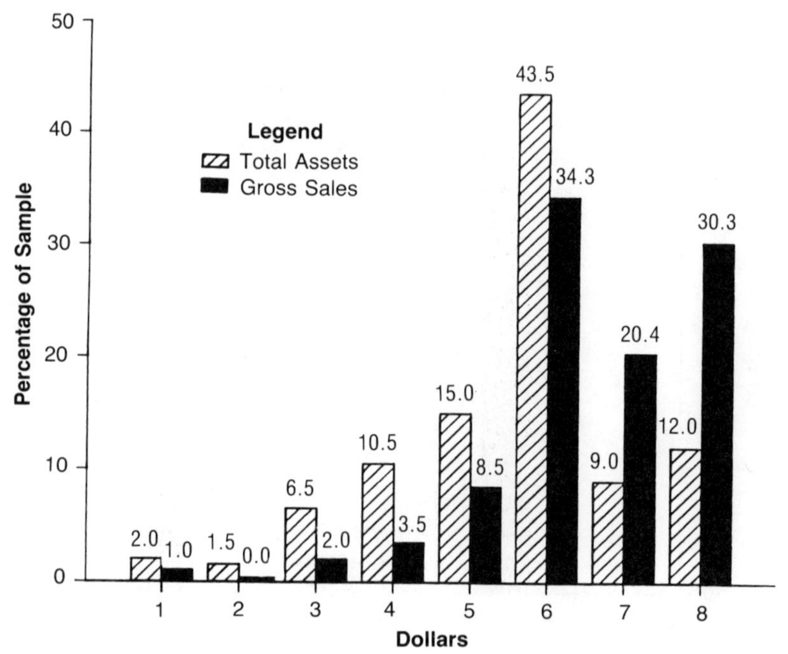

	Dollar Amount Key	Valid Cases Assets	Valid Cases Sales
1 =	Under $50,000	4	2
2 =	$50,000 to $99,000	3	2
3 =	$100,000 to $249,000	13	2
4 =	$250,000 to $499,000	21	7
5 =	$500,000 to $999,000	30	17
6 =	$1,000,000 to $4,999,000	87	69
7 =	$5,000,000 to $10,000,000	18	41
8 =	Over $10,000,000	24	61
		200	201

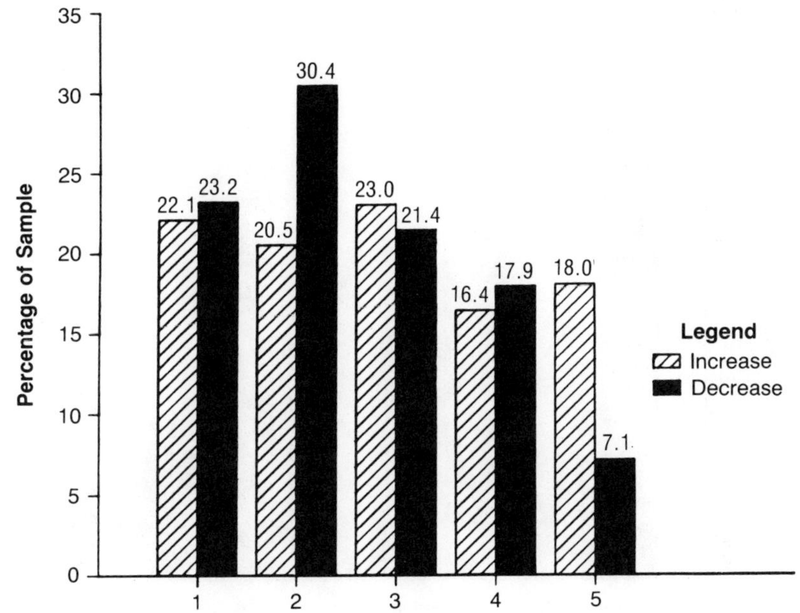

		Valid Cases	
Change in Gross Sales Key		Increase	Decrease
1 = 1–10%		27	13
2 = 11–20%		25	17
3 = 21–30%		28	12
4 = 31–50%		20	10
5 = Over 50%		22	4
	Total	122	56

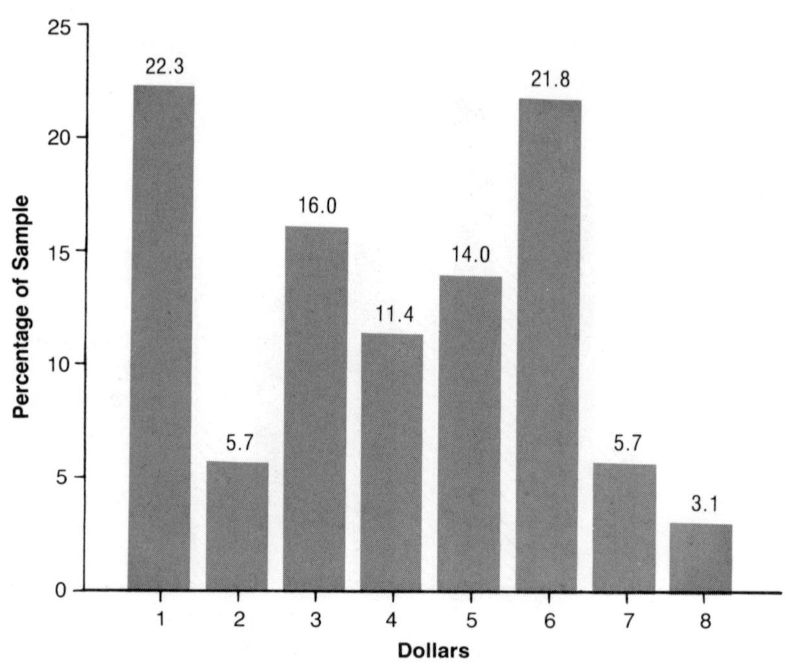

Dollar Amount Key	Valid Cases
1 = Under $50,000	43
2 = $50,000 to $99,000	11
3 = $100,000 to $249,000	31
4 = $250,000 to $499,000	22
5 = $500,000 to $999,000	27
6 = $1,000,000 to $4,999,000	42
7 = $5,000,000 to $10,000,000	11
8 = Over $10,000,000	6
Total	193

values for total assets and total debt (we used the ranges indicated), 10 firms (4.9%) indicated that their total debt exceeded their total assets, and 46 firms (22.7%) indicated that total assets were about equal to or somewhat greater than total debt. Thus some 28% of the responding small businesses are insolvent, or nearly so. An additional 27.9% said that their debt-to-asset ratios were very high. Together, these figures indicate that a substantial percentage of small firms have a very small cushion of owner's equity, if any, to fall back on. And as much of the debt in small businesses is of a fairly short-term nature, while a major portion of total assets are noncurrent (particularly for the construction and manufacturing firms), many firms are illiquid.

As long as the cash flow from operations remains sufficient and stable enough to pay the obligations as they come due or to act as a financial foundation for refinancing the debt, this situation is tolerable. In fact, during good economic times many small businesses operate on the assumption that short-term debt will be refinanced continuously to some degree or another, and to that extent will act, in effect, as more or less permanent capitalization for the firm.

However, when sales drop, or at least do not increase in real terms; when interest costs and other out-of-pocket expenses increase, at times more rapidly than the general inflation rate; and when the cash flow from operations decreases substantially, as has happened generally during the past three years, it becomes difficult to pay the debt. Even when refinancing is possible (and often it is not), it must be done at a continuously increasing cost, because of the higher-risk premiums firms must pay.

To survive under such conditions, firms often make up the short-fall in cash by liquidating receivables, inventories, and other assets, and by cutting back on the number of employees, reducing salaries and wages, and otherwise reducing operations requiring cash out-flows. Many small businesses, which often are not highly liquid even in the best of times, do not have the buffer to weather a depression without cutting back operations substantially, and sometimes not even then, as we have indicated. Our data indicate that there is a tendency for firms with fewer than 100 employees to have higher debt-to-asset ratios and to be less liquid than those with 100 to 499 employees, although the evidence is not conclusive. Generally, the breakdowns of firms by total assets for Michigan and Colorado were similar (although the variations in observations for Michigan are somewhat higher), but Texas firms in the sample tended to be considerably larger in terms of total assets, as the data in Figure 3-12 indicate.

Comparisons of the total debt to total assets of firms by states reflect percentages almost identical to those previously stated. Considering that the economy in Texas was relatively strong while Michigan was in a recession during the period covered, this supports the conclusion that small businesses typically carry a high debt-to-asset ratio in any economy. In good times they turn over the debt and use it as a portion of the "permanent" capitalization of the firm. In bad times they reduce debt by liquidating assets and reducing operations or they go out of business.

Changes in Productivity

In the face of generally severe productivity declines during the past decade, one might expect that the period 1979–1982 (the most difficult of the decade) would show a precipitous decline in productivity in small businesses. At first glance, it appears that this was not the case. In answer to the question "Over the past three years, has your firm's productivity decreased significantly, decreased slightly, stayed the same, increased slightly, or increased significantly?" we received the answers illustrated in Figure 3-13. More than 52% of the firms indicated that productivity increased, and 16.8% said the increase was significant. Only 29.9% indicated a decrease, which was perceived by 9.1% to be significant. Although there was some variation between close categories on the ordinal scale for the different states, on balance the results by state paralleled the general results fairly closely, as shown in Figure 3-14.

To understand these results, one must keep in mind that we dealt with survivors; we did not include in our survey firms that had gone bankrupt or had ceased operations for other reasons.[12] Had a representative sample of such firms been included, undoubtedly productivity would have shown a substantial decrease during the period 1979 through mid-1982.

Those answering the questionnaire are those who, to that point, had been able to take the actions necessary to prevent collapse. They offset—at least to the extent necessary to survive—the cash flow problems generated by decreases in sales and in the selling prices of their products and services and increases in labor costs, interest rates, and other costs, by liquidating receivables and inventories,

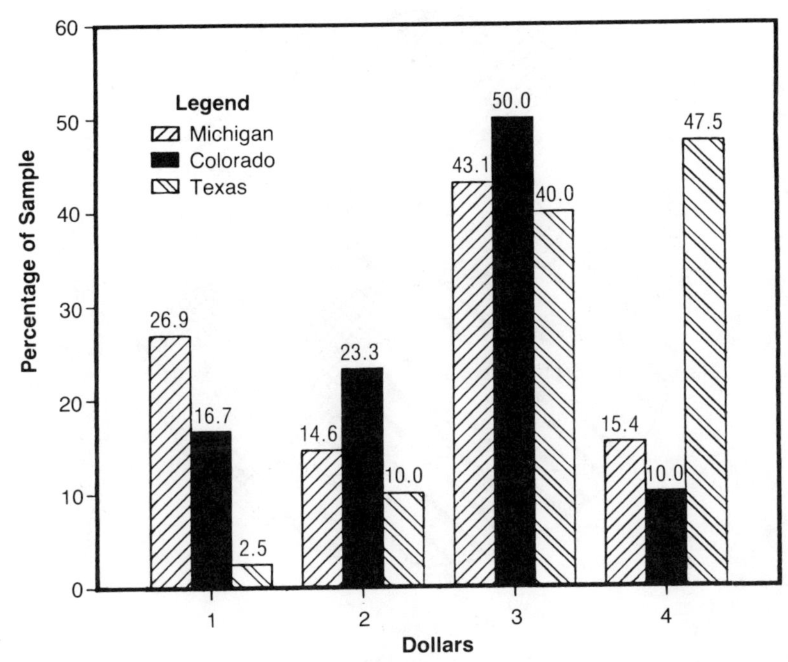

Dollar Amount Key	Valid Cases			
	Michigan	**Colorado**	**Texas**	**Totals**
1 = Under $500,000	4	5	1	10
2 = $500,000 to $999,000	50	7	4	61
3 = $1,000,000 to $5,000,000	56	15	16	87
4 = Over $5,000,000	20	3	19	42
Totals	130	30	40	200

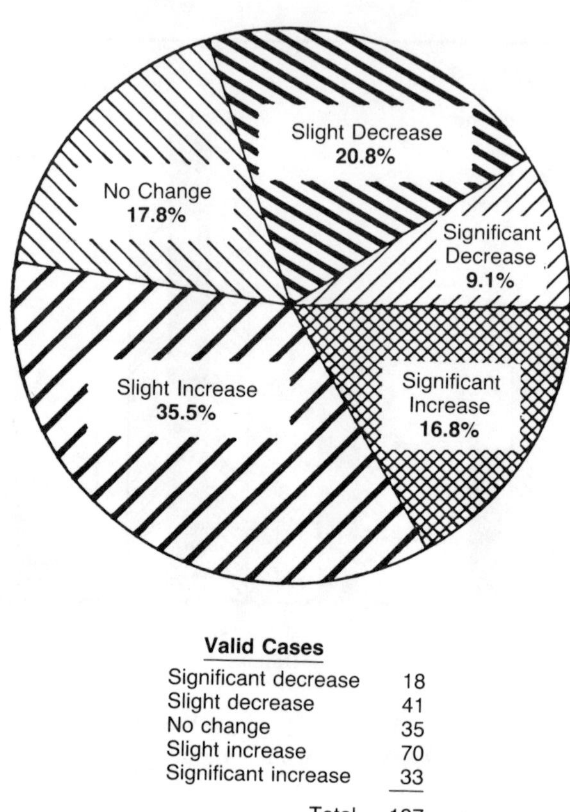

Valid Cases

Significant decrease	18
Slight decrease	41
No change	35
Slight increase	70
Significant increase	33
Total	197

FIGURE 3-14
Change in Productivity: Comparison by State

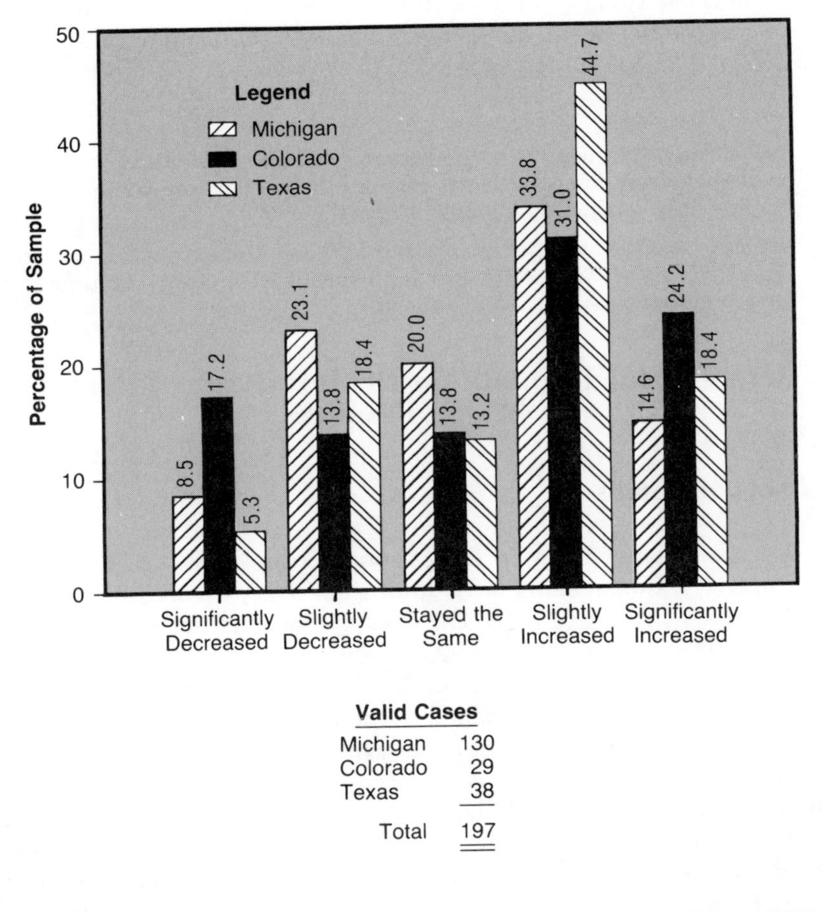

Percentage of Sample
50
40
30
20
10
0
Legend
Michigan
Colorado
Texas
8.5
17.2
5.3
23.1
13.8
18.4
20.0
13.8
13.2
33.8
31.0
44.7
14.6
24.2
18.4
Significantly Decreased
Slightly Decreased
Stayed the Same
Slightly Increased
Significantly Increased
Valid Cases
Michigan   130
Colorado   29
Texas   38
Total   197

cutting employment, and increasing the productivity of the labor force that remained. As Professor Dunkelberg stated, "They're holding garage sales to keep from going out of business. Many of these actions resulted in lower breakeven points for these firms, and most are reflected in increased productivity."[13]

Thus, even though economic conditions are bad—or perhaps partially because this is true—small businesses have been forced to become more efficient in their operations just to survive; this should provide a firm base when expansion of the economy ultimately takes place.

> One of the bright aspects of the generally bleak small-business scene . . . is that many companies have lowered their breakeven points. That is, they have learned to manage more efficiently.
>
> In fact, . . . companies that have survived these most extreme economic conditions since the Great Depression constitute a strong, lean force for promoting the eventual expansion.[14]

Detrimental Impacts on Productivity of Certain Major Factors

Effects of Unions

Another focus of this investigation was the impact of unions on productivity. Considering only unionized firms, we obtained the results shown in Figure 3-15. On average, unions are seen as moderately detrimental, with 67.2% viewing them as moderately to highly detrimental and 32.8% indicating no impact or only a slight one. Interestingly, no respondent to the questionnaire indicated that unions have any beneficial impacts. During our personal interviews we found one case, under special circumstances, in which union influence was felt to be beneficial. Many of the employees had been with that firm for a long time and had become like family members to the owner, who found it difficult to establish and enforce work rules because of these close personal ties. When his firm became unionized, the union, with his input, established some discipline. He felt productivity increased as a result, at least initially.

Comparing the overall changes in productivity with the changes in firms that are unionized, we obtained the results shown in Table 3-2. We observe important differences when the results in Table 3-2 dealing with overall changes in productivity are compared.

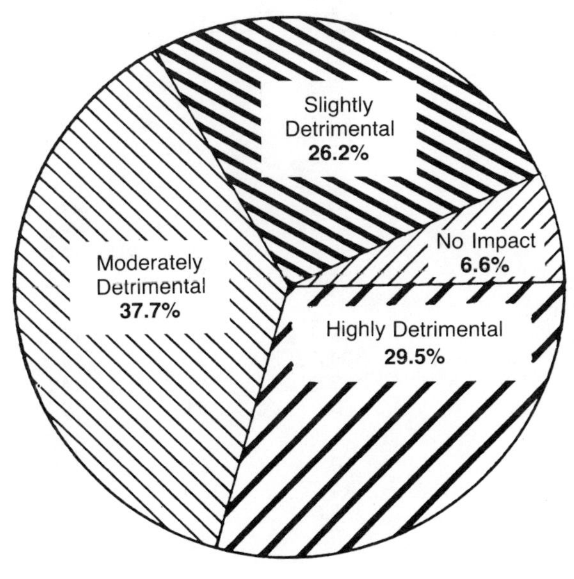

Valid Cases

Highly detrimental	18
Moderately detrimental	23
Slightly detrimental	16
No impact	4
Total	61

Table 3–2
Productivity Changes Related to Degree of Unionization

Count Change in Productivity	Degree of Unionization			
	Yes, to a Great Extent 1.	Yes, to a Lesser Extent 2.	No, Not at All 3.	Row Total
1. Decreased Significantly				
Count	3*	2	13	18
Row, %	16.7**	11.1	72.2	9.1
Column, %	7.1***	10.5	9.6	
Total, %	1.5****	1.0	6.6	
2. Decreased Slightly				
Count	15	2	24	41
Row, %	36.6	4.9	58.5	20.8
Column, %	35.7	10.5	17.6	
Total, %	7.6	1.0	12.2	
3. Stayed the Same				
Count	12	4	19	35
Row, %	34.3	11.4	54.3	17.8
Column, %	28.6	21.1	14.0	
Total, %	6.1	2.0	9.6	
4. Increased Slightly				
Count	10	8	52	70
Row, %	14.3	11.4	74.3	35.5
Column, %	23.8	42.1	38.2	
Total, %	5.1	4.1	26.4	
5. Increased Significantly				
Count	2	3	28	33
Row, %	6.1	9.1	84.8	16.8
Column, %	4.8	15.8	20.6	
Total, %	1.0	1.5	14.2	
Column Count	42	19	136	197
Total, %	21.3	9.6	69.0	100.0

  * Count is the number of observations.
  **16.7 of the 18
 ***7.1 of the 42
****1.5% of the total 197 observations

Whereas productivity increased for 52.3% of the firms and decreased for 29.1% of the firms overall, productivity increases and decreases for unionized firms were as follows:

    A. Firms Unionized to a Great Extent (21.3% of respondents).
       1. Only 28.6% indicated productivity had increased.
       2. 42.8% indicated productivity had decreased.

B. Firms Unionized to a Lesser Extent (9.6% of respondents).
   1. 57.9% indicated productivity had increased.
   2. 21.0% indicated productivity had decreased.

C. Firms Not Unionized at All (69.0% of respondents).
   1. 58.8% indicated productivity had increased.
   2. 27.2% indicated productivity had decreased.

These statistics indicate that unions had a slight to moderate negative impact on productivity overall and, more importantly, that productivity *increases* generally were substantially less in unionized firms than in nonunionized firms. There were no important differences between states regarding changes in productivity as influenced by unions.

We asked about specific detrimental impacts of unions, and received answers as reflected in Figure 3-16. All specific effects were seen to be more than slightly detrimental, with wage and fringe benefit demands being the most detrimental (between moderately and highly detrimental). The effects of union work rules and seniority systems are important, but somewhat less so, while time spent on union matters, on average, was felt to be only little more than slightly detrimental.

As Figure 3-17 shows, the specific type of impact by state follows the same general overall pattern reflected in Figure 3-16, except that Texas and Colorado firms felt that time spent on union matters had a slightly more detrimental effect than union seniority systems, a slight difference from the overall pattern. In every case except wage demands, Colorado felt the specific impacts of unionization less severely than Texas or Michigan. In every category except time spent on union matters, Michigan felt the impact more severely than Colorado and Texas. Michigan's plight is indicated in the following:

High wages and generous workers' compensation outlays deter new businesses from moving into the state [Michigan], says a comprehensive new University of Michigan report on the state's economic and fiscal health.

. . . At the same time, lawmakers need to be concerned with the high labor costs, accounting for 70 percent of business expenditures. This, said the report, "is a major determinant of the state's competitive position."

Part of that high cost goes for unemployment insurance and workers' compensation benefits. Some of these costs can be controlled by the government [and] . . . reform is called for.

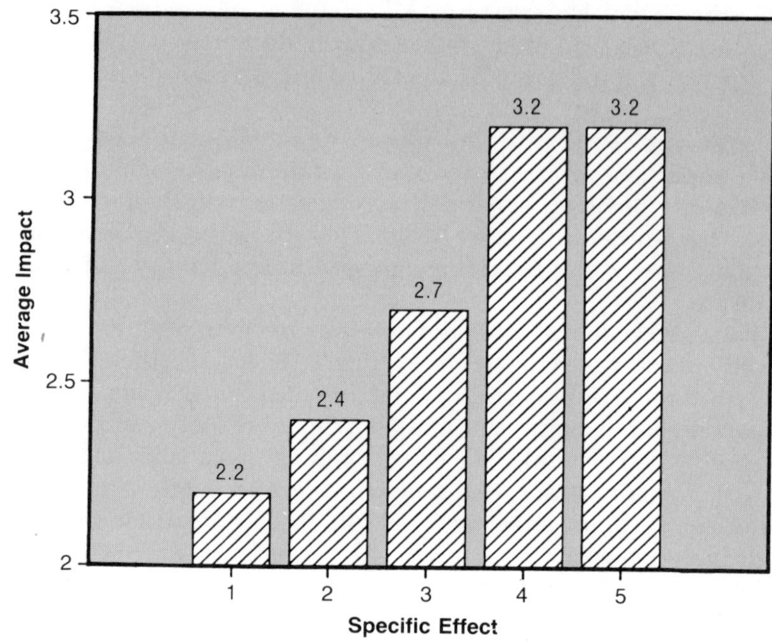

Average Impact Key

1 = No impact
2 = Slightly detrimental
3 = Moderately detrimental
4 = Highly detrimental

Specific Effect Key

1 = Time spent on union-related matters
2 = Seniority systems
3 = Work rules
4 = Wage demands
5 = Fringe benefit demands

Valid Cases

Time spent on union-related matters	61
Seniority systems	62
Work rules	62
Wage demands	62
Fringe benefit demands	62

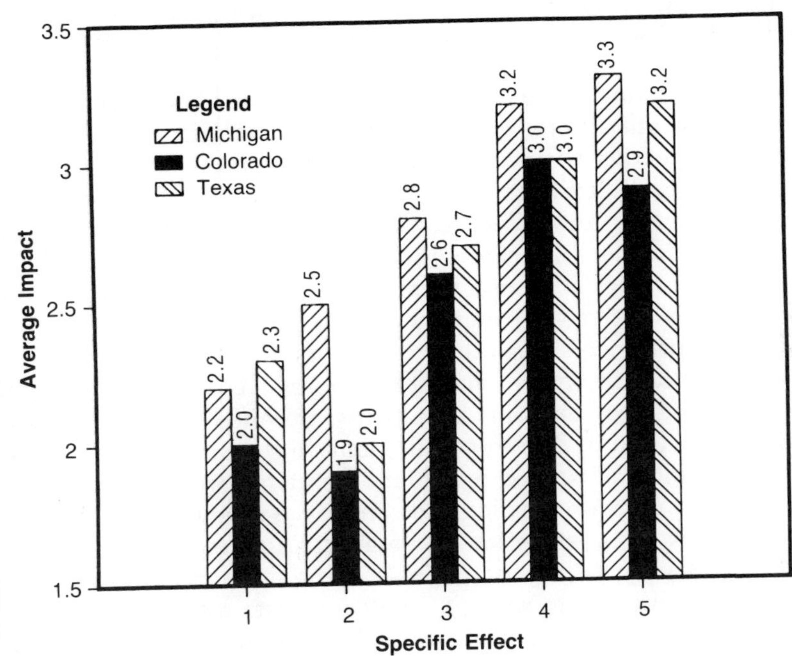

Average Impact Key

1 = No impact
2 = Slightly detrimental
3 = Moderately detrimental
4 = Highly detrimental

Specific Effect Key

1 = Time spent on union-related matters
2 = Seniority systems
3 = Work rules
4 = Wage demands
5 = Fringe benefit demands

Valid Cases

Michigan   48
Colorado   8
Texas   6
TOTAL   62

. . . But because of the high labor costs, the state may face a difficult
choice. . . . A high wage structure—25 or 30 percent above the national
average in manufacturing—will mean a continued high risk of unemployment and slow growth. . . . A low wage structure would mean
a low risk of unemployment and rapid growth.[15]

When we compared specific impacts by industry groups (Figure
3-18), significant differences emerged. (Financial firms are excluded
because not one of the respondents was unionized; the service industry was excluded because we received too few responses to be
regarded as important.) Wholesale and retail firms are affected more
severely by the more direct and immediate impacts of unions—wage
and fringe benefit demands—because such firms generally are in a
stronger competitive environment, which makes it more difficult to
pass along such increases to their customers. Furthermore, they tend
to be more labor-intensive, so that total employee costs are a higher
percentage of total costs in these firms. Because workers in these
industries tend to be more unskilled and to turn over more rapidly
than those in construction and manufacturing, we were surprised
to find that union work rules and seniority systems affect them as
much as they do construction and manufacturing.

Manufacturing and construction, on the other hand, tend to be
more capital-intensive, so that employee costs are a smaller percentage of their total operating costs. More of these firms are likely
to be able to pass price increases along to their consumers, particularly where they have carved out a niche for themselves and consequently do not have much competition, where the government is
an important customer, or where (in the case of some manufacturers)
they are producing a product that is to become a component of another product and its price is a relatively small part of the total cost
of the final product.

In construction and manufacturing one person can often perform
more than one task: for example, maintaining and making minor
repairs as well as operating machinery or equipment; operating more
than one machine or piece of equipment, particularly where they
are used at different times; or working in lower-skilled areas when
there are temporary shutdowns. Union work rules frequently prevent
such dual uses of the labor force and therefore generally have a more
severe impact in those areas than in wholesale and retail firms. And
seniority systems frequently prevent the use of the most competent,
and often lower-paid, individual, leading to higher costs and reduced
productivity, particularly in highly skilled functions.

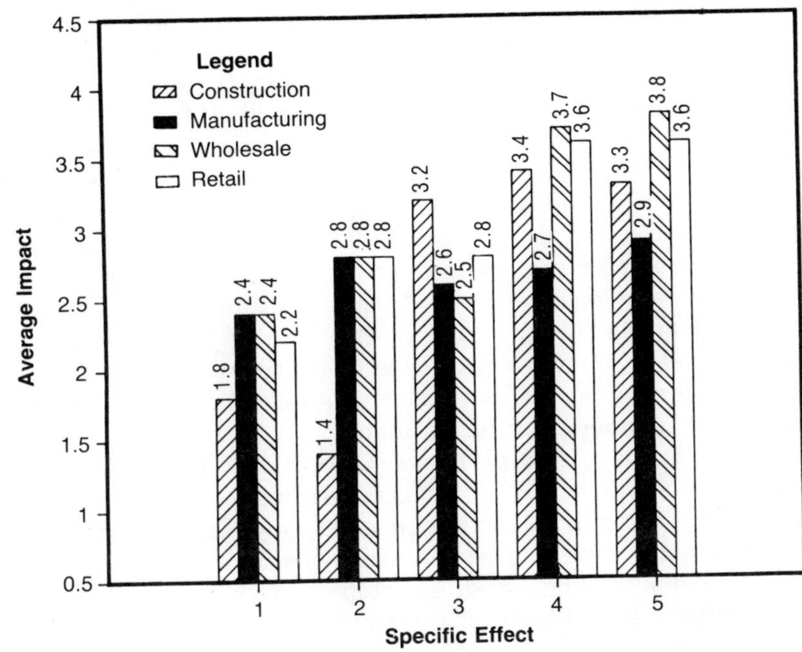

Average Impact Key

1 = No impact
2 = Slightly detrimental
3 = Moderately detrimental
4 = Highly detrimental

Specific Effect Key

1 = Time spent on union-related matters
2 = Seniority systems
3 = Work rules
4 = Wage demands
5 = Fringe benefit demands

Valid Cases

Construction	17
Manufacturing	23
Wholesale	13
Retail	5
TOTAL	58

Most of our interviewees from unionized firms mentioned this lack of flexibility in using workers due to union rules as having an important detrimental impact on productivity. On the other side, a number of those in nonunionized firms indicated they could make more effective and efficient use of their workers because the workers could perform more than one function or do more than one job. One stated that he had stopped hiring workers laid off from automobile assembly plants because those he had hired didn't work out: they were either unable or unwilling to adjust to a more flexible work environment after their previous experiences under union control. As one would expect, firms in the Houston area gave a substantial amount of credit for their success to the fact that they are not unionized. One stated that success depended primarily on hard work, which in turn depends primarily on the right mental attitude—the work ethic—and unions are antithetical to this mental attitude.

We asked respondents how frequently over the past three years their firms' suppliers have been unable to meet delivery schedules because of union-related problems. On average, it happened only occasionally and, when it did happen, the impact was only slightly detrimental. Keep in mind that these are averaged responses. As respondents and interviewees indicated, the impact on a particular firm can be devastating, slowing or stopping production or construction and making it difficult or impossible to meet deadlines agreed on with their customers. All of these things translate into decreased productivity and increased costs for the firm, which often cannot be passed on to the customers.

When economic conditions during the period covered are considered, the detrimental impact of unions on productivity is more important. Under depressed conditions, the influence of unions tends to decrease. In answer to the question "As economic conditions worsened, did the union's influence decrease, stay the same, or increase?" 39.3% indicated a decrease, 50.8% indicated no change, and 9.8% indicated an increase in influence. By state, union influence decreased slightly more in Colorado and Michigan than in Texas, but the differences are minor. By industrial classification, union influence decreased substantially more in retail and wholesale operations than in manufacturing and construction. (The number of unionized financial and service firms that responded was too small to be useful in the analysis.) Because retail and wholesale firms tend on average to be smaller than construction and manufacturing firms, they are likely to receive less attention from union representatives. More importantly, workers tend to be less skilled and more easily replaceable than in construction and manufacturing.

When profits fall, firms reduce production and sales, and unemployment increases. Unions are less successful in obtaining wage and fringe benefit increases and work slowdown agreements and often, in fact, are forced into making various wage and work-rule concessions. During such times, job security becomes the overriding consideration, and the productivity of the remaining workers often increases. If, under such conditions, the overall impact of unions is a slight to moderate decrease in productivity, the impact during prosperous times, when unions do have considerable influence, is likely to be even more detrimental.

Some of our responses from interviewees are interesting. One felt that high wages and fringe benefits were not the major detrimental effect of unions. The major problem he saw was in union rules, mainly those dealing with seniority, which limits the ability of supervisors to discipline employees, to advance those doing outstanding work, and to demote those who aren't, all of which adversely affects productivity. He also felt that union officials are out of touch with reality in that they represent the 30% or so of radical employees who make unrealistic, unjustifiable demands, rather than the 70% or so whose demands are realistic.

A quotation from an unsolicited letter we received summarizes the feelings of many of those we interviewed:

> Most compensation programs have no direct tie to productivity. Productive and unproductive workers are many times paid as a class rather than on individual results. Why should a worker work hard for results when he doesn't have to, and if he does he won't receive any extra compensation. Many workers that don't show up on the job at all are, in fact, paid. Under these circumstances the *unproductive* are *rewarded* and the productive are not. The trend in productivity is, therefore, downward.

> Union leadership, in order to keep control of their members, has convinced their members that business would not take care of them if it were not for the union. Union leaders have convinced their membership that they must act as a group and not as individuals if they are going to have power. The workers are paid based on a negotiated contract that has nothing to do with productivity. The worker knows that he has job security because of the union. He also knows that if he works harder that there will be no additional reward based on his extra productivity. He may, in fact, get harassed by union leadership if he tries to produce too much because it makes other workers look bad. Here again the unproductive are rewarded and the productive are not.

Inflation and Small Businesses

Inflation is considered by small businesses to be a severe problem, as indicated in Figure 3-19. Of the 88% of the respondents who felt inflation had a detrimental effect on their firms, a little over 38% felt the impact to be highly detrimental, about 31% said inflation had a moderate effect, and 18% indicated a slight impact. When we consider the overall effects of inflation by states (see Figure 3-20), these results are not substantially different from the general results, although there are some differences in perceived severity between close categories on the ordinal scale.

Interestingly, nearly 8.5% of the respondents indicated that inflation had had beneficial effects on their firms. They felt that their firms had become more cost conscious, controlled costs better, and had better inventory control; that inflation had encouraged their firms to concentrate more on improving worker productivity; and that it had helped to improve their cash flow procedures. In a few cases, they felt that the increased cost of investment helped keep competitors out of the market.

Figure 3-21 shows the specific detrimental effects of inflation on all small businesses in the three states sampled or surveyed, while Figure 3-22 reflects the breakdown by state.

The 3.6 average level of impact for "increases risk and uncertainty" indicates that small businesses generally are affected by inflation, regardless of their nature or size (within the size limitation as defined). The ultimate effect of a decrease in the purchasing power of the dollar is that consumers' selectivity increases and they buy less, especially in the luxury or nonessential categories of goods and services. People change their consumption patterns. They eat at restaurants less often, buy fewer household goods and clothes, and shift from more expensive to less expensive goods and services. These changes are felt first by retail firms and are then communicated through wholesale firms to manufacturers (note the 3.2 average for "increases customer selectivity"). All these factors and others create a general atmosphere of increased risk and uncertainty. Important parts of this scenario are the inability to pass price increases on to customers (3.1) and the inability to make timely collections from customers who buy on credit (3.0).

Nor is it surprising that "higher wages and salaries" was at or near the top of the rankings of the detrimental effects of inflation. During periods of persistently high inflation rates, people develop

FIGURE 3-19
Effect of Inflation on Small Businesses

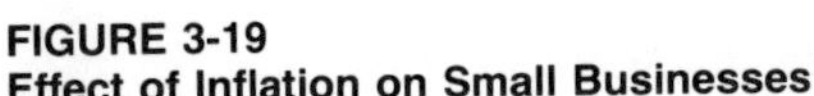

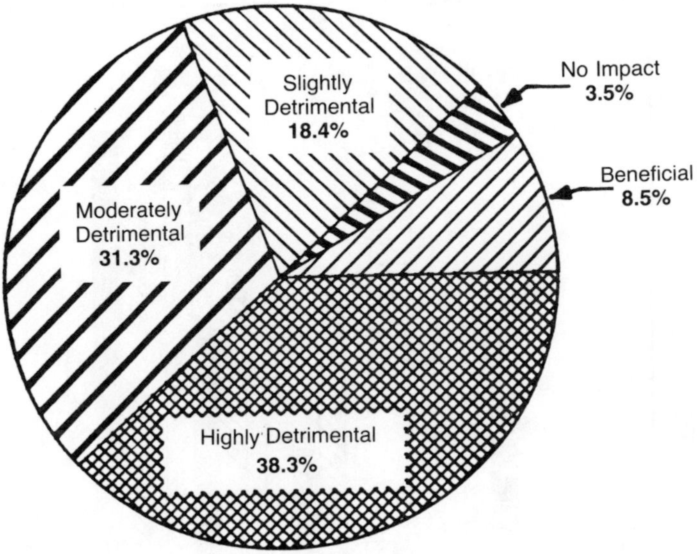

Valid Cases	
Highly detrimental	77
Moderately detrimental	63
Slightly detrimental	37
No impact	7
Beneficial	17
TOTAL	201

FIGURE 3-20
Impact of Inflation: Comparison by State

Legend
Michigan
Colorado
Texas

Percentage of Sample

60
50
40
30
20
10
0

6.8
13.3
10.3

3.8
3.3
2.6

21.2
10.0
15.4

28.8
26.7
43.6

39.4
46.7
28.2

1
2
3
4
5

Degree of Impact

Degree of Impact Key
1 = Beneficial
2 = No impact
3 = Slightly detrimental
4 = Moderately detrimental
5 = Highly detrimental

Valid Cases
Michigan   132
Colorado   30
Texas   39
TOTAL   201

80

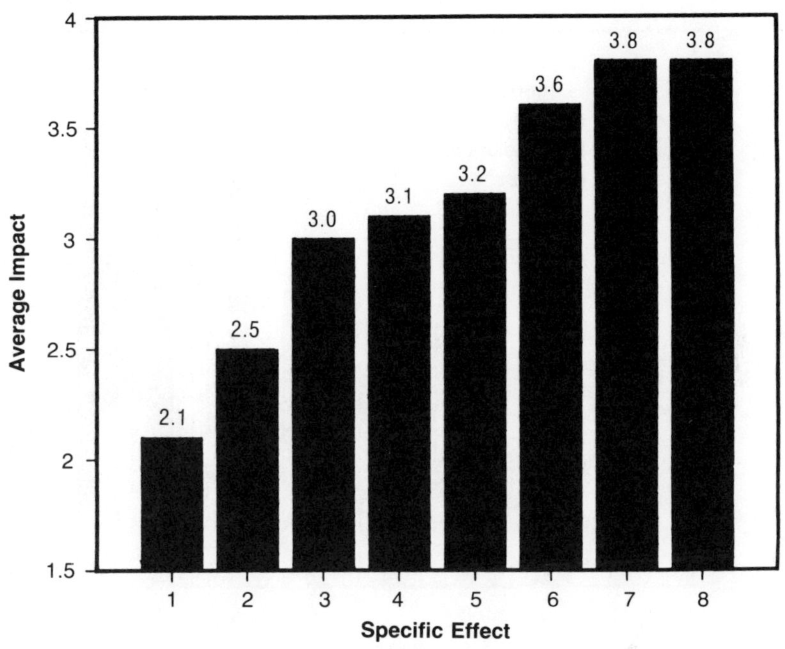

Average Impact Key

1 = No impact
2 = Slightly detrimental
3 = Moderately detrimentai
4 = Heavily detrimental
5 = Very severely detrimental

Specific Effect Key

1 = Stops innovation and technological advances
2 = Places firm at competitive disadvantage
3 = Increases difficulty of timely collection
4 = Hampers ability to pass along price increases
5 = Increases customer selectivity
6 = Increases risk and uncertainty
7 = Causes higher wages and salaries
8 = Makes it difficult to quote long-term prices

Valid Cases

Stops innovation and technological advances	135
Places firm at competitive disadvantage	189
Increases difficulty of timely collection	182
Hampers ability to pass along price increases	187
Increases customer selectivity	178
Increases risk and uncertainty	196
Causes higher wages and salaries	202
Makes it difficult to quote long-term prices	153

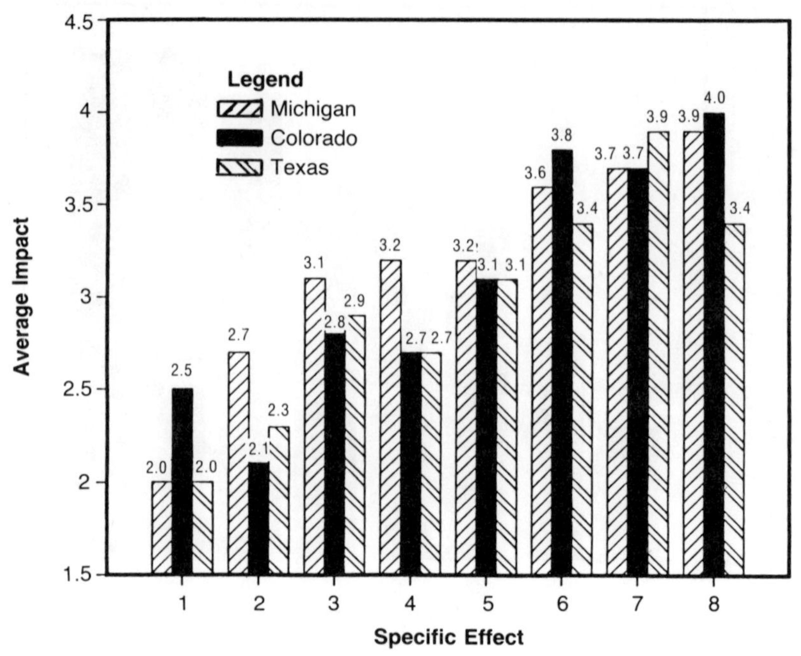

Average Impact Key

1 = No impact
2 = Slightly detrimental
3 = Moderately detrimental
4 = Heavily detrimental
5 = Very severely detrimental

Specific Effect Key

1 = Stops innovation and technological advances
2 = Places firm at competitive disadvantage
3 = Increases difficulty of timely collection
4 = Hampers ability to pass along price increases
5 = Increases customer selectivity
6 = Increases risk and uncertainty
7 = Causes higher wages and salaries
8 = Makes it difficult to quote long-term prices

Valid Cases

	Low	High	Mean
Michigan	84	132	114
Colorado	19	30	26
Texas	32	40	38

what might be called an "inflation psychosis"—they come to expect price increases and to feel that their wages and salaries should increase at least enough to maintain a constant purchasing power. And managers often think in these terms when considering employees for pay increases. Union and other contracts promote and perpetuate such attitudes. With cost of living allowances (COLA) in such contracts, wages increase automatically by some agreed-upon formula for adjusting for general price level changes. Such adjusted basic wages become the starting point for negotiations on wage and salary increases. Social security payments and many government retirement benefits are indexed to changes in the general price level, ultimately reflected in increased total wages and salaries through increased social security taxes and retirement benefit costs.

Such agreements and procedures have important indirect effects throughout the economy. For example, in order to compete for labor in many locations, nonunionized firms must meet or beat union scale, particularly for skilled labor. In some firms, the wages of supervisory and management personnel are tied closely to the results in union contracts.

The respondents generally felt that inflation affected their firm's ability to compete only slightly. The perception is that all firms in a given area of activity are affected fairly uniformly by inflation, and therefore inflation creates very few competitive advantages or disadvantages.

On average, small business managers and owners also felt that inflation affected innovation and technological advances only slightly. Actually, one way to decrease inflation is to increase productivity through innovative ideas and rapid technological advances.

When we considered the overall effects of inflation by states, we found no important differences from the general results, although there are some differences as to the perceived severity between close categories on the ordinal scale. When we compared effects by industry groupings, we found that "difficulty of timely collection of accounts" has less detrimental effect on construction than on any other industry groupings; and "increases customer selectivity" has the second greatest effect, exceeded only by its effect on retail firms.

Many firms that make or sell high-cost items constructed or built over an extended period of time are having cash flow problems because of the depressed economic environment. Once demand is reduced, firms compete fiercely for jobs, often reducing prices in the process. Knowing this, buyers have reduced advance payments on such projects, often requiring the builder to finance 100% of the costs to completion. The inflation problems mentioned exacerbate the situation. Consequently, it is not surprising that difficulty in quoting long-term prices was reported to be the most important detrimental effect of inflation, particularly given the significant portion of the questionnaire returns that came from construction and manufacturing firms.

These conclusions are supported by Figure 3-22, which illustrates the detrimental effects of these various factors on small businesses in Michigan (heavily represented by manufacturing firms), Colorado (heavily represented by construction firms), and Texas (heavily represented by wholesale firms). The mean level of effect on quoting long-term prices increased from 3.8 for all small businesses to 3.9 for Michigan and 4.0 for Colorado, and decreased to 3.4 for Texas, which has a disproportionate number of wholesale firms. This difference in types of businesses also partially explains the difference in importance attached to the more general detrimental effect, "increases risk and uncertainty."

In general, our interviewees supported these conclusions. The problems they mentioned most were the upward push on salaries and wages brought about by inflation, the difficulty in quoting prices on long-term contracts, and the inadequacy of depreciation allowances for tax purposes. One said that inflation had reduced his sales substantially both because buyers became more careful and thoughtful in their selections—impulse buying decreased—and because higher prices meant some potential buyers were unable to afford the products. One owner said inflation has helped him. He entered the business when costs were low, and the subsequent dramatic increase in prices has helped keep out potential competitors.

Impact of High Interest Rates on Small Businesses

High interest rates have an even worse effect on small businesses than inflation, as Figure 3-23 indicates. Well over 50% of the respondents felt that high interest rates were highly detrimental to the effective operations of their firms, and 87.2% felt they were detrimental to some degree. The fact that small firms generally are heavily leveraged is one explanation of this strong impact. Many use a significant amount of debt as a permanent form of capitalization, refinancing it as circumstances dictate. As interest rates escalate, debt turnover is at higher and higher cost, frequently reaching

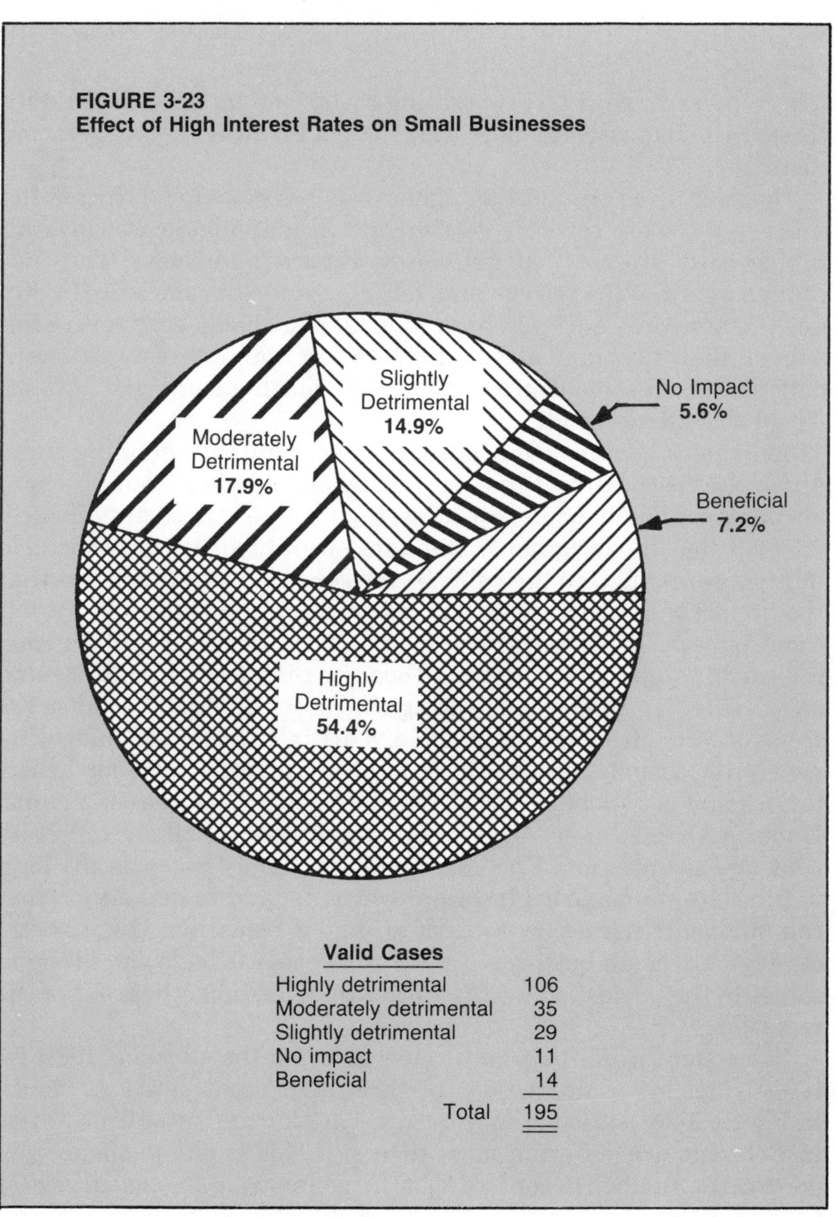

FIGURE 3-23
Effect of High Interest Rates on Small Businesses
Slightly Detrimental 14.9%
No Impact 5.6%
Moderately Detrimental 17.9%
Beneficial 7.2%
Highly Detrimental 54.4%
Valid Cases
Highly detrimental 106
Moderately detrimental 35
Slightly detrimental 29
No impact 11
Beneficial 14
Total 195

a high percentage of total operating costs. One interviewee said interest costs had risen to more than 23% of his firm's total operating costs.

However, even though the higher costs associated with increasing interest rates are severely detrimental in individual cases, overall higher costs are not that critical, as Figure 3-24 shows. Thus, although 54.4% of the respondents felt high interest *rates* were highly detrimental, only 8.9% felt high interest *costs* had a very severe impact on their firm, and although 87.2% felt high interest *rates* were detrimental to some degree, only 37.5% felt high interest *costs* affected their firms at all.

The major general effect of high interest rates explaining these differences is the uncertainty caused by not only high, but also generally unpredictable, interest rates. Figure 3-25 reflects this. Nearly 25% felt that the uncertainty associated with high and unpredictable interest rates affected their firms very severely. Two thirds felt that the impact was moderate to very severe, and a whopping 83.7% felt some impact. If not certainty, businessmen desire (need) at least reasonable stability if they are to operate their firms efficiently and effectively. Otherwise, projecting consumer demand becomes extremely difficult, if not impossible. This in turn makes budgeting nearly impossible because there is no reasonable basis for expectations and projections. Everything becomes a mere guessing game. Under such conditions, owners and managers are likely to take a wait-and-see position. The risk premium simply becomes too high to innovate, to make capital improvements, and to make the other commitments necessary to turn around a recession. Owners and managers of small businesses generally appear to have placed themselves in the mode of following rather than leading others out of the recession.

Some significant differences emerge when the effects of high interest rates are compared for the three states considered, as shown in Figure 3-26. Although interest rates are hurting most firms, those in Colorado are suffering most severely. This is due to the disproportionate number of construction firms included in the survey for Colorado. Texas is hurt the least because the state is in a better economic position, requiring less borrowing, and because there is a high proportion of wholesalers and retailers in the survey, firms that normally need less leverage than manufacturers and construction firms.

Another general explanation can be found in the indirect effects

FIGURE 3-24
Effect of Higher Interest Costs on Small Businesses

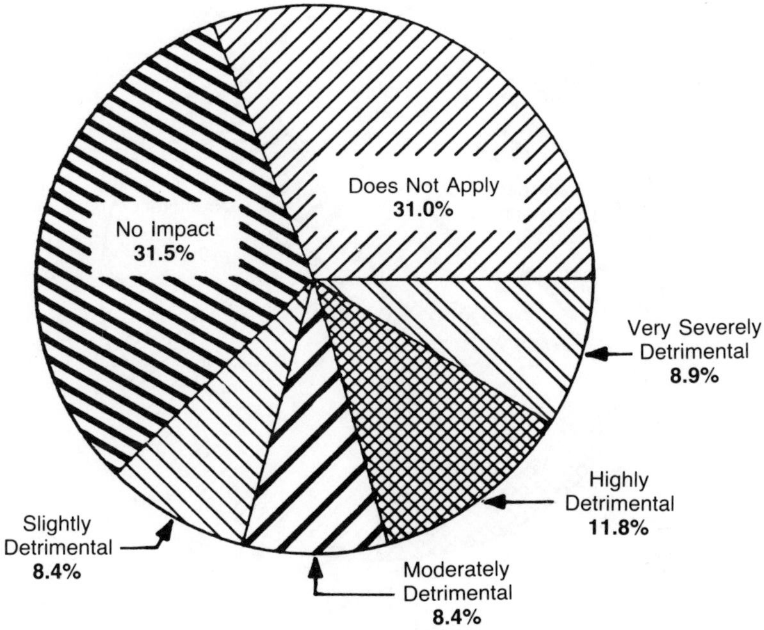

Valid Cases

Very severely detrimental	18
Highly detrimental	24
Moderately detrimental	17
Slightly detrimental	17
No impact	64
Total	140

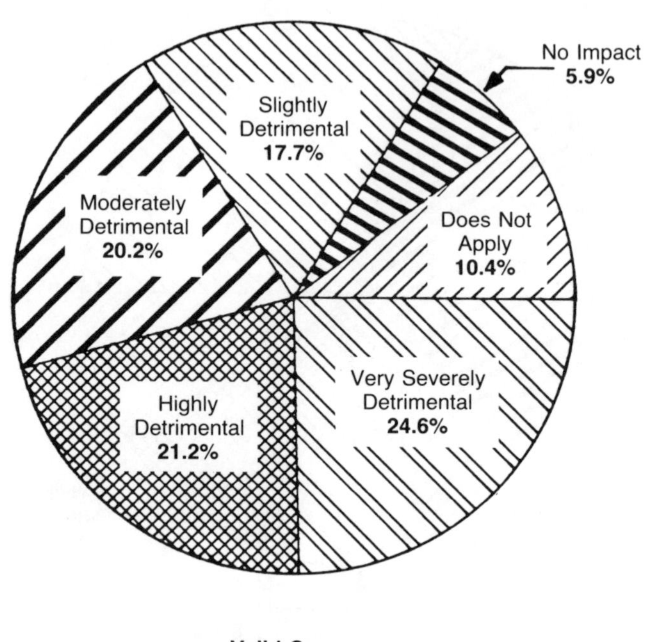

Valid Cases

Very severely detrimental	50
Highly detrimental	43
Moderately detrimental	41
Slightly detrimental	36
No impact	12
Does not apply	21
Total	203

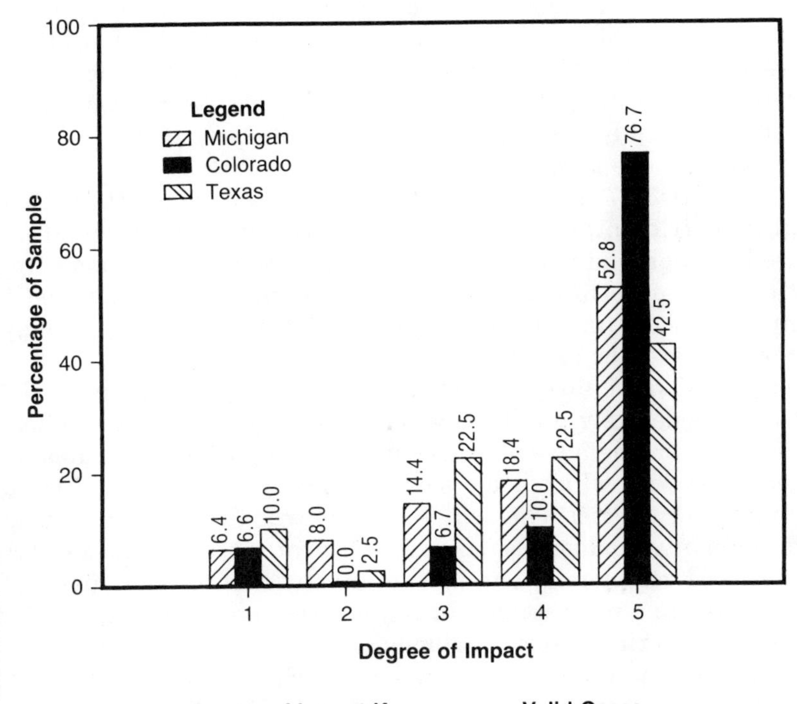

FIGURE 3-26
Impact of High Interest Rates: Comparison by State

100

Legend
Michigan
Colorado
Texas

Percentage of Sample

80

60

40

20

0

76.7
52.8
42.5
6.4
6.6
10.0
8.0
0.0
2.5
14.4
6.7
22.5
18.4
10.0
22.5

1
2
3
4
5

Degree of Impact

Degree of Impact Key

1 = Beneficial
2 = No impact
3 = Slightly detrimental
4 = Moderately detrimental
5 = Highly detrimental

Valid Cases

Michigan   125
Colorado   30
Texas   40
TOTAL   195

of high interest rates, often more important than the direct effects. These indirect effects (frequently called derived, or second-order, effects) are the result of close ties and dependence upon other industries adversely affected by high and variable interest rates—the automotive and construction industries, for example. As Figure 3-27 reflects, the only direct effects more severe overall than the second-order effects are the slowing of customer payments and the uncertainty caused by high and variable interest rates. Weighted together, these second-order effects caused problems for firms as reflected in Figure 3-28. Together, 41.8% of the firms felt that these second-order effects were highly to very severely detrimental, and 65.5% felt that they caused some problems.

As Figure 3-27 indicates, each of the specific effects is at least slightly detrimental, with the most severe being the uncertainty caused by high and variable interest rates. As discussed under inflation, such uncertainty makes it nearly impossible to plan meaningfully for the future, and firms having substantial difficulties may or may not even be around in the future.

The third most severe effect, nearly tied for second, and rated between moderately and highly detrimental, is the indirect effect resulting from the adverse consequences of high interest rates on other firms with which some small businesses are closely related (second-order effects). This is particularly true for the construction and automotive industries. High interest rates are the basic factor that slowed commercial and private construction in most parts of the country to a near standstill. As construction decreases, the demand for materials, labor, equipment, and supplies also decreases. The logging and lumber industry is affected almost at once. Even those in various service industries, such as lawyers and accountants who perform services for lumber, construction, wholesale, and retail firms, find the demand for their services falling off.

Because the construction industry in Colorado is represented heavily in the sample, it is not surprising that, of the three states, Colorado firms rated increased uncertainty as having the most severe effect (3.9—highly detrimental). For the same reason, Colorado firms rated slower progress payments higher than Michigan and Texas (2.8—close to a moderately detrimental impact). Interestingly enough, this also explains why Colorado firms rated the effect that high interest rates on other firms have on their firms the lowest of the three states (2.5—between slightly and moderately detrimental).

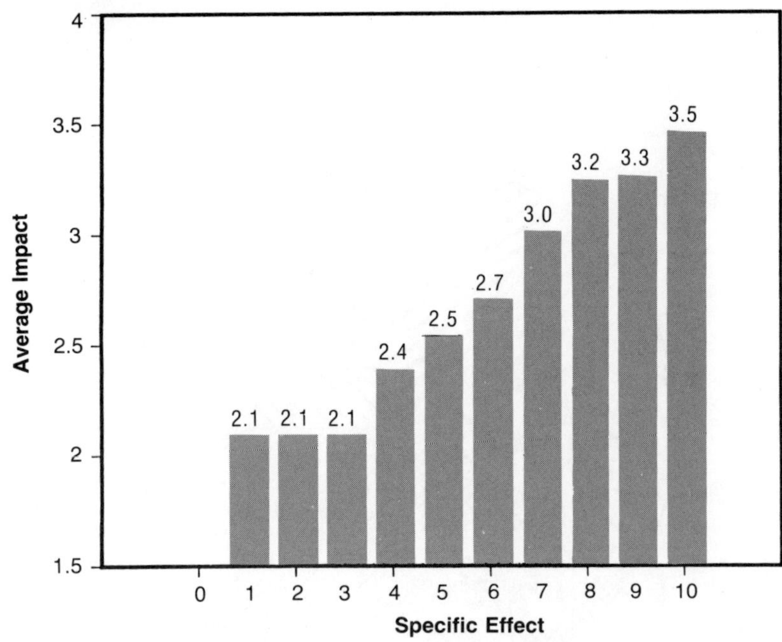

Average Impact Key

1 = No impact
2 = Slightly detrimental
3 = Moderately detrimental
4 = Heavily detrimental
5 = Very severely detrimental

Specific Effect Key

1 = Lowers credit rating
2 = Slows innovation and technological advances
3 = Places firm at competitive disadvantage
4 = Causes higher interest cost
5 = Slows progress payments
6 = Causes overemphasis on financial aspects of business operations
7 = Postpones capital investments
8 = Has second-order effects
9 = Slows customer payments
10 = Increases uncertainty

Valid Cases

Lowers credit rating	173	Causes overemphasis on financial aspects of business operations	165
Slows innovation and technological advances	168	Postpones capital investments	174
Places firm at competitive disadvantage	148	Has second-order effects	170
Causes higher interest cost	140	Slows customer payments	183
Slows progress payments	127	Increases uncertainty	182

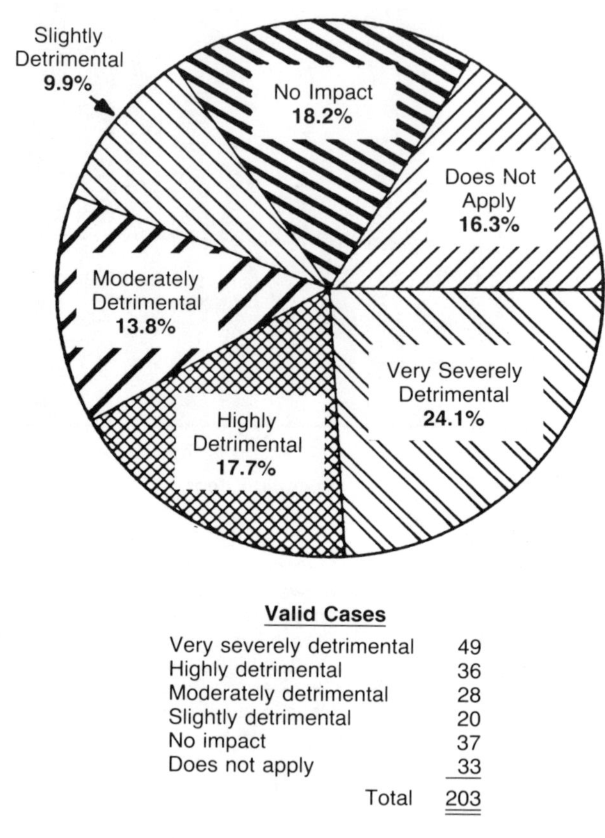

Valid Cases

Very severely detrimental	49
Highly detrimental	36
Moderately detrimental	28
Slightly detrimental	20
No impact	37
Does not apply	33
Total	203

The effect of high interest rates on construction hurts other firms, not the reverse.

Michigan, of course, is heavily tied to the automotive industry and has large numbers of firms supplying parts, subcomponent materials, and services to firms that construct and assemble automobiles. High interest rates are one of the main factors decreasing the demand for automobiles, and thereby decreasing the demand for the products and services of the firms closely tied to the manufacturers and assemblers. This explains why Michigan firms rate as a moderate to heavily detrimental impact both uncertainty (3.4) and the effect that high interest rates for other firms have on their firms (3.5). In Michigan, because of the size limitation in our survey, the manufacturers of automobiles (General Motors, Ford, etc.) were not included, but many suppliers of automotive parts and services were. The impact on manufacturers starts the dominoes falling, not the reverse.

Except for uncertainty and slower progress payments, each of the effects was rated as more severe by Michigan firms than by firms in Colorado or Texas. With two exceptions—and in those two the differences were not important—Texas firms rated each as less severe than Michigan or Colorado. These findings reflect not only that Michigan is the most economically depressed state in the union, but also that the economic depression has psychological effects. Many owners and managers of firms in Michigan, certainly more than those in Texas, have lost a great deal of faith and confidence that prospects will improve substantially in the future, particularly in the near term.

Because of the high interest rates, many managers felt they had to spend a disproportionately large portion of their time on the financial aspects of their firms, taking time away from what they perceived to be more productive tasks—manufacturing and selling the products and services of their firms (2.9—a near moderately detrimental effect). Michigan firms rated this effect higher than those in Texas (2.2) or Colorado (2.6).

Interviewees' responses generally followed the same pattern. One firm, closely tied to the automotive industry, felt that unstable or fluctuating interest rates were a greater problem than high interest rates because of the uncertainty they create, making it very difficult to quote prices two or more years in advance. He also said capital investment was dramatically reduced in his firm because of high interest rates. This lack of capital investment hurts quality, he felt, because technological advances are slowed down. He has also post-poned automating certain production functions and acquires old, re-built machinery and equipment rather than investing in new equipment.

Another interviewee, engaged in selling and renting copiers, entered the era of high interest rates financing his heavy investment in inventory with short-term debt. High interest rates have been devastating to him. He stated that he cannot earn, net of taxes, a rate of return on his investment higher than interest cost, net of taxes. He also feels these pressures have caused him to spend a disproportionate part of his time on the financial aspects of the business, reducing the time he feels should be spent on marketing and sales efforts.

Because of a heavy debt structure, due mainly to the high interest rates, one firm's cash flow has become so critical that most of its vendors will only sell to the firm COD. High interest rates and a reduced volume of work spread among a number of competitors also have reduced progress payments the firm receives down to near zero. The firm used to receive a substantial amount of money up front for the work it did, but now must finance 100% of the investment in most projects until the customer is billed and pays. Cash flow problems have become so severe that an employee is sent to local customers to pick up checks for payments on account because the firm cannot wait the two or three days required for mail delivery. In turn, customers are now wondering about the firm's viability—will it be able to stay in business long enough to complete the work?—and sales have been lost.

Another firm had leveraged heavily to expand and modernize its facilities just prior to the rapid increase in interest rates. The owner indicated that interest is now 28% of the total costs of operations.

One firm did not borrow, so interest costs do not affect the firm directly. The owner felt, however, that sales had dropped significantly, and cash flows with it, because customers could no longer afford to finance acquisitions.

The increase in interest rates also has substantially slowed customer payments, one owner told us. Customers are playing a number of games to delay payment, such as calling after 29 days, when payment is due in 30, to complain about something in order to delay payment. The owner said he must then do the same thing to his creditors.

High interest rates, however, were perceived as having certain

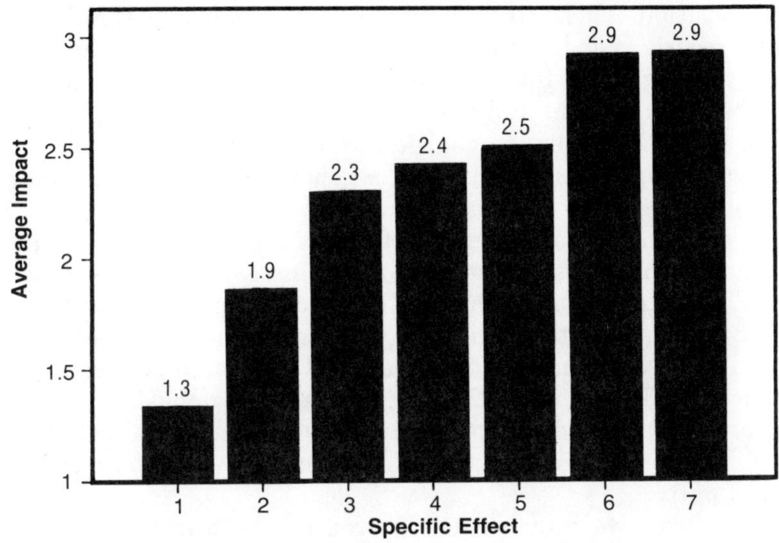

Average Impact Key

1 = No impact
2 = Slightly beneficial
3 = Moderately beneficial
4 = Highly beneficial

Specific Effect Key

1 = Use of industrial revenue bonds
2 = Competitive advantage of being larger than competitors
3 = Good returns on investments
4 = General competitive advantage of entering high-interest era in highly liquid position
5 = Encouragement of better control of receivables and inventory
6 = Encouragement of emphasis on increasing worker productivity
7 = Encouragement of better cost control generally

Valid Cases

Use of industrial revenue bonds	70
Competitive advantage of being larger than competitors	121
Good returns on investment	133
General competitive advantage of entering high-interest era in highly liquid position	153
Encouragement of better control of receivables and inventory	163
Encouragement of emphasis on increasing worker productivity	192
Encouragement of better cost control generally	191

beneficial effects, as reflected in Figure 3-29 (p. 95). A number of firms entered the era of rapidly increasing interest rates in a highly liquid position. These firms have been able to invest their excess cash in securities and certificates with higher returns than they could earn by using these funds in their business operations. This was rated between a slight and moderately beneficial effect (2.3). In addition, it allowed them to charge lower prices than their heavily leveraged competitors, giving them a general competitive advantage (2.4—slight to moderately beneficial effect).

The most important beneficial effects of high interest rates, however, are in the areas of cost control and increasing worker productivity. The category of "encourages better cost control generally" was rated nearly moderately beneficial (2.9), while the more specific category of receivable and inventory control was rated between slight and moderately beneficial (2.5). The increased emphasis on improving worker productivity was a moderately beneficial effect (2.9). Except for minor differences, the results for each state followed this general pattern.

Three firms we interviewed entered the high-interest era in a strong liquidity position and are realizing good returns on their investments. Almost all the interviewees indicated that high interest rates had encouraged them to control costs and investments in inventory much more closely than they had before.

Impact of Government Regulations

Government regulations in total—federal, state, and local—are perceived as having serious detrimental effects on small businesses, as shown in Figure 3-30. Some 62% of the respondents felt government regulations were moderately to highly detrimental, while nearly 26% saw them as slightly detrimental, making a total of about 88% viewing them as having some detrimental effect. Only 3.0% said regulations had beneficial effects.

When we asked about the relative effects of federal, state, and local regulations, we received the replies reflected in Figure 3-31. Figure 3-31 reflects the belief that federal government regulations are having the greatest detrimental effects on small business, although the mean effects of state and federal regulations are quite close. Keep in mind again that these are weighted responses. To an individual firm, such as a bar, state or even local regulations related to selling alcoholic beverages frequently have the most adverse ef-

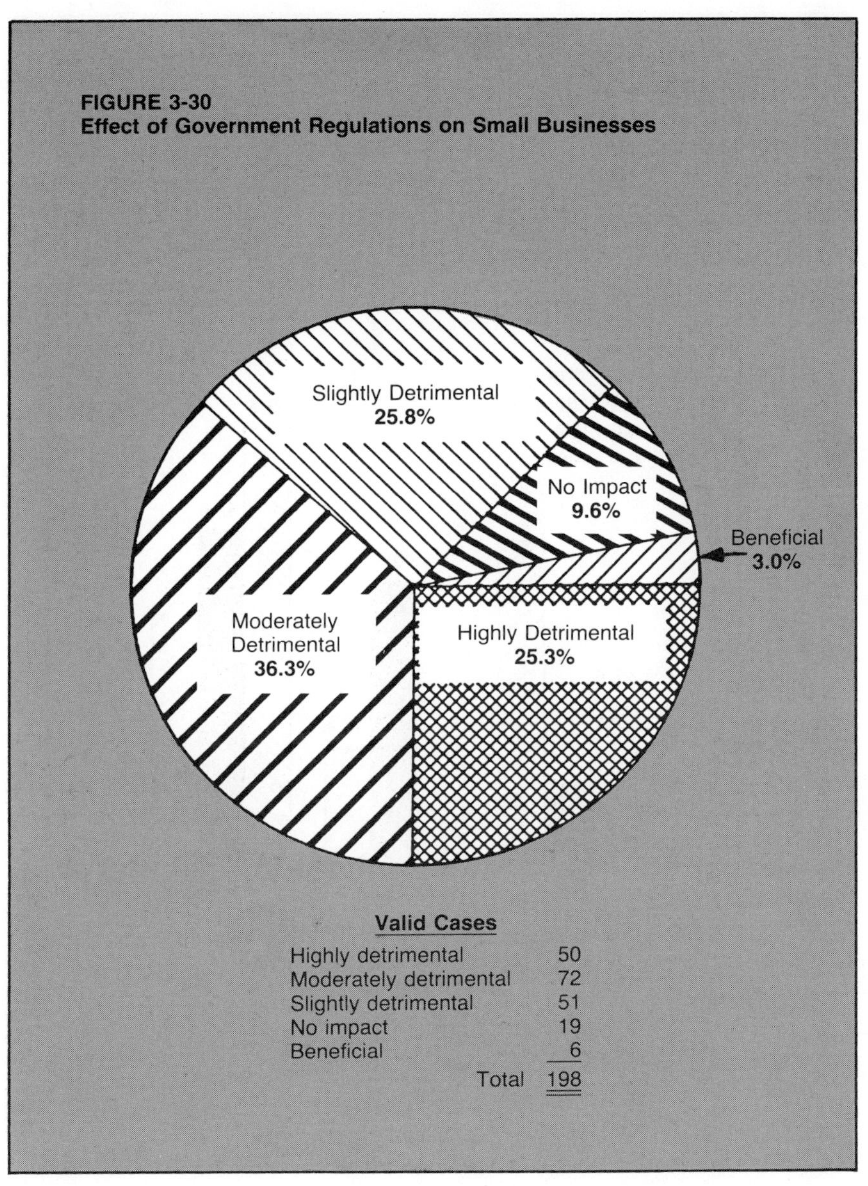

FIGURE 3-30
Effect of Government Regulations on Small Businesses

Slightly Detrimental
25.8%

No Impact
9.6%

Beneficial
3.0%

Moderately
Detrimental
36.3%

Highly Detrimental
25.3%

Valid Cases
Highly detrimental   50
Moderately detrimental   72
Slightly detrimental   51
No impact   19
Beneficial   6
                 Total   198

FIGURE 3-31
Relative Importance of Federal, State, and Local Regulations on
Small Businesses

80

Legend
Federal
State
Local

Percentage of Sample

62.3

60

46.3

47.6

40.5

40

37.3

23.6

20

14.2

16.4

11.9

0

Low

Medium

High

Degree of Importance

Valid Cases
Federal   106
State   84
Local   67
Total   257

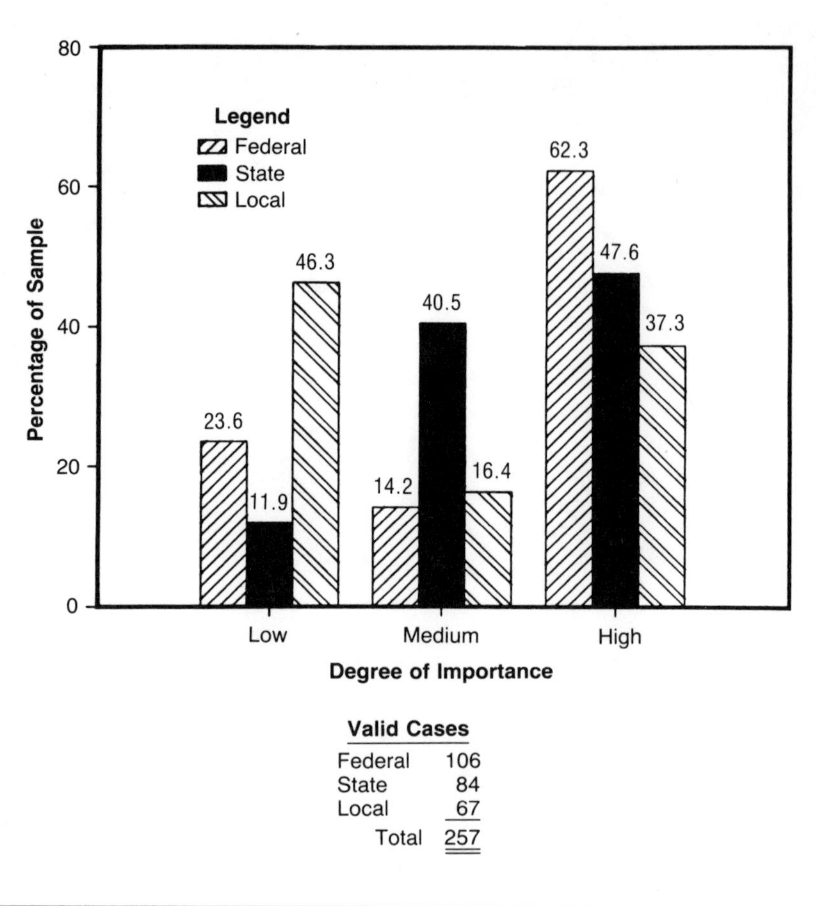

98

fects. The effects of regulations depend on the nature of the business activities and the degree of control exercised by the state or city in which the firm is located.

Nevertheless, 62.3% of the respondents felt that federal government regulations had the greatest adverse effects; this percentage dropped to 47.6% for state governments, and 37.3% for local. However, only 11.9% of the respondents felt that state government regulations had the least impact; this percentage increased to 23.6% for the federal government and 46.3% for local governments.

We asked the respondents to weight five factors that are part of the detrimental effects of regulations: duplication of requirements between regulatory agencies, inconsistent requirements within and between regulations, lengths of forms to be filled out, complexity of complying with regulations, and unnecessary requirements. Figure 3-32 gives the results. Although length of forms, complexity of complying with regulations, and unnecessary requirements rate substantially higher than duplication of requirements and inconsistent regulation requirements in terms of the severity of their effects, all had some impact, ranging from slightly detrimental to more than moderate. Considering that we are dealing with averages, the figures are substantial and indicate that all these factors need to be taken into consideration in revamping regulatory requirements.

Moreover, because these are averages, it must also be kept in mind that the severity of each factor depends upon the type of business activities a firm is engaged in, the importance of each factor with regard to the particular regulatory requirements for a particular business, and, again, how extensive and complex regulations are in the state and local area in which the firm is domiciled. In other words, the severity of these factors can vary considerably between individual firms. Consequently, a substantial number of individual firms might be affected severely, even when the average impact is slight to moderate. Using unnecessary requirements as one example, note the results in Figure 3-33. More than 21% of the respondents felt that unnecessary requirements had a very severely detrimental effect on their firms, and 67.5% felt the impact to be between moderate and very severe.

Using industry breakdowns as another example, note the variations that unnecessary requirements have on firms in different industry classifications, as shown in Figure 3-34. The range drops from nearly a heavily detrimental impact for construction firms (3.9) to a slight to moderate impact for wholesale firms (2.4). This pattern

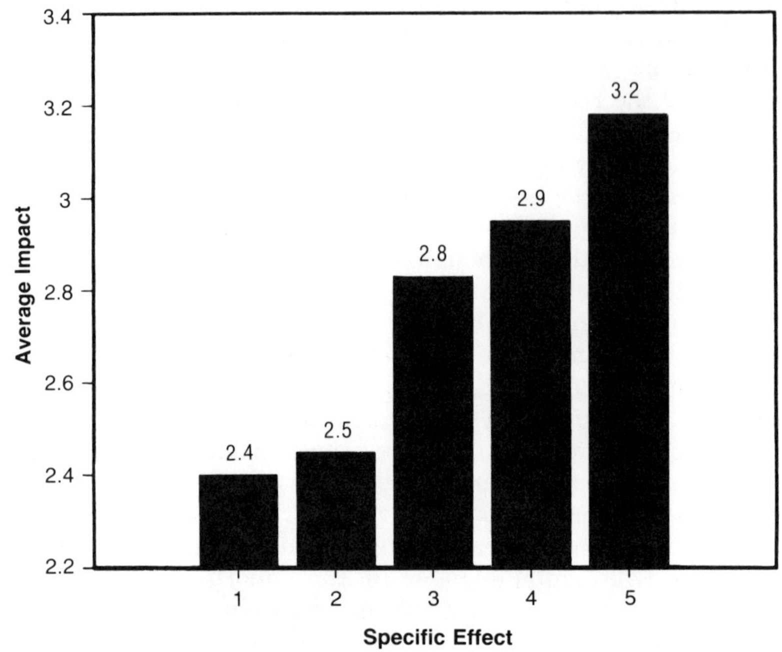

FIGURE 3-32
Effects of Specific Regulations on Small Businesses

Average Impact Key

1 = No impact
2 = Slightly detrimental
3 = Moderately detrimental
4 = Heavily detrimental
5 = Very severely detrimental

Specific Effect Key

1 = Duplicate requirements
2 = Inconsistent requirements
3 = Form length
4 = Requirement complexity
5 = Unnecessary requirements

Valid Cases

Duplicate requirements	198
Inconsistent requirements	197
Form length	197
Requirement complexity	198
Unnecessary requirements	197

FIGURE 3-33
Effects of Unnecessary Requirements on Small Businesses

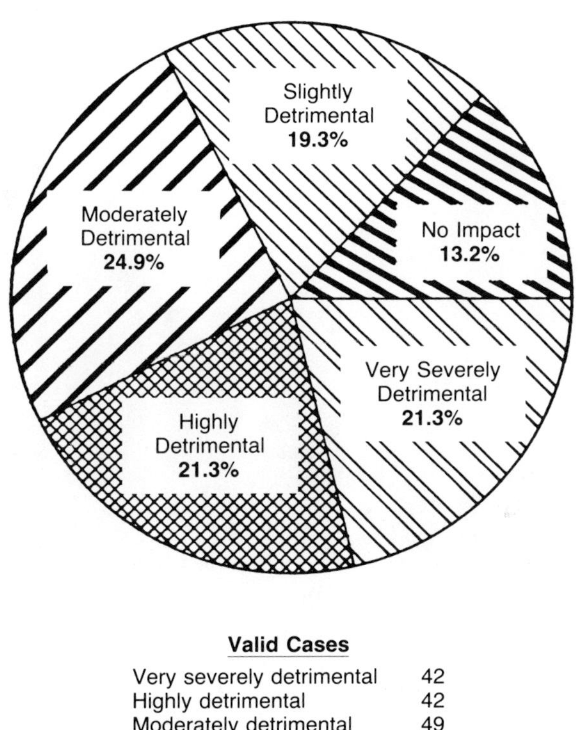

Valid Cases

Very severely detrimental	42
Highly detrimental	42
Moderately detrimental	49
Slightly detrimental	38
No impact	26
Total	197

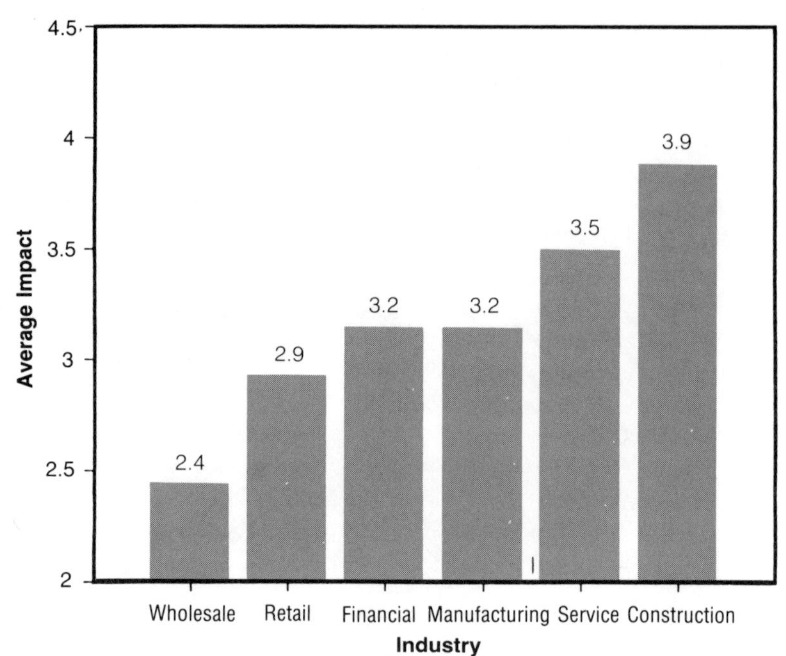

FIGURE 3-34
Detrimental Effects of Unnecessary Requirements:
Comparison by Industry
4.5
4
3.9
3.5
3.5
3.2
3.2
3
2.9
2.5
2.4
2
Average Impact
Wholesale Retail Financial Manufacturing Service Construction
Industry
Average Impact Key
1 = No impacct
2 = Slightly detrimental
3 = Moderately detrimental
4 = Heavily detrimental
5 = Very severely detrimental
Valid Cases
Construction 26
Manufacturing 81
Wholesale 25
Retail 28
Financial 13
Service 18
Total 191

typically follows for each of the other factors; and, in total, construction and manufacturing are affected substantially more than wholesale and retail firms, as Figure 3-35 reflects.

The severity of the effects of the various factors for Texas are consistently lower than for Colorado and Michigan, as reflected in Figure 3-36. Although a part of these variations can be explained by the differences in industry groups in each state, the fact that Texas typically has fewer state and local regulations than either Colorado or Michigan is another important factor.

Most of the interviewees in Michigan felt that some regulations were necessary to maintain an orderly environment—to get the "bad" guys. However, they were unanimous in feeling that most of the benefits—one interviewee said 80 to 90%—could be attained with fewer regulations and substantial reductions in cost. Most said that regulations were overdone, redundant, and overly complex. Interestingly, one interviewee felt that regulations affected larger businesses more because they have more employees and are in the limelight more. Most, however, felt that the opposite was true.

The interviewees in Texas did not feel the burden of regulation nearly as much as those in Michigan because of fewer state and local regulations in Texas. One firm owner in Texas, who does business in a number of states, said that regulations were devastating everywhere except Texas, which was the best state in the union in which to do business.

Taxes and Small Businesses

Taxes, on average, are viewed as being more detrimental than regulations to small businesses. In answer to the question "How would you describe the impact taxes have on your firm?" we received the responses illustrated in Figure 3-37. More than 94% felt that taxes had some detrimental effect on their firms, while 75.9% felt the impact to be moderately to highly detrimental.

We listed some potential problems created by high taxes and asked respondents to describe how seriously each problem had affected their firms' operations. The results are shown in Figure 3-38. The reduction of profits was viewed as the most serious detrimental effect, rated slightly higher than moderately detrimental (3.1). This effect is rated most serious for two reasons. First, many small businesses are highly competitive and are therefore unable to pass all the taxes through to their customers in the form of higher prices. This reduces

FIGURE 3-35
Specific Detrimental Effects of Regulation: Comparison by Industry

Average Impact

4.5

4

3.5

3

2.5

2

1.5

1

3.3 2.5 1.8 1.9 2.4 2.2
3.3 2.4 1.8 2.1 2.8 2.2
3.5 2.8 2.6 2.4 3.2 2.6
3.4 3.0 2.5 2.7 3.2 2.9
3.9 3.2 2.4 2.9 3.2 3.5

1   2   3   4   5

Specific Effect

Legend
Construction
Manufacturing
Wholesale
Retail
Financial
Services

Average Impact Key
1 = No impact
2 = Slightly detrimental
3 = Moderately detrimental
4 = Heavily detrimental
5 = Very severely detrimental

Specific Effect Key
1 = Duplicate requirements
2 = Inconsistent requirements
3 = Form length
4 = Requirement complexity
5 = Unnecessary requirements

Valid Cases
Construction   27
Manufacturing   81
Wholesale   25
Retail   28
Financial   13
Services   18
Total   192

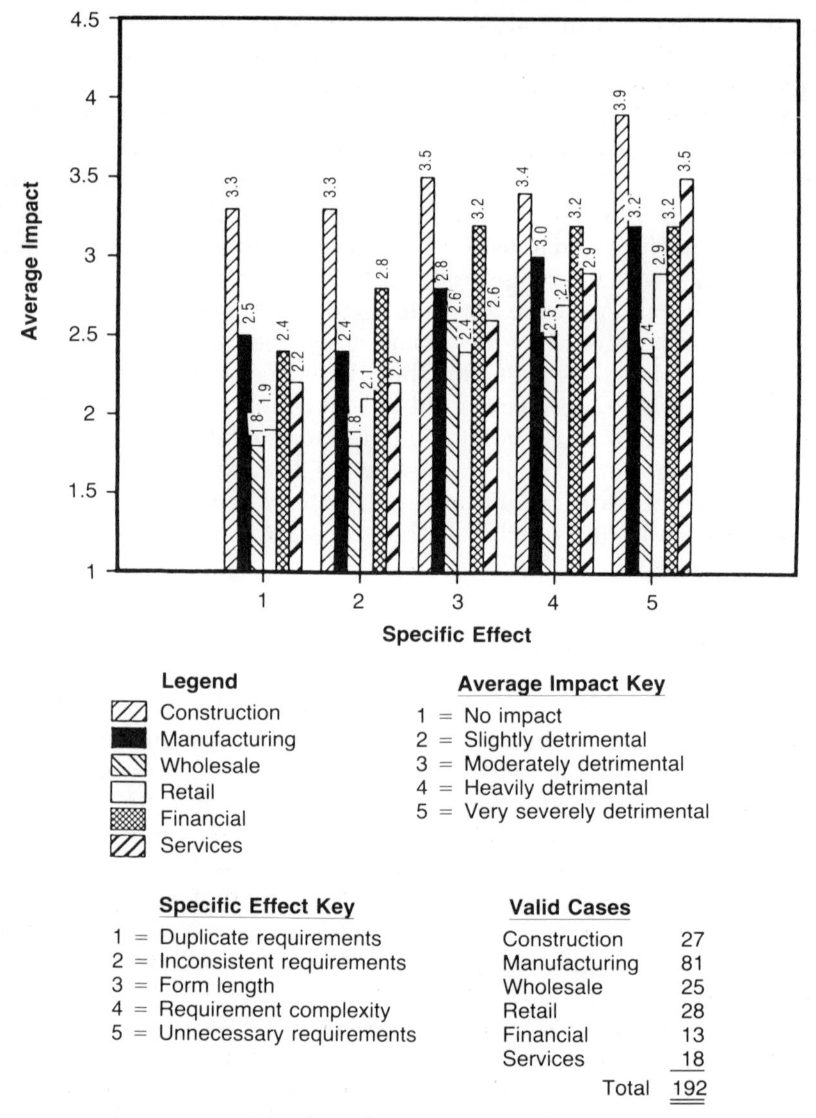

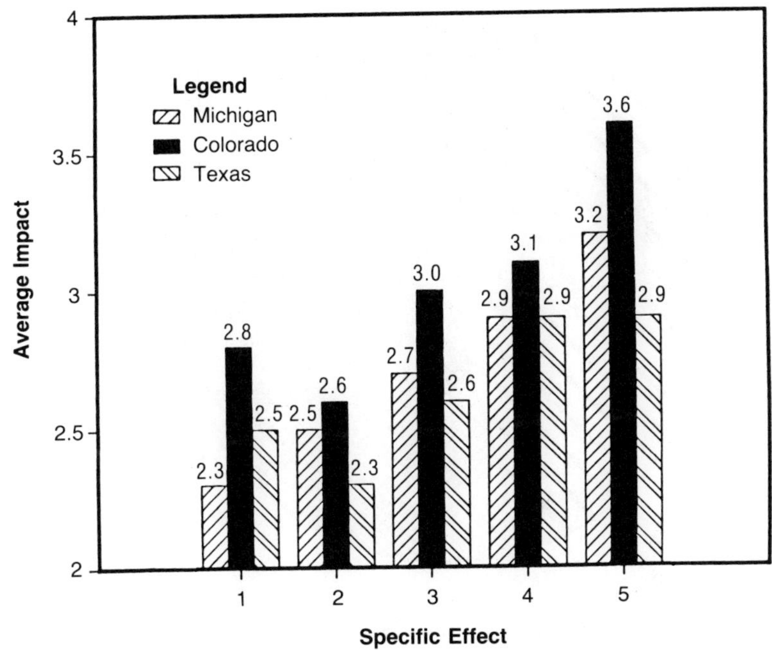

FIGURE 3-36
Detrimental Effects of Regulation: Comparison by State

Average Impact Key

1 = No impact
2 = Slightly detrimental
3 = Moderately detrimental
4 = Heavily detrimental
5 = Very severely detrimental

Specific Effect Key

1 = Duplicate requirements
2 = Inconsistent requirements
3 = Form length
4 = Requirement complexity
5 = Unnecessary requirements

Valid Cases

Michigan	128
Colorado	30
Texas	40
Total	198

FIGURE 3-37
Effect of Taxes on Small Businesses

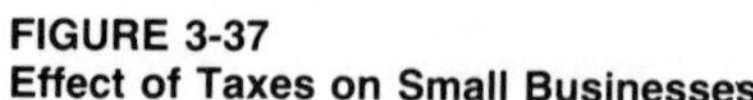

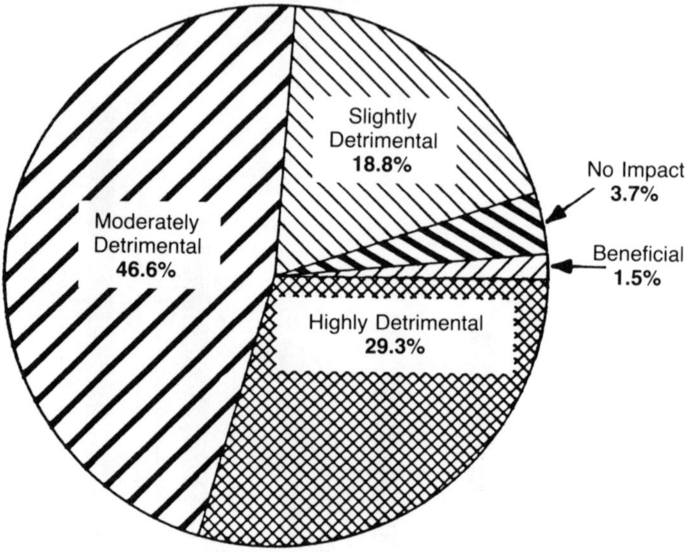

Valid Cases

Highly detrimental	56
Moderately detrimental	89
Slightly detrimental	36
No impact	7
Beneficial	3
Total	191

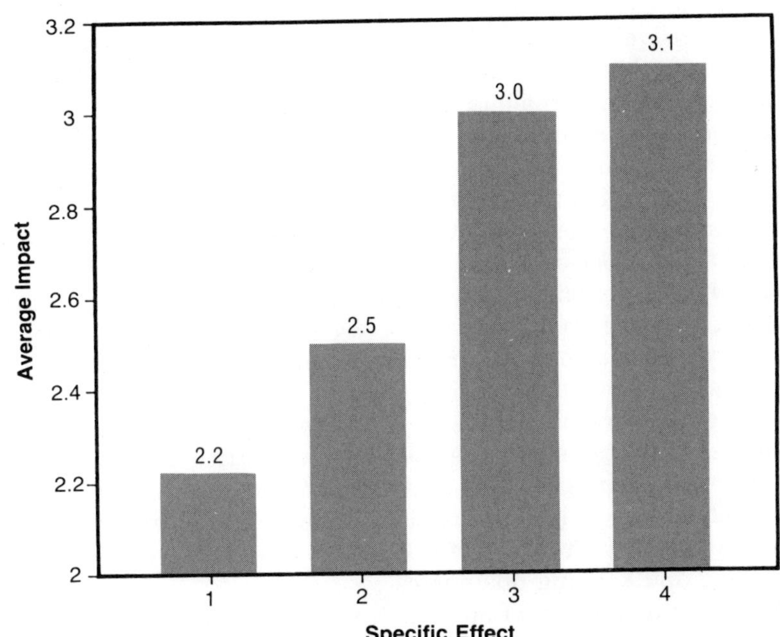

FIGURE 3-38
Specific Detrimental Effects of Taxation on Small Businesses

<u>**Average Impact Key**</u>

1 = No impact
2 = Slightly detrimental
3 = Moderately detrimental
4 = Heavily detrimental
5 = Very severely detrimental

<u>**Specific Effect Key**</u>

1 = Competitive disadvantages of high
    state taxes
2 = Decreases workers' incentives
3 = Hurts small business disproportionately
4 = Reduces profits

<u>**Valid Cases**</u>

Competitive disadvantages of high state taxes	<u>201</u>
Decreases workers' incentives	<u>200</u>
Hurts small business disproportionately	<u>200</u>
Reduces profits	<u>202</u>

the return on investment and/or the return to owners for services performed to below what are perceived to be acceptable levels. Second, high taxes (for the reasons given) reduce net cash flow from operations, leaving insufficient funds to be plowed back into the business for expansion and renovation.

Many owners and managers felt that small businesses were hurt disproportionately by high taxes. Part of the harm was the result of the intensive competition of small businesses and the consequent reduction of profits mentioned in the preceding paragraph. Therefore, these owners and managers argued, small businesses are paying a disproportionate share of the taxes. Also, some taxes are viewed as inequitable for small businesses. For example, Michigan has a single business tax, which is determined largely by labor costs. In effect, it is a value-added or excise type of tax closely related to the labor costs of a firm. Because many small businesses are more labor-intensive than larger businesses, this tax is perceived to be inequitable.

When we compared these effects by state, we found significant differences, as shown in Figure 3-39. Michigan felt the impact of all four types of effects more severely than Colorado and Texas, partly because of the severely depressed economy in Michigan and the psychological impact of such an economy on the attitudes and outlooks of owners and managers. But this sharp impact also reflects the fact that Michigan taxes businesses more heavily than most other states, which is one of the reasons states like Michigan have difficulty in attracting and keeping businesses.

We listed a number of specific taxes and asked respondents to indicate the severity of the effect of each of these taxes on their firms' operations. We obtained the results shown in Figure 3-40. On average, the effects ranged from slightly detrimental for estate taxes (1.9) to almost heavily detrimental for workers' compensation (3.7). Unemployment compensation, state business taxes, and workers' compensation are perceived as having the greatest detrimental effect.

When we compare the effect of various taxes by states, we see some significant differences, as reflected in Figure 3-41. The managers and owners of firms in Michigan rate the impact of all taxes other than estate and federal income taxes as more severe than do managers and owners in Colorado or Texas, for the same reasons previously cited in connection with the specific types of effects of high taxation.

Because we are concerned with causes for productivity declines, we need look into only one aspect of the Michigan situation more

FIGURE 3-39
Specific Detrimental Effects of Taxation: Comparison by State

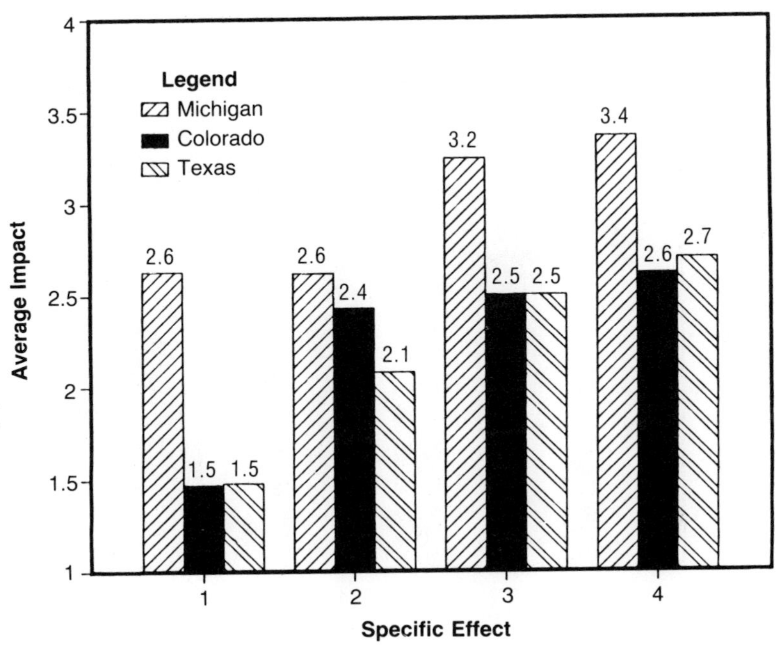
Legend
Michigan
Colorado
Texas
Average Impact
4
3.5
3
2.5
2
1.5
1
2.6
1.5
1.5
2.6
2.4
2.1
3.2
2.5
2.5
3.4
2.6
2.7
1
2
3
4
Specific Effect

Average Impact Key

1 = No impact
2 = Slightly detrimental
3 = Moderately detrimental
4 = Heavily detrimental
5 = Very severely detrimental

Specific Effect Key

1 = Competitive disadvantages of high
    state taxes
2 = Decreases workers' incentives
3 = Hurts small business disproportionately
4 = Reduces profits

Valid Cases

	Low	High	Mean
Michigan	130	132	131
Colorado	28	30	29
Texas	40	40	40

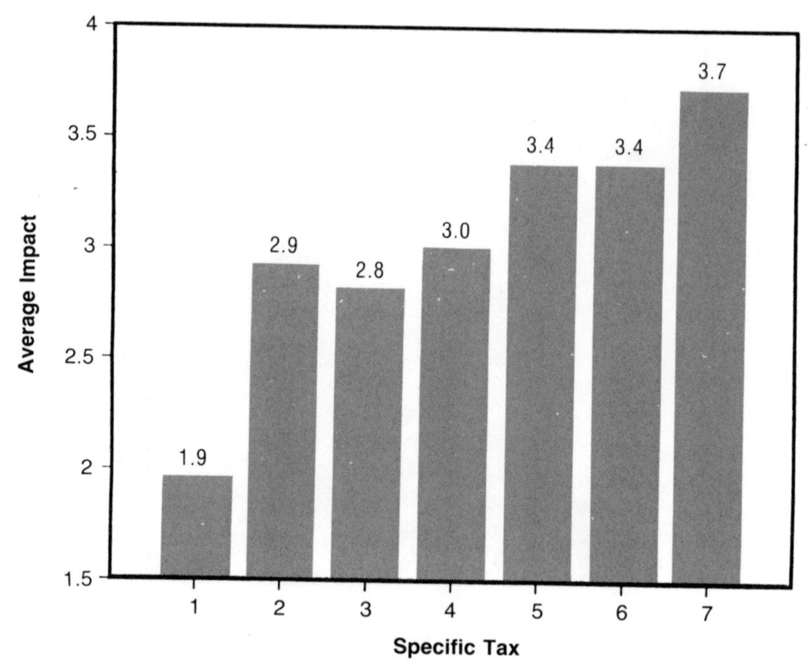

Average Impact Key

1 = No impact
2 = Slightly detrimental
3 = Moderately detrimental
4 = Heavily detrimental
5 = Very severely detrimental

Specific Tax Key

1 = Estate taxes
2 = Federal income tax
3 = State income tax
4 = Social security
5 = Unemployment compensation
6 = State business tax
7 = Workers' compensation

Valid Cases

Estate taxes	103
Federal income tax	200
State income tax	145
Social security	202
Unemployment compensation	203
State business tax	193
Workers' compensation	200

110

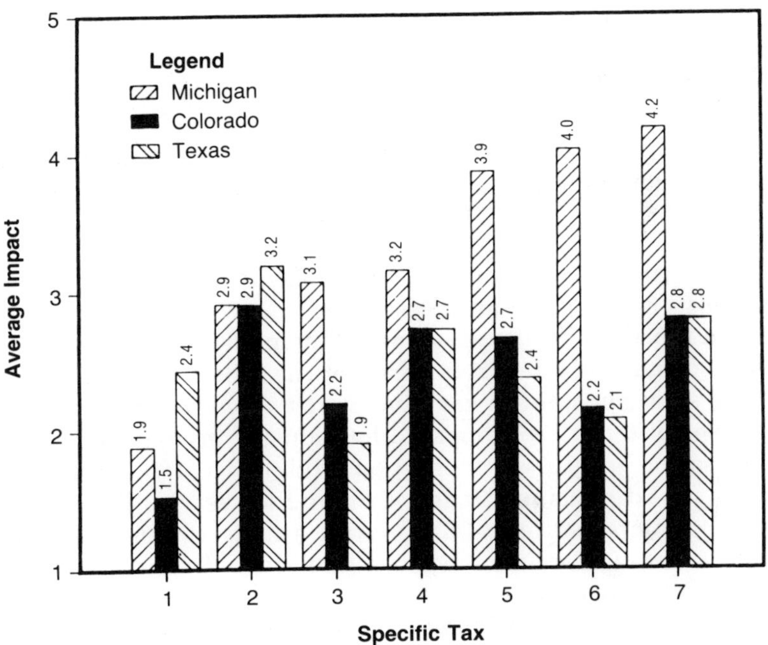

Average Impact Key

1 = No impact
2 = Slightly detrimental
3 = Moderately detrimental
4 = Heavily detrimental
5 = Very severely detrimental

Specific Tax Key

1 = Estate taxes
2 = Federal income tax
3 = State income tax
4 = Social security
5 = Unemployment compensation
6 = State business tax
7 = Workers' compensation

Valid Cases

	Low	High	Mean
Michigan	63	133	118
Colorado	17	30	27
Texas	11	40	32

fully to perceive the problem. Figure 3-41 supports what many have been saying for a number of years.

> Michigan's deficit-ridden unemployment compensation system is a costly program that provides the highest average weekly jobless benefits of any major state. . . . Unemployment taxes on employers in Michigan are also relatively high, although not high enough to cover the costs of benefits. Michigan's average jobless benefit payment of $153 is highest of 14 states with more than 5 million people—the average for the other 13 is $109. . . . Michigan has the highest total benefit cost per worker as a percent of total payroll and the highest maximum tax rate on wages. . . . Michigan workers receive benefits for a longer period—19.7 week average—than any state except New York, which is the same. . . . The cost of benefits per covered worker was $351 . . ., the highest among the major states and more than double the average of the other 13 largest states.[16]

The same general conditions prevail in Michigan regarding workers' compensation and state business taxes.

When types of effects are compared by industry grouping, we observe a substantial amount of variation, as reflected in Figure 3-42. And the same substantial variations exist when the impacts of various types of taxes are compared by industry groupings. Workers' compensation has the worst effect on retail firms (4.3). For financial firms it is state business taxes (4.4), and for service firms, unemployment compensation (3.2). Overall, the detrimental effects of various types of taxes are felt more severely by financial and retail firms and less by service firms.

A number of small businesses headquartered in Michigan are involved in interstate operations. The managers of those firms indicated that high Michigan taxes—particularly workers' compensation and unemployment compensation—create severe competitive problems with firms located in states in which these taxes are much lower. A number felt that the single business tax in Michigan was not equitable in that an unprofitable firm might still pay taxes because of the add-backs to get the tax base. Most felt that this tax is discriminatory against labor-intensive firms because wages are one of the add-back items. We received one unsolicited letter from the manager of a firm in Michigan that read in part as follows:

> Many government programs provide income security. In this case, the government is redistributing income from the productive to the unproductive. This is accomplished by excessively taxing the producers (income, property, social security, etc.). Why produce and generate

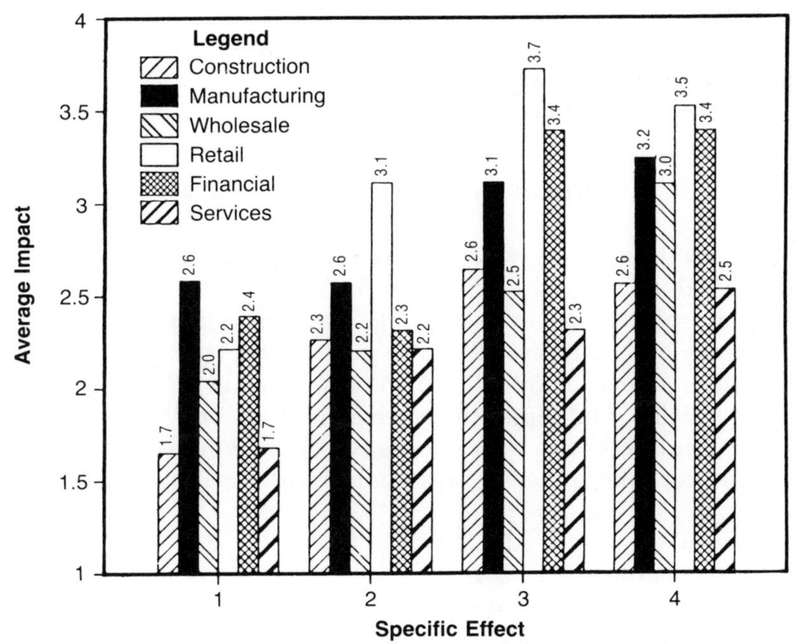

Average Impact Key

1 = No impact
2 = Slightly detrimental
3 = Moderately detrimental
4 = Heavily detrimental
5 = Very severely detrimental

Specific Effect Key

1 = Competitive disadvantages of high state taxes
2 = Decreases workers' incentives
3 = Hurts small business disproportionately
4 = Reduces profit

Valid Cases

	Low	High	Mean
Construction	25	27	26
Manufacturing	82	83	83
Wholesale	25	26	25
Retail	28	29	29
Financial	13	13	13
Services	19	19	19

additional income when the government seems bent on taking an excessive share? This applies to workers and business alike. Again, the trend in productivity is downward because the *unproductive* are *rewarded* and the *productive* are *penalized.*

Most of those in Texas, on the other hand, were fairly well satisfied with the tax situation. They stated that workers' compensation was a good system in Texas. Others stated that state taxes are minimal and that Texas provides a good business environment in which to operate. By far the majority agreed that they would rather operate in Texas than anywhere else.

Summary and Conclusions

All the major issues we considered in Chapter 2 appear to have substantial detrimental effects on the productivity of small businesses. If only responses indicating heavy detrimental effects are considered, high interest rates are clearly the strongest at 54.4%, inflation is second at 38.3%, unions are third at 29.5%, taxes are fourth at 29.3%, and regulations are fifth at 25.3%. When moderate detrimental effects are added to heavy detrimental effects, a shift in weighting takes place—taxes jump from fourth place to first.

1. Taxes   75.9%
2. Interest rates   72.3%
3. Inflation   69.6%
4. Unions   67.2%
5. Regulations   61.6%

It appears that inflation and high interest rates—particularly the latter—have the strongest detrimental effects, but that overall, taxes have the greater total detrimental impact. Certainly, however one wishes to interpret these figures, all of them will need to be addressed continuously and reduced substantially if productivity increases are ever to return to previous levels.

The detrimental effects of inflation and high interest rates appear to be relatively uniform across state lines, indicating that these are almost exclusively national problems and efforts to overcome them will need to be continued basically at the federal level. The impacts of both do vary, at times considerably, between industry groupings. Thus, the adverse effects are not felt uniformly by construction, manufacturing, service, financial, wholesale, and retail firms. The price of high inflation and interest rates is not paid equitably by various groups in the economy.

All the effects have not been detrimental, however. High interest rates and inflation have caused owners and managers to become more efficient in operating their firms, because to survive they have had to reduce costs and control operations better. Frequently, the break-even point in businesses has decreased and more cost-conscious management has built a firm foundation for future productivity increases as the economy recovers.

Union influence has had a fairly severe detrimental effect on productivity, dwindling during depressed times and increasing during periods of growth and prosperity. Thus, unions appear to hold back productivity advances when they should be increasing at the fastest rate. For example, even though productivity increased in 52.3% of the firms surveyed, of those firms unionized to a great extent only 28.6% reflected productivity increases, while 57.9% of firms unionized to a lesser extent and 58.8% of firms not unionized at all reflected productivity increases. The most severe effects of unions relate to wage and fringe benefit demands.

All taxes except estate taxes are perceived as having substantial effects on small business firms, but workers' compensation, state business, and unemployment compensation taxes have the strongest detrimental effects and need the most attention.

The most detrimental effects of regulations are unnecessary requirements, requirement complexities, and form length, in that order. These attributes should receive immediate attention in order to reduce the adverse effects of regulations. Construction and service industries appear to suffer most from regulations, while wholesale firms are the least affected. Which attribute of regulations has the greatest effect varies by industry.

Also, the detrimental effects of high taxes and regulations vary considerably across state lines; in fact, it appears that the adverse effects of certain state taxes are more severe than those of federal taxes, certainly for some types of firms. Thus, the problem needs careful consideration by individual states and local units, as well as by the federal government. And high taxes do affect various industry groupings differently in many cases.

Federal regulations have the greatest overall effect on small business, but state and local regulations do have severe effects on certain subgroups of firms in the various industry groupings, and these vary considerably by state. Thus, although one can allege in general terms, with justification, that taxes are too high and there are too many regulations, solutions will have to be based to a large degree on analysis of the effects of specific taxes and regulations, at the federal, state, and local levels, on subgroups of the general industry groupings.

Certainly states like Michigan, with relatively higher taxes and more regulations than many other states, are finding it difficult to compete with other states to attract new firms and industries, and to keep those they have. These states will have to adjust and alter their taxation and regulation policies substantially if they are to compete successfully. One positive effect of the recession is that they have been forced to start working along these lines. Whether they will go far enough remains to be seen.

Finally, we did ask in the questionnaire and during our interviews about other items stated in Chapter 2 as problems. such as federal procurement, international trade, product liability, and health and accident insurance costs. Although these are probably substantial problems for specific firms and groups of firms in the total economy, perhaps because of our selection process or for other reasons, none of these was reflected as a major problem in our survey data, and we are therefore not able to provide empirical data in an informed manner regarding them.

Notes

[1]"U.S. Business Failure Rate Fastest Since the Depression," *The Ann Arbor News,* April 19, 1982, p. B4.

[2]*Ibid.*

[3]Ann Reilly, "The Bankruptcy Explosion," *Dun's Business Month* (May 1982), p. 52.

[4]"U.S. Business Failure Rate Fastest Since the Depression," p. B4.

[5]Arlene Hershman et al., "The Big Bankruptcy Scare," *Dun's Business Month,* Vol. 120, No. 3 (September 1982), p. 37.

[6]*Ibid.,* p. 36.

[7]Kathy Williams, "Small Business—1983: A Good Year for Entrepreneurs?" *Management Accounting,* Vol. 64, No. 7 (January 1983), p. 18.

[8]John Cunniff, "Cut It—Small Businesses Chop Inventories, Jobs, Borrowing," reporting conclusions of Prof. William Dunkelberg, Purdue University economist, *The Ann Arbor News,* August 18, 1982, p. E8.

[9]John W. Tukey, *Exploratory Data Analysis* (Reading, Mass.: Addison-Wesley, 1977), pp. 1 and 3.

[10]Leonard Curry, "On the Economic Seesaw, Michigan Goes Up When Texas Goes Down," *The Ann Arbor News,* April 24, 1983, p. B1.

[11]Cunniff, p. E8.
[12]We usually found it impossible to determine which firms had gone out of business, and, even when we did, it was impossible to locate the previous owners or managers.
[13]Cunniff, p. E8.
[14]*Ibid.*
[15]Kathy Hulik, "U-M Study Says High Labor Costs Are Hurting the State," *The Ann Arbor News,* October 31, 1981, pp. A1 and A5.
[16]Citizens Research Council of Michigan, "Jobless Pay Highest Among Major States," *The Ann Arbor News,* October 21, 1982, p. A13.

Chapter 4

Applying a Basic Philosophy: The Key to Maximizing Productivity

Increased productivity is the key to economic progress. It allows the nation to raise its standard of living, to support such social goals as education and health care, and to contribute to other aspects of the general welfare; it is an essential underpinning of the nation's security. Higher productivity allows these "noneconomic" objectives to be achieved without absolute reduction of workers' living standards.[1]

General Overview

As indicated in Chapter 2, most writers hypothesize some single factor as being the major, or only, cause for productivity declines in the United States. For example:

> While U.S. productivity remains the highest in the world, we face problems at the national level. Our labor productivity during recent years has been declining. Real incomes can rise, and the nation's standard of living can improve, only when productivity per worker increases at a rate that is at least equal to increases in wage rates. If the present situation persists, however, and productivity continues to decline, our expectations about rising living standards cannot be met.[2]

Certainly all these writers cannot be correct; and even if one or a few factors are the major problems, there is little concurrence among them as to exactly which factors these are. On the basis of our research, we agree in principle with the following statement:

> Our productivity problem is akin to death by a thousand cuts. . . . We have literally dozens and dozens of problems that are causing productivity to decline . . . together, they signify at the very least that we need multiple cures. And that is where it gets difficult, because everyone is looking for this one magical solution.[3]

We agree for two reasons. First, we feel that the empirical data in Chapter 3 show that decreased productivity has many causes,

119

even though we were primarily concerned only with those at the macro level. With all the possibilities at the industry and firm levels—worker relations, cost control, management performance, technological advances, among many others—it is not hard to conceive of "dozens and dozens" of problems needing solution. Therefore, there are enough blame and responsibility for all of us to share equitably.

Second—although not an ideal approach, as we discuss later—on balance we probably wouldn't lose if we attacked some or all the problems individually, regardless of whether each is major or minor. Solutions to any of them are likely to improve productivity to some degree. There are probably few instances in which an individual, group, firm, industry, or the nation as a whole cannot improve the existing conditions, and continuing evaluation and reevaluation are necessary for continuing advancements. The nature of the total environment ensures that when advancement stops, regression takes over; i.e., it is not possible to maintain the status quo, to stabilize at any position.

Two major, basic conclusions follow from acceptance of the idea that "our productivity problem is akin to death by a thousand cuts." First, it means that most, if not all, of us must share the blame. The responsibility is on all our shoulders. If we are objective and responsible, this fact should change our approach from one that is accusatory, diversionary, and divisive to one of sharing a common objective and working together in harmony to accomplish that objective.

Second, it makes it clear that a basic philosophy is needed, to which we must dedicate ourselves and which must be followed consistently if all the problems are to be solved. Even though we stated that attacking problems individually is likely to bring some *net* advancement in improving productivity, from an ideal viewpoint we should approach all the problems from the vantage point of a basic philosophy, a set of ideals. To attack each of a multitude of problems individually without reference to such a basic unifying philosophy for guidance could very well result in solutions that are inconsistent and counterproductive. Even if there is some *net* advancement, productivity is not likely to be maximized. We feel our research has shown this to be true.

We don't need to develop that basic philosophy. It exists, and has existed for 210 years or so; but for a variety of reasons we have forgotten, or have come to overlook, its basic tenets. Equally important—perhaps even more so—systems have developed over the years that produce actions that run counter to the tenets of that basic philosophy. Our purpose in this chapter is to describe that philosophy, indicate what we need to follow it, and show that it is basic to solving the productivity problem. Once that philosophy is understood, dedication to its ideals and consistency in their application are the keys to maximizing productivity increases.

Placing the Problem in Perspective

Even though our average standard of living (in terms of dollars of constant purchasing power) has improved little, if any, during the last decade, on the whole and on the average we live well. On the other hand, we should be concerned. Chapters 2 and 3 do indicate that we have substantive problems that must be recognized, attacked, and solved if, in real terms, we are to improve our standard of living in the future. The longer such problems are allowed to exist unsolved, the more difficult they will be to solve. Moreover, despite the fact that 1983 and up to mid-1984, the date of this writing, the United States has had gains in productivity, we must not fall into the trap of assuming that the problems have gone away. Those gains are due primarily to emergence from a recession, not to any specific act or program designed to improve productivity. We still face severe problems related to productivity. We must start to solve these problems now; and they should be evaluated, reevaluated, and altered where necessary, on a continuing basis, so that we do not slip back into the bad habits of the past.

We should not be lulled into the belief that we can remain at a relatively high standard of living without working very hard at it. It may be possible to conceive of a *stable* high standard of living, but in practice this is difficult, if not impossible, to achieve. In the long run our standard of living, however it is defined, will either increase or decrease. Even if we consider the United States by itself, the causes of productivity changes are too complex, too interrelated and interdependent, to expect any degree of stability. When we consider the United States in the context of competing nations, it is too much to hope that all the factors will somehow balance out to a stable high standard of living. For example, as the productivity growth of other nations outstrips ours, we lose competitiveness in the world markets. Declining productivity is often accompanied by rising inflation and unemployment. The dollar cheapens relative to other nations' currencies, and foreign firms are able to buy up

American businesses. These and other factors usually translate into a decreased U.S. standard of living.

Chapters 2 and 3 clearly indicate that there is a problem and that the root causes for this problem go back perhaps 40 or 50 years (we will discuss the root causes further later in this chapter), even though the consequences of those causes were not grave until the last decade or so. Given that the problem is substantial and has had a heavy impact on our economy, the United States is not in a critical economic crisis; we are not about to go down the economic drain—at least not yet. But we must be positive and optimistic that the problem can be solved, and that we have enough time to solve it. Otherwise, we are not likely to devote enough effort to the problem. A total effort is needed, and needed now.

Reasons for Lack of Progress

During the past few years not many subjects have been discussed at such length as productivity with so few results. Why? There are a number of reasons for this lack of progress.

Complexity

Productivity is a complex subject in terms of both concept (meaning) and measurement. Unless we have at least a general understanding of its meaning, we can't develop a common objective toward which to work. And unless we understand how to measure productivity and changes in it, it is difficult to determine if the objective is being attained. To understand a difficult concept, it is sometimes best to go back to fundamentals. Productivity, for example, entails *output* and *standard of living.*

In its broadest sense, *output* refers to whatever is produced. Output could be material things such as automobiles and homes, artistic productions such as ballets and operas, or services such as cleaner air and water or improved safety standards for workers. *Standard of living,* in its broadest sense, refers to each individual's well-being, as he or she measures it. One person may be perfectly content to live in the wilds of a forest, surviving on berries and nuts, communing with nature, and having few of the rights and responsibilities attached to urban living. That person may think he has the highest possible standard of living. Another person might measure his well-being strictly by number of material possessions. Most people fall somewhere between these extremes. The major point is that *anything* that increases someone's standard of living, as that person perceives it, could be viewed as an increase in productivity. Consequently, it is easy to see that an increase in national output, whatever it may be, does not necessarily represent an increase in productivity from one particular person's point of view.

As we move from the individual's point of view to consider sectors of the U.S. economy, the entire U.S. economy, or other aggregates, the concept and measurement of productivity become more complex. It becomes necessary to consider the *aggregate* average change in standard of living related to the *aggregate* output for the group or sector being considered—a business, a grouping of industries, all manufacturing concerns in the United States, a city, a state, a country, or the entire world. However, no matter which level we consider beyond that of the individual, if the aggregate output increases the aggregate average standard of living, there has been a growth in productivity.

We can see immediately a number of the problems that are inherent in the measurement and interpretation of productivity changes.

1. "Standard of living" changes cannot be measured directly when we are considering large groups or total populations. Surrogate measures, such as bushels of wheat per acre, number of automobiles per auto worker, or the like, must be used.

2. On the output side, some items that might have an impact on the standard of living either cannot be measured at all or can be measured only quite inaccurately (for example, the benefits associated with a cleaner environment or with increased safety for workers), and thus are very difficult, or impossible, to include in productivity measures at the present time.

3. A number of important input factors, such as capital, are usually not included by many who measure changes in productivity. This has led the Bureau of Labor Statistics (BLS) to attach the following caveat to the productivity statistics it publishes:

> . . . these measures relate output to employment and employee hours; they do not measure the specific contribution of labor, capital, or other factors of production. Rather they reflect the joint effect of a number of interrelated influences such as changes in technology; capital in-

vestment per worker; level of output; utilization of capacity; layout and flow of material; managerial skill; and skills and effort of the work force.[4]

In other words, although productivity is determined by many factors, it is measured by the BLS only in terms of employment and employee hours. We expand on this in a subsequent section devoted to measurement problems.

4. Problems of measurement and interpretation increase as statistics are aggregated for industries and the total U.S. economy. For example, firms and industries are not all affected in the same way by inflation, high interest rates, and taxes. Neither do specific solutions apply equally to every industry or firm. Increasing depreciation deductions for tax purposes might help capital-intensive industries but have little impact on labor-intensive industries, and the impact of other solutions varies also.

The data and considerations in Chapters 2 and 3 lead to three broad possibilities:

1. Some things may be done on the broad macro level (total U.S. economy) that can help to solve the productivity problem for business firms generally, and for small businesses in particular.

2. Other things done specifically for the "small business sector" may help it to overcome productivity problems.

3. Specific segments of the small business sector may have different problems calling for different solutions. Firms in the small business sector range from capital-intensive to labor-intensive, from financial to manufacturing, and so on. Even though all small firms may have some common problems, they also undoubtedly differ in terms of their needs and the appropriate approaches to satisfy their needs.

In the course of this study, we will be concerned primarily with the first possibility. All three are critically important, of course, in solving the productivity problem completely. It is simply beyond the range of reasonable possibility to cover them all in one writing. Certainly we will consider data related to small businesses, but basically only as a stepping-stone to the establishment of conclusions and recommendations at the broad macro level.

Thus, objectives must be defined and the means for attaining those objectives must be included in the determination of whether productivity has changed, and in which direction. Economists define average productivity, in its simplest terms, as "output divided by input." Our discussion indicates the necessity of coming to some agreement on the desired objectives (outputs); only then can decisions be made as to which inputs are necessary to reach those desired objectives. In addition, data are needed to provide indications of how well the inputs have been utilized. This has led one writer to remark that "it is essential to clarify and to distinguish between the terms *efficiency* and *effectiveness* which, in essence, combine to form productivity. . . . Effectiveness refers to achieving desired ends without paying attention to how many inputs it took to do so. Efficiency refers to achieving desired results with minimum inputs or obtaining maximum results from a limited amount of input."[5] One might produce 10,000 widgets in the most efficient manner possible, but if there is no demand for widgets, one could hardly declare that the undertaking was effective or that productivity improved.

Questions such as the following must therefore be answered. How many resources should be allocated to pollution abatement equipment? Because resources are limited (we don't live in a utopia), and the resources used to produce a clean environment are therefore not available to produce other products and services, the question becomes, "How important is a clean environment, and how many of our resources are we willing to commit to achieve it?" This is only one of the many such societal questions that must be answered. In a democracy those decisions are ultimately made by the citizens: they set the objectives and determine what they wish the balance to be. In general, citizens in a democracy determine the average standard of living they want, given the scarce resources available. Not everyone will necessarily be happy with the result, of course, but it reflects the will of the majority. Once the objectives are defined, an attempt is made to obtain them in the most efficient manner, with the minimum use of scarce resources.

In this writing, we will not attempt to answer such societal questions as how many resources ought to be devoted to such things as workers' safety and pollution control. We will present data reflecting the costs of such programs with implications on the decreases in the production of other goods and services brought about by them, so that readers are in a better position to judge whether their costs exceed the benefits. Only with such knowledge can rational decisions be made.

Measurement Problems

Measurement difficulties related to productivity are another significant reason the problem has not been solved. Because we are primarily concerned with the policy level and the conceptual problems involved at that level, we will spend little time on this issue; nevertheless, it must be placed in perspective to understand the total picture.

There is disagreement, or at least uncertainty, as to what should be considered in both sides of the equation: outputs and inputs. As factors are added to or subtracted from either side, the final measurement of productivity also changes, and with it interpretations are altered, both deliberately and accidently. As a consequence, incorrect conclusions might be reached, resulting in inappropriate recommendations for solutions.

In the past, the BLS in the U.S. Department of Labor has been the organization most involved in measuring productivity. In essence, the BLS measures productivity by dividing the output of goods and services in the private economy by the hours of labor paid for. Three important sources of error come into the BLS measures of output:

1. The output of about 5% of private business firms is measured indirectly—by proxy output variables.

2. The outputs of government and nonprofit institutions are excluded because they can't be measured.

3. Output is deflated to correspond with the "base" or real value. In the process, the deflators exclude the real productivity of some industries, such as computers and aircraft, in which rising prices have been accompanied by extremely rapid technological changes.[6]

There are measurement problems on the input side as well:

1. BLS productivity indexes do not explicitly include the input factors of capital, energy, and materials.

2. The indexes measure hours paid for, not hours actually worked.

3. They do not measure productivity at the plant level.

4. BLS publishes productivity measures for only 75 out of about 400 industries.[7]

Of course, an ideal productivity index would divide *all* goods and services from all sectors of the economy by *all* the input factors used in creating the output. To be most useful, an index measuring *output* should have the following characteristics:

- It should relate output to the volume of imputs from all basic factors of production—labor, capital, and purchased materials and services—in other words, it should be a "total factor" measurement system.
- It should relate output to the investment in intangibles such as research and development.
- It should relate output to the investment required to comply with government regulations.[8]

These things are more easily said than done. In the first place, even if it were possible to measure all the factors affecting both the input and output sides objectively, the cost of accumulating the necessary data could be prohibitive. As businesses would not be likely to collect this information on their own, more regulations would have to be forthcoming from the federal government to get the job done.

In the second place, certain important sectors of the economy affecting the standard of living are either excluded or included only indirectly in these measures. Most service industries such as insurance companies, hospitals, most schools, police, and postal services fall in this category. Developing and implementing measures of productivity for these sectors at a reasonable cost would be difficult.

Another long-standing problem with which the Bureau of Labor Statistics has been contending in constructing the consumer price index is how to exclude quality changes and technological improvements so that the index will reflect changes in the *general* price level—inflation or deflation—more accurately. In a broader sense, the problem is really how to adjust for all *specific* price changes that are brought about by changes in supply and demand factors relating to the good or service, as opposed to price changes brought about by other factors that cause inflation. To begin with, distinguishing between the two is extremely difficult; then, measuring them with any reasonable degree of reliability for the entire economy, or even selecting representative goods and services out of the total as a surrogate, would be a large and complex task. Nevertheless, such differences are critical in measuring real changes in productivity accurately.

Finally, even though some promising research has been done on measuring output, accurate measurement of benefits from items such as environmental and research and development expenditures still appears to be on the distant horizon.

An ideal index measuring *inputs* would have the following characteristics:

- It would distinguish between various skill levels because one assumes that if all other factors were kept equal, the more highly skilled person would be more productive than a less-skilled employee.
- It would assess the effect that increasing numbers of female and younger workers have on productivity at the macro level, though the time and effort to make this calculation accurately would be enormous.
- It would include the currently excluded "white-collar" workers, who make up about 35% of employees in manufacturing industries.
- It would include capital, energy, and intermediate goods and services as inputs in the calculations of productivity changes.[9]

In sum, when only the input of production workers is included in the calculations of productivity, all items included in the output side are attributed to their efforts. The unsophisticated user of such statistics is likely to give production workers all the credit for productivity increases and all the blame for productivity decreases. As indicated earlier in the caution given by the BLS, other inputs do have an impact on productivity and should be considered when interpreting productivity statistics. However, this is like saying, "Here is the statistic, but don't believe what it tells you. I cannot show you exactly why it is not true, but I can make a few broad generalizations about other things that do have an effect on productivity." Interpretation is difficult—or impossible—under such circumstances, and considerable caution is needed.

It is encouraging to note that a number of economists and others outside government are experimenting with measurements of what is often called "multifactor productivity." For instance, the American Productivity Center now publishes a quarterly Total Factor Productivity Index that includes capital investment input as well as labor effort in measuring productivity. Although the center itself admits that lack of data keeps the index from being highly accurate, the Total Factor Productivity Index reflects an even greater decline in U.S. productivity than indexes that include only labor input.[10] Others are also discussing "total factor productivity" and how to apply it to business settings.[11]

The lack of progress in solving the measurement problems may be due in part to the fact that productivity declines generally were not observed until the late 1960's or early 1970's, and substantial effort was not put into it until a few years ago. It will take time.

Such uncertainties in measurement create disagreements as to *specific* causes of productivity changes and therefore make it difficult to arrive at an agreement on the *specific* solutions that are needed when productivity declines. This is particularly troublesome at the macro level, but it is also a problem in comparing the productivity of sectors and of firms at the plant level. However, no matter how productivity is measured, there is a consensus that total productivity is declining (at the macro level), and "the slowdown . . . is by no means confined to special parts of the business economy."[12] Consequently, the measurement problems will not seriously affect the goals and objectives of this monograph.

Lack of Agreement Among Economists

One of the most important reasons the productivity problem has not been solved can be laid at the doorstep of economists. Most disciplines have areas of contention and disagreement, but none has more than economics. Each economist appears to have his own pet theories about the problems that exist and their solutions. These vary greatly, so it is no wonder the rest of us—politicians, business leaders, labor unions, and all the others—who depend on these economists as experts in the area are confused and have difficulty in selecting rationally from the potpourri of recommended solutions those most likely to work.

From the 1930's until about a decade ago, most economists probably adhered to the philosophy of John Maynard Keynes, who felt output, employment, income, and prices are determined by aggregate spending. He believed that there is a trade-off between inflation and unemployment and that government action is needed to stabilize the economy, primarily through fiscal policy. Monetary policy he considered as secondary. Keynesian economists believe inflation is caused when the demand for goods and services exceeds the supply and wage and price increases exceed productivity increases.

It became clear to many in the early 1970's that Keynesian theory could not explain stagflation, a situation of high unemployment, reduced demand, and increased inflation. Many adherents dropped by the wayside as a result.

Monetarists believe that the economy has an inherent tendency toward stability and that changes in the money supply—not fiscal policy—have the primary impact on economic activity. They believe changes in the money supply cause changes in economic activity through changes in quantity, price, or both. They believe all inflation is demand-pull, caused by a growth in money supply in excess of growth of output, and that fiscal policy has little impact on economic activity. Yet many business leaders in the automotive industries contend that high wages have pushed prices beyond the point where their products can compete effectively [cost-push inflation]. A few months ago the money supply was increased beyond the growth in real GNP, interest rates fell, and the stock market soared, while inflation continued downward. Again, the point is that monetary theory, like Keynesian theory, does not explain all changes in economic activity under all circumstances.

We have seen the rise of so-called neo-Keynesians who borrow and combine what they believe to be the best ideas of Keynes and monetarists such as Milton Friedman to explain economic activity. Neoliberals have come into being, preaching that even more government intervention, government planning for the future, and social spending are necessary. Some critics have said that "the neoliberals understand everything but reality, because they assume that the U.S. economy is static—that people's behavior will not change significantly just because we alter their incentives.[13]

A number of economists, different in certain respects from the neoliberals, have one common theme they emphasize—"national industrial policy"—"the government should play a greater role in managing the economy."[14] Although individuals in this group—Robert Reich, Thomas Weisskopf, Lester Thurow, and Robert Lekachman—differ on particulars in terms of where and how government influence should be directed, all want to inject the government more and more into the pattern and structure of economic activity. They want certain industries targeted—mainly the so-called smokestack industries—for government help and influence in competing with foreign competitors, although their recommendations in this regard are still hazy and not well developed.

It is obvious as one reads the writings of these and some other economists that they, too, lack a basic philosophy from which their ideas spring or, if they do have a philosophy, it is not one that derives from a representative democracy as we later describe it. Certainly political feelings influence economic theories, as we have stated, and certainly these writers have a right to their political feelings. We are not alleging that those economists don't agree with representative democracy—only that if they do, they don't understand it. But whether they disagree or don't understand is unimportant. What is important is that the people who are considering their recommendations understand where those recommendations are at variance with the dictates of representative democracy so that they may evaluate accurately what the cost of following those suggestions might be.

Time Lapse in Representative Democracies

Another reason the productivity problem has not been solved is the necessary delay, in representative democracies, between the time an emerging problem is observed and the time action is taken to solve the problem. First, it takes time before enough citizens become aware of the problem to pressure their representatives to make the necessary changes. Second, it often takes time—and sometimes dramatic events—before the representatives become aware of the citizens' desires and feelings.

For example, consider government expenditures and regulations, which have been increasing for at least 50 years. During much of that time, the average standard of living in the United States also was increasing, and most of the citizens supported representatives who voted for increased spending and regulations. In other words, as long as productivity is great enough to increase the average standard of living to an acceptable degree, the citizens are not concerned about the amount of resources diverted to government use. When productivity increases are not great enough to do this, when citizens perceive that their standard of living is decreasing or not increasing at the rate they desire, they make their dissatisfaction known. Likewise, citizens seldom feel concerned about the increasing number of regulations until those regulations impinge on fundamental rights or, again, negatively affect their standard of living. The election of President Reagan and a more conservative House of Representatives and Senate are reflections of the reaction of citizens to these factors, among others.

Thus, even though the present productivity problem is rooted in thinking and actions that occurred many years ago, the impact was not apparent until the early 1970's, and citizens did not react until late 1979. As a result of their reaction, President Reagan was able to get through Congress a budget and tax cut program he hoped would start to reverse the trends of the last 50 years.

The Essential Reason for Failure

But the essential reason we have a productivity problem and have failed to solve it is that we have swerved away from following a number of the major tenets of democracy, and have developed systems (in business organizations, in nonbusiness organizations, with special-interest groups, and in governments at all levels) that have aided and abetted these deviations. Before discussing these assertions in more detail, we will provide needed perspective with a brief historical review.

A Brief Historical Review

People have been interested in productivity since at least the Industrial Revolution. In the early part of the twentieth century, pioneers in productivity research such as Frederick Taylor and Frank and Lillian Gilbreth sought to improve productivity through time and motion studies. They sought to establish the most efficient production methods, and then to use them as standards against which to gauge the performance of the workforce. Their effort was at the plant level.

Life was much simpler during that era, and people generally agreed that increasing production of products was a desirable objective. Government at all levels was much smaller and taxation was low. (Remember, the federal income tax didn't come into existence until 1913.) The amount of resources used for services was low relative to the amount used to make products; and a general philosphy of *laissez-faire,* or noninterference by government, permeated the land. In such an atmosphere, government units at all levels have little impact on productivity. The emphasis on improving productivity appears at the company or plant level, and some combination of these measurements of productivity at the plant level would indicate what productivity is and how it is changing at the industry level and at the macro level—say, for the entire United States.

After the stock market crash, beginning with the start of the

"Roosevelt era" in 1932, the government began taking a more active role in the lives of individuals. Government work programs such as the WPA came into existence; the social security program was started; and in myriad ways, government regulation of individuals and businesses increased. Although the role of government has been defined and redefined since that period, it has continuously grown during the past 50 years, particularly at the federal level. Transfer payments, such as welfare, have increased. Regulations have increased. Administering them costs money, so taxes have increased, thus removing from the private economy money that could have been used for capital investment and other purposes.

A critical point, needing emphasis, is that the structure of the workplace has undergone three significant changes during the last 50 years. First, farm productivity has increased rapidly as a result of capital replacing labor on the farms. Technological advances in farm production have taken place at a rapid pace. As a consequence, the average farm size has increased significantly, and the number of farm workers needed has been reduced. From a high of approximately one fourth of the population in the United States living and working on farms in 1929, the number has steadily decreased to about 4% at the present time. The first big exodus from the farms to the cities took place during the economic crises of the 1930's when millions of agricultural jobs were lost. This is when the United States moved from a primarily argicultural to a manufacturing economy. Displaced farmers moved to cities in the hopes of finding work. Most of these people did not have the necessary skills to perform the required tasks in the factories, even when work was available in the plants.

The second major change in the structure of the workplace probably started in the mid-1950's but was not felt significantly until the mid- to late-1970's. Service industries expanded rapidly, much more than production industries, as reflected in Figure 4-1. "During this period, manufacturing decreased from 33 percent of national income to about 23 percent, while service functions increased from 10 to 15 percent. In late 1982, the number of service industries surpassed those in industrial employment."[15] One reason for this was that productivity was increasing significantly during much of the period from 1945 through the late 1960's; more industrial goods were being produced by fewer and fewer people, releasing people to work in the service and other industries. The percentage of white-collar workers increased compared with that of blue-collar workers.

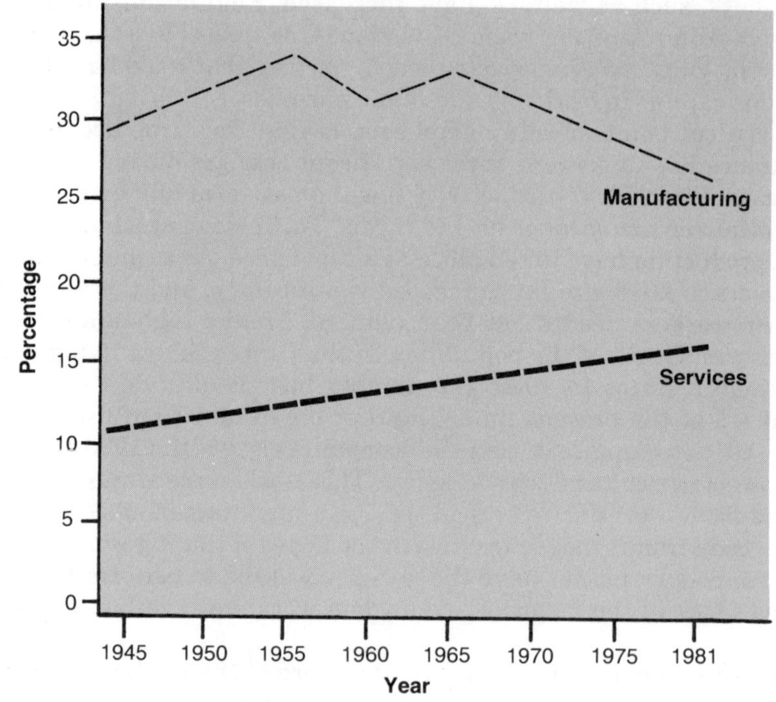

FIGURE 4-1
National Income from Manufacturing and Services, 1945–1981
Source: U.S. Bureau of Economic Analysis.
35
30
25
20
15
10
5
0
Percentage
Manufacturing
Services
1945
1950
1955
1960
1965
1970
1975
1981
Year
Manufacturing includes autos, fabricated metals, furniture, wood products, food, printing, chemicals, petroleum, and textiles.
Services includes hotels, restaurants, auto repairs, amusements, health, education, and legal aid.

A third major change is our loss of competitive advantage in the smokestack industries. "As late as 1979, the steel industry was producing over 3 million more tons of steel than it had a decade earlier, but with 75,000 fewer workers."[16] Nevertheless,

> Foreign competitors with modern factories can produce more steel more cheaply than U.S. producers with 20th century open-hearth furnaces, despite the added expense of shipping the product halfway around the world. . . .

> Lack of investment in new facilities has left the industry with an aged capital stock. Aggressive investment by foreign producers, in contrast, provided some countries not only more modern plants, but also larger plants with the accompanying economies of scale.[17]

The consequence has been that foreign producers have maintained their share of the U.S. market at approximately 20 million tons of steel during the last three years of recession, while production of U.S. companies has fallen by about 16 million tons.

Steel and automotive companies have closed their most outmoded, least efficient plants, and are beginning to adopt new technologies to increase productivity.

> At the Chrysler Corp. plant in Newark, Del., a Chrysler spokesman says 30 robots under the direction of an electrician have taken the jobs of 30 workers while increasing production from 60 cars an hour to 100.

> General Motors Corp. will have 14,000 robots at work by 1990, says GM economist H. Paul Root. The robots will improve quality control and lower production costs, Root says.

> The steel industry is undergoing similar changes.[18]

Labor costs are the major reason for closing inefficient plants and developing new technologies. "In 1972, the wages and health and welfare benefits of a steelworker averaged $7.08 per hour. By 1981, the union had negotiated wages and benefits worth $20.16 per hour—70 percent higher than the inflation rate for that 10-year period. By knocking more than 100,000 workers off the payroll, the industry reaped savings of $1.3 million an hour."[19] Similar wage increases took place in the automotive and other industries.

Thus, during the last 50 years we have gone from a primarily agrarian economy, to a production or manufacturing economy, to a service-oriented economy. Blue-collar workers have decreased significantly, while white-collar workers have increased. Important technological advances have been made in many areas, and we have probably only seen the beginning. In some areas we have lost our technological advantage and are fighting to regain it. In a word, we have seen dramatic structural changes in the economy, and history teaches that they are likely to continue. All such changes affect productivity and its measurement.

During this period, we also have seen the rise of environmental protection groups. Labor union power and influence have increased, with resulting pressure for increased wages, better retirement benefits, and greater emphasis on job design and enrichment. Consumer advocates have come to the fore. These changes and their impact on the thinking and attitudes of society are reflected in the 1975 legislation to establish the now defunct National Center for Productivity and Quality of Working Life. The purpose of the center was "to establish a national policy which will encourage productivity growth consistent with needs of the economy, the natural environment, and the needs, rights, and best interests of management, the work force, and consumers."[20]

All the above factors, as well as many others, affect productivity and increase the difficulties of measuring it. And, as we see later, a great deal of the discussion at the government level during the past decade regarding productivity turns out to be nothing more than lip service; i.e., there has been a great deal of discussion with little substantive accomplishment. Admittedly, there has been a turnaround regarding some major factors during the last few years—but more about that later.

In summary, government is now often seen as having two basic functions: (1) to do for citizens those things they desire but are unable to do for themselves and (2) to redistribute the wealth of the country. The first function includes such things as building highways and providing protection through the military, among many others. Although income distribution might be altered indirectly by these actions, their primary goal is to provide services that citizens desire, and that consequently contribute to their standard of living as they perceive it. If the government would take on only the first function, the pricing system would be allowed to distribute wealth as well as to determine what is produced.

As we mentioned, until the 1930's citizens perceived their standard of living as being increased primarily by the increased production of goods and services in the private economy. The shock of the depression in the 1930's led many people to demand more of government because they perceived that their standard of living would improve as a result.

At the same time, and in the years since, a great deal of emphasis in American society has been directed at redistributing income in accomplishing the second function of government. Many citizens believed that their standard of living would be higher if wealth were redistributed in what was perceived to be a more equitable fashion. Thus, we saw the rise of the minimum wage law, unemployment compensation, welfare payments, and the like. Private organizations, such as unions, certainly have played a role in wealth redistribution as well.

The critical point is that it's an entirely different ball game when there are influences outside the business venture that have a substantial impact on its productivity, compared with situations in which there are fewer external influences. In the latter case, about the only concern is to increase productivity at the micro level—the level of the firm. In the former case, those outside influences can be so extensive that productivity will decline no matter what is done at the firm level. When that is true, the first task is to alter policies so that increased productivity is encouraged, or at least so that the outside influences are neutralized and firms can work toward improving productivity. That, in fact, is our primary goal in writing this monograph.

We will discuss these things more fully later, but here we wish to make a broad point or two to clarify the essential meaning of productivity. First, as long as citizens *on the average* support government programs for income redistribution, it is clear that they believe these programs are bettering their average standard of living at the national or macro level. In this broad sense, then, government programs are productive as long as desired objectives are being attained. When citizens reach the point of feeling that programs have gone too far, that the costs exceed the benefits in terms of the standard of living, they will insist on cutbacks until an acceptable level is reached. In this sense, income redistribution reduces the majority's share of the output of measurable goods and services below acceptable levels, and they are therefore perceived to be unproductive.

But measurement techniques are easier to use and to interpret at the firm, or micro, level. For example, if employees at a factory work faster and produce more of a given type of shoe per hour, thereby reducing price, people desiring that type of shoe would conclude that productivity has increased, other things remaining equal. Whether this represents an increase in productivity from the point of view of the entire economy, however, is another matter. Nevertheless, we must consider productivity questions at all levels if productivity is to be maximized. At the same time we need to keep potential conflicts, interrelationships, and interdependencies of cause and effect in clear focus.

Productivity Is a Political Issue

These considerations lead us to conclude that how, where, and how much to increase productivity are primarily political issues, in terms of both output and input. Whether this is good or bad depends upon how "political" is visualized. In a pure democracy, people would decide every issue by vote, given that basic rights were appropriately protected. For example, the Bill of Rights gives Americans the right to worship as they see fit. It implies strongly that *each* American has that right, and that it cannot be taken away from him by majority vote. Many feel, in fact, that one of the Constitution's main fuctions is to preserve and protect the rights of individuals and minority groups, to protect them against the tyranny of the majority.

In a republic, such as the United States, citizens elect representatives whose primary responsibility is to act on behalf of the people. Citizens no longer decide each issue by direct vote, as in a pure or direct democracy, but the election of representatives who act on their behalf supposedly produces a similar result—representative democracy. Thus, indirectly, most issues are decided by majority vote (or, at least, by the majority of those who vote).

We need to understand the basic differences in political systems if we are to understand how the inclinations of persons toward these systems (or at least toward some of the attributes of the systems) are likely to affect their beliefs about what causes declining productivity, the weighting they give to each of these causes, and the solutions they recommend. For example, one author, in describing the causes of the U.S. productivity slowdown, listed and discussed the following divergent views:

1. The "mainstream" position of the neoclassical economists
2. The "war economy" argument . . .
3. The "neo-Marxist" interpretation that is espoused by radical economists

4. The "doomsday" stance derived from the writings of those who predict, and often advocate, an end to economic growth

5. The "noninterventionist," or free market, perspective of the libertarian economists . . .[21]

This indicates that the importance given to certain causes varies, just as the importance given to solutions will depend on the economic and political philosophies held by the individuals. It makes it difficult to arrive at a consensus on the causes of declines in productivity; perhaps more importantly, the differences in philosophies make it hard to agree on the best approaches to reverse the trend and the relative weights or emphasis that ought to be given to them.

As we stated earlier, we accept as a given that the vast majority of citizens in the United States want representative democracy. The problem is that (1) we are not following some of the major basic tenets of that philosophy and (2) we do not perceive how the considerations of productivity, particularly at the macro level, tie into this philosophy. Consequently, we need to spend some time on these matters.

The Basic Tenets of Representative Democracy

Webster's Third New International Dictionary[22] defines "democracy" and "republic" as follows:

Democracy. Government by the people . . . a form of government in which the supreme power is vested in the people and exercised by them directly [absolute, or pure, democracy] or indirectly [representative democracy] through a system of representation. . . .

Republic. A state in which supreme power resides in a body of citizens entitled to vote and is exercised by elected officers and representatives responsible to them and governing according to law; also a political unit (as a nation or state) having such a form of government.

In order to continue the discussions of the political aspects of productivity, we also need the following definitions from *Webster's*[23]:

Communism. A totalitarian system of government in which the state . . . through the medium of a single authoritarian party controls in large measure the economic, social, and cultural life of the society.

Fascism. Any program for setting up a centralized autocratic national regime with severely nationalistic policies, exercising regimentation of industry, commerce, and finance, rigid censorship, and forcible suppression of opposition.

Socialism. Any of various theories or social and political movements advocating or aiming at collective or governmental ownership and administration of the means of production and control of the distribution of goods.

Representative democracies and republics are essentially the same (we'll use the term *representative democracy* in the rest of this discussion) and both forms of government stress *individualism,* which *Webster's*[24] defines as:

The ethical doctrine or principle that the interests of the individual himself are or ought to be paramount in determination of conduct. . . . A theory . . . maintaining the political and economic independence of the individual. . . . The conception that all values, rights, and duties originate in individuals and that the community or social whole has no value or ethical significance not derived from its constituent individuals.

How do the essential differences in political systems affect productivity questions? Although there are many ideological and philosophical differences between systems, for our purposes the essential difference is the degree of freedom and power individuals have under the various systems, particularly the amount of *economic freedom and power.*

Implications for the property rights of individuals are clear. In pure communism, individuals have no property rights; they cannot own private property, nor can they own the means of production and distribution. As a significant consequence, the pricing mechanism is not allowed to work on either the production or the distribution side. The party (more particularly, the leaders in power—the dictators) decides what will be produced and how the output will be distributed (a centrally planned economy).

In fascist countries (Germany under Hitler, for example, or Italy under Mussolini), there are some differences in terms of property rights, but they are insignificant from the viewpoint of society as a whole. Individuals are allowed to own property in fascist regimes, but only at the will of the dictator. Essentially this means that they can own property but only as long as they support the dictator and use the property in an approved way. Nevertheless, under fascism the pricing mechanism is not allowed to operate to any significant degree on either the production or the distribution of goods, because individuals generally do not have the right, through their investment and consumption patterns, to decide what will be produced and how it will be distributed.

Most of the same points can be made regarding socialist countries, but to a lesser degree. Although private property can be owned by individuals, the governments in such countries own the essential means for the production and distribution of goods and services, such as the steel and railroad industries. Therefore, and in spite of the ideal that socialism is to provide for "democratic management of the essential means for the production and distribution of goods," a few individuals make many of the basic production decisions, deciding which firms will stay alive, which will die, and which will contract or expand. Beyond this, socialist governments are heavily involved in the distribution of goods and services, deciding who will be able to obtain the goods and services produced.

The very essence of capitalism as opposed to these other systems, and one of its main strengths from an economic viewpoint, is its flexibility.

> . . . . The great merit of capitalism and the secret of its past successes was its great flexibility, imparted to it by the automatic forces of the market.
>
> In general, there are two kinds of economic flexibility. The first is the flexibility of the economy's individual members: the flexibility of consumers in adapting their expenditure patterns, of producers in modifying methods of production and utilizing the most available inputs, and of the owners of productive services in providing the services most in demand. The second and more drastic kind is the ability of the system as a whole to . . . increase its reliance on those best adapted or able to adapt to changed circumstances and [to get rid of] those unadapted and unable to adapt. . . .
>
> Market prices and earnings were an excellent means of assuring both kinds of flexibility.[25]

A number of important and interrelated aspects of capitalism are contained in the above statement. First, the consumer is king. By casting their individual votes in the marketplace each time they buy a product or service, consumers communicate what and how much they want produced. Owners and managers react to such signals by increasing or decreasing production, or by changing the goods and services they produce. Consequently, and importantly, consumers get timely and direct feedback from the market regarding products and services available, and the prices at which they are available, to aid their decision-making process. But prices also fulfill a distributive function. Those producers who are able to anticipate market demand, those most able to adapt to changing circumstances, those most effective and efficient, will receive the greatest rewards. Those least able to do these things will be weeded out of the market.

Second, if capitalism is to work and survive, the market must remain essentially free of outside controls so it can adjust to these responses. Sometimes such adjustments are hardly noticeable, but at other times they are dramatic and traumatic. Capitalists, in other words, believe essentially in the "invisible hand" doctrine of Adam Smith. Paraphrased, it says that if each individual is left to pursue economic objectives in his own best interest, an "invisible hand" is present that will ensure that society as a whole will be better off economically.

For people to act in this manner, anticipated rewards must exceed anticipated risks. If all risks are removed, all chances for success are also removed. The future is unknown. In order to reap benefits, risks must be assumed. When anticipated rewards are reduced below anticipated risks, entrepreneurship is destroyed. If the rewards for accepting risk are reduced by devices such as heavy taxation, or the risk/reward relationship becomes altered by government regulations, transfer payments to redistribute wealth, and high taxes, for example, capitalism becomes less flexible. Carried far enough, such devices could destroy capitalism. Thus, expectations are critical in the process.

> It makes a difference in the results of the economic behavior of businessmen and consumers, whether at a given time most people expect similar future trends or whether the average expectations result from many [people] expecting much higher rates of change in the future [while] many others expect much lower ones.[26]

Third, and strongly implied by the first two, capitalism requires people to have a long-range view. Although some necessary adjustments may hurt some people in the short run, the more effective and efficient use of resources will more than make up for that in the long run. As no one can foresee the future, mistakes will be made in the short run, but they will be more than counterbalanced in the long run.

For example, what if someone puts his entire life savings into a restaurant? He would do so only in the belief that he would earn enough profit to compensate for the risks he takes. But there is no guarantee—nor should there be—that he will make a profit. What if he is driven out of business because of poor location, bad food, poor service, incompetent management, or some combination of these and/ or other reasons? Certainly he is hurt economically; he has used his resources inefficiently and ineffectively. No one wishes to lose money or waste resources but, in effect, short-run failures become or are a necessary cost of long-run success.

Thus, when we consider the *economic* attributes of different political systems and plot them on an ordinal scale, we get:

	Decreases	Individual	Increases	

$$\longleftarrow \text{—————— Economic Freedom ——————} \longrightarrow$$

			Representative Democracies		Radical Individualism
Communism	Fascism	Socialism	(Republics)	Pure Democracies	(Anarchy)
|________|	|____|	|______|	|______|	|______|	|____|

It really makes little difference whether communism and fascism are placed to the right or left on the scale, or which one is placed before the other. The critical point is that they are very similar in terms of control of the production and distribution facilities of a country, of the property rights of individuals, and of the other factors we have discussed that are part of the productivity issue.

During the past 50 years, city, state, and federal governments, labor unions, consumer groups, and others have attempted to fine-tune the economy in the hope of easing the short-term economic hurt. They have done this through massive regulations, welfare payments, unemployment compensation, and a variety of other methods that will be discussed later. In so doing, they have substantially reduced the flexibility of capitalism to adjust to imbalances in the economy. Such approaches have caught up with us and are reflected in the decreasing growth in productivity over the last 10 to 15 years.

In the last 50 years we have become more concerned with distribution than with production, evidently not realizing, or at least ignoring, that you can only distribute what is available, and production must come first. We started preaching egalitarianism. We became unwilling to accept the short-run consequences of competition.

> Capitalism never got high marks for equity, although it was good not only to capitalists. *Its fast growth benefited the average person and with him the majority* [emphasis added]; but it did so at the cost of great fluctuations and a wide dispersion of incomes around the fast-growing average. . . . Flexibility and the systems' viability were well maintained as long as the public accepted the inequality of incomes and the wide scatter of winnings and losses as manifestations of the immutable laws of the market.
>
> In time . . . [the more] we learned how to correct, suppress, overrule, or supplement the distributive functions of prices and price changes; and the better we learned to divorce income distribution from market forces, the more reluctant we became to accept the economic inequalities imposed by the market.[27]

As a consequence, we have moved progressively farther to the left on the scale as we have presented it.

However, we emphasize that as a country moves toward the form of government that corresponds with its economic beliefs, it will consequently move toward the associated social and political beliefs as well, and vice versa. Often this is not understood, and recommendations are made without taking this into account. From a policy viewpoint, we must consider this if we want to understand the total costs associated with any given position or change in position.

> Nevertheless Americans concerned for the future of their personal and political freedoms should not assume that they can indefinitely survive the erosion of economic freedom. There is a link between economic freedom and other freedoms. In recent years the American economy, once the most vibrant and vigorous in the world, has acquired an astounding distinction. It has the lowest percentage of capital investment, the lowest rate of productivity growth, and one of the highest percentages of obsolete plants among major industrial countries.[28]

The variety of factors imputed to have an impact on productivity indicates the importance of these discussions of the various types of political systems and the economic ideas inseparably attached to them. This does not mean that any political system necessarily exists in the pure forms in which we have described them. Each system has borrowed and implemented some of the social, political, and economic ideas of one or more of the others. A good example of this is the change going on in China with regard to farm production. At one time, food was grown only in communes and disposed of in accordance with the directives of the leaders of the Communist Party. Now, some farmers are allowed to grow their own "side" crops and sell them in the towns and cities for whatever prices they can obtain:

to this very limited extent, the market has become "free" and the pricing mechanism is allowed to operate.

We are not alleging that socialistic, communistic, or fascist countries cannot have increases in productivity. Over the short run such increases might even exceed those in capitalistic countries. We are alleging that over the long run, productivity will be maximized only if the free market system is allowed to operate in accordance with the tenets we have discussed. We elaborate on this more fully in the following chapters.

Summary and Conclusions

Our productivity problem has many causes, some broad and general, others narrow and specific. And although some headway has been made in improving productivity, the problem has not been solved. We feel that the basic, most important step to be taken, if productivity is to be maximized, is to dedicate ourselves to the basic philosophy already in place and to follow the tenets of that philosophy consistently.

The basic philosophy is representative democracy. Shenfield clearly summarized the ideas discussed in the preceding pages when he listed the following four principles (tenets) of American freedom.

First, the state is not society. Society and the state are two different entities, even though their members may be the same and even though they may intermesh with each other intimately. The state is the entity charged with the task of protecting society, but the society overflows the bounds of the state into fields where the state has no right to go. A society cannot be free if it is synonymous with the state. For if it were, all human activity would not only be governed by law. It would also be prescribed and licensed by law, which is the meaning of totalitarianism.

Secondly, liberty is a negative, not a positive, concept. . . . The negative concept teaches us that liberty is freedom from coercion, not power over desires or desired resources. It includes the freedom to seek the satisfaction of one's wants, subject to the like freedom of others, but not the power to command that satisfaction.

It follows that freedom and welfare are separate, and may be opposing, conditions. In a free society it is hoped, with great practical and historical justification, that freedom will be the fountain of men's welfare, and welfare is therefore sought through freedom. As a general rule welfare may not be sought by state action which offers itself as benevolent and compassionate, for that means the intrusion of the state upon the people's [individuals'] freedom. . . .

Thirdly, the only form of equity which may be sought by the state is equality before the law. With equality before the law, the goddess of justice is rightly depicted as blind as she holds the scales evenly; blind because she is no respecter of persons. To her all, rich or poor, strong or weak, high or low, come for equal protection.

Per contra, the state pursuit of equality of income or wealth is poison to justice and freedom. So too is equality of opportunity if that means, as unfortunately it has increasingly come to mean, that life's races [pursuits] must be fixed so that all start equal. . . .

Notice that though the free society does not seek equality of opportunity, it does produce abundance of opportunity; and in that abundance there is a closer approach to equality of opportunity than is know in any unfree society.

It follows that, though even the modest taxation of the limited state may have some incidental income-redistributive effect, the deliberate pursuit of redistribution of incomes or wealth by the state is absolutely impermissible. . . .

Fourthly, the state may not command, direct, control or regulate the economic activity of the people, except where it can be convincingly shown that such a measure is an essential means of preventing the people from encroaching upon each other's liberty or rightful property.[29]

Underlying these four principles are two basic assumptions. First, people in the United States want power divided such that no one individual, or small group of individuals, can control all, or any significant portion, of it. This means that economic institutions (business and others) must be separated from the state as surely as the press, churches, and universities must be separated from the state. It is this desire for power to be divided among individuals that makes democracy and capitalism (the free market system) necessary.

Second, people generally, and basically, are moral, ethical, and rational. It is doubtful if any society could last long if these things are not true; certainly a representative democracy could not. In other words, it is this assumption that makes democracy and capitalism possible. This does not mean that every individual is moral, ethical, and rational, of course. The system can survive and prosper with a little bit of larceny in the hearts of many, and a great deal of larceny in the hearts of a few. But it cannot survive with a great deal of larceny in the hearts of many.

And a number of subtenets flow from these four principles (some are the basis for further discussion in Chapter 5). These are not stated in any particular order of importance.

1. Primary emphasis is placed on individuals and their rights and responsibilities. Government's primary function, in addition to protecting people generally, is to see to it that rights are preserved and responsibilities fulfilled. For example, we have the right to free speech, but that does not include yelling "fire" in a theater. Everyone claiming a right must stand ready to support and defend that right for everyone else if freedom is to be preserved. It is the government's ensuring that individual rights are preserved and individual responsibilities fulfilled that prevents anarchy.

2. The institutions and systems designed and developed by governments to carry out their legitimate functions, as well as those developed by businesses, nonbusiness organizations, and all others, must be based on the assumption that most people are moral, ethical, and rational; and the procedures in the systems should encourage, promote, and sustain moral, ethical, and rational behavior, not work at cross-purposes with them.

This is not inconsistent with the basic assumptions themselves. As we discuss more fully later when we talk about the free enterprise system, a system cannot be either moral or immoral, but the system can encourage or discourage moral, ethical, and rational conduct.

Also, most people are willing and able to work hard—they wish to be productive members of society. Such attitudes should be promoted. Certainly, systems should not thwart productivity.

3. From a societal viewpoint there cannot be any hierarchical structure of rights. Certainly each individual can decide which rights are of greatest importance to him or her, but to society as a whole, all rights are equal. The right to vote is equal to the right to worship as one pleases. Property rights are equal to these, and so on.

This must be so in a representative democracy, since a reduction or elimination of any right places increased power in the hands of a few and moves a society toward socialism or a totalitarian form of government. In addition, placing rights in any perceived order of importance is divisive and ultimately destructive to the structure of a representative democracy.

And Krushchev, a contemporary Soviet prime minister, said: "We cannot expect Americans to jump from capitalism to Communism, but we can assist their elected leaders in giving Americans doses of socialism until they suddenly awake to find out they have Communism."[30]

4. In terms of abilities, there is a virtually unlimited amount of variation between people. Such differences must be recognized and

promoted, not thwarted by an unrealistic assumption of egalitarianism.

5. Fairness is a nonoperational concept except in the sense that if rights are preserved and responsibilities fulfilled, what results is fair.

Support for a free market economy—the free enterprise system—flows naturally and logically from these tenets and subtenets of representative democracy. As stated earlier, a system cannot be moral, ethical, or rational:

> Like a society, the economic system called capitalism is a system of relationships. It is a composition of markets, and markets are by definition systems of relationships, not purposive bodies. It follows that we can apply the tests of morality to capitalism only by considering the behavior of individuals who operate within it, not as a system capable in itself of being moral or immoral. Is it compatible with just individual behavior? Is it more compatible with just than unjust behavior, or the reverse? Does it nuture or reinforce just or unjust individual behavior? These are the questions which we need to set if we subject capitalism to an examination in morality.[31]

Capitalism, or the free market system, is a system of voluntary relationships in which each individual seeks to maximize his or her own economic self-interest. But we can do this only by reacting with others having the same purpose. This is a compelling force to treat others with respect, for if we don't, ultimately we must be driven from the market.

> This leads us to the most fundamental change in the human condition that has been wrought since the birth of our species. Men have always wanted to be rich, whatever the precepts of their religion may have been. Until the rise of capitalism the most effective way to become rich was to seize men's bodies or land. Submission to conquest of territory, enslavement, or reduction to serfdom were the common experience of the greater part of mankind. . . . Capitalism was the first system in human history to harness the desire to become rich to the peaceful supply of men's abundance. This is the most striking and beneficent change in human affairs of all those produced by the Industrial Revolution. . . .
>
> First, there is the institution of private property, basic to the whole system . . . on balance it is a powerful force for moral training. Every time we treat property with diligence and care, we learn a lesson in morality. We see this in the behavior of the good husbandman, who has traditionally aroused our admiration. . . .

> Secondly, there is the sanctity of contract. There are many who have no respect for it. But the trust of the capitalist system is to favor those who keep their contracts and to hamper those who do not. Sanctity of contract is one of the most important elements in the cement which binds a civilized society together, and it tends to arise naturally in a society where private property is respected. At the same time it has an elevating effect on men's character.
>
> Thirdly, there is the work ethic . . . it is in fact a prime agent of moral training and character evaluation. To know that we must work for what we want, that there are few free goods in the world, that almost everything has a cost which must be met, is to understand the fundamental truth of our situation as human beings. Under capitalism this is brought home to everyone. In a world of collectivism everything still has a cost, but everyone is tempted, even urged, to behave as if there is no cost or as if the cost will be borne by somebody else. This is one of the most corrosive effects of collectivism upon the moral character of the people.[32]

Our right is freedom to pursue our own purposes, with the concomitant responsibility to accord the same freedom to others.

> This is the fundamental morality which capitalism requires and which it nurtures. It alone among economic systems operates on the basis of respect for free, independent, responsible persons. All other systems in varying degrees treat men as less than this.[33]

This does not mean that individuals cannot cooperate in ventures, of course. Without social cooperation, many worthwhile objectives could not be attained. It does means that objectives and procedures to attain them must remain within the tenets of democracy and the dictates of a free market economy.

In three sentences we can summarize these thoughts in terms of the objectives of this monograph. Without a representative democracy, the free enterprise system cannot exist, and the opposite is just as true. A representative democracy can exist over the long run only if all the rights of individuals are preserved and strengthened. Only by following the dictates of the free enterprise system can productivity be maximized.

In the next two chapters we present numerous examples to support these assertions and clarify the meaning and results of the application of the dictates of the free enterprise system to some specific circumstances.

Notes

[1] Deloitte Haskins & Sells, quoting the Committee for Economic Development in "Productivity Policy: Key to the Nation's Economic Future," *The Week in Review,* June 3, 1983, p. 4.

[2] Charles Steele, *The Week in Review,* November 20, 1981, p. 1.

[3] David Gilman, Interview with Lester Thurow, *World,* Vol. 15, No. 1 (Winter 1981), pp. 26–27.

[4] Bruce L. Baggaley, "How Do You Measure Productivity?" *World,* Vol. 15, No. 1 (Winter 1981), p. 12.

[5] Ervin Schoenblum, "Overview and Perspective on Productivity," *Management Focus,* Vol. 25, No. 6 (November–December 1978), p. 13.

[6] Albert Rees, "Improving Productivity Measurement," *The American Economic Review,* Vol. 70, No. 2 (May 1980), p. 340.

[7] Statement of American Productivity Center at the Hearing before the Subcommittee on General Oversight and Minority Enterprise of the Committee on Small Business, House of Representatives, Ninety-Sixth Congress, First Session, on *Productivity and the U.S. Economy,* Washington, D.C., March 14, 1979 (Washington, D.C.: U.S. Government Printing Office, 1979), p. 23.

[8] Baggaley, p. 12.

[9] *Ibid.*

[10] Statement of American Productivity Center at the Hearing before the Subcommittee on General Oversight and Minority Enterprise of the Committee on Small Business, p. 23.

[11] Gary D. Poe and Leon E. Mechem, "How Total Factor Productivity Works," *Management Accounting,* Vol. 64, No. 12 (June 1983), pp. 44–46.

[12] Edward F. Denison, "The Puzzling Setback to Productivity Growth," *Challenge,* Vol. 23, No. 5 (November–December 1980), p. 8.

[13] Louis Rukeyser, "Neoliberalism Is Nonsense," *The Ann Arbor News,* December 5, 1982, p. E2.

[14] Constance Crump, "Democrats Grope for an Economic Guru," and "Profiles," *The Ann Arbor News,* August 14, 1983, pp. C1, C2, and C10.

[15] Leonard Curry, "Good-bye Jobs—A Second Revolution Leaves Industrial Workers in the Cold," *The Ann Arbor News,* October 31, 1982, p. F13.

[16] *Ibid.*

[17] *Ibid.*

[18] *Ibid.*

[19] *Ibid.*

[20] Ervin Schoenblum, p. 15.

[21] Cambell R. McConnell, "Why Is U.S. Productivity Slowing Down? *Harvard Business Review,* Vol. 57, No. 2 (March–April 1979), pp. 36–37.

[22] *Webster's Third New International Dictionary,* Merriam Co., Springfield, Mass., 1981.

[23] *Ibid.*

[24] *Ibid.*

[25] Tibor Scitovsky, "Can Capitalism Survive?—An Old Question in a New Setting," *The American Economic Review,* Vol. 70, No. 2 (May 1980), p. 2.

[26] George Katona, "How Expectations Are Really Formed," *Challenge,* Vol. 23, No. 5 (November–December 1980), p. 33.

[27] Scitovsky, p. 4.

[28]Arthur Shenfield, "A Durable Free Society: Utopian Dream or Realistic Goal," *Imprimis,* Vol. 12, No. 3 (March 1983), p. 3. These quotations are from a paper presented at Hillsdale College's Ludwig Van Mise's Lecture Series and are reprinted by permission of *Imprimis,* the monthly journal for Hill's Center for Constructive Alternatives and its Savano Institute for National Leadership.

[29]*Ibid.,* pp. 1–2.

[30]Libor Brom, "Where Is Your America?" *Imprimis,* Vol. 11, No. 8 (August 1982), p. 3.

[31]Arthur Shenfield, "Capitalism Under the Test of Ethics," *Imprimis,* Vol. 10, No. 12 (December 1981), pp. 1–2.

[32]*Ibid.,* pp. 4–5.

[33]*Ibid.,* p. 6.

Chapter 5

Essentials in the Philosophical Foundation

The essential requirement for overcoming productivity problems is easy to state philosophically. We must follow the dictates of a representative democracy, which has as an essential element the free market system. Basic to this must be a change in attitude of the members of society, and through them, a change in attitude of the politicians who serve them. Such changes will not come rapidly. In this chapter we discuss what is necessary to change those attitudes. In the next chapter we show how those changed attitudes will direct us toward solutions to more specific problems, such as inflation, high interest rates, and regulations.

Overview of Conceptual Foundation

Individually and collectively, businesses have had to overcome many problems; success does not come without considerable struggle. The most notable general obstacles, as indicated by our research, have been excessive regulation and taxes, union influence, and the effects of high interest rates and inflation. These things have created an uncertain environment, making efficient and effective management of businesses difficult, if not nearly impossible. Best efforts are often thwarted. The demands of an increasingly complex, changing, interactive society and the uncertainty that accompanies such changes have made the businessman's job of maintaining and increasing productivity a challenging one, to say the least.

More specifically, our research has indicated productivity problems resulting from interactive processes related to excessive regulation; persistently high inflation, interest rates, and taxes; inability to obtain enough capital; inability to promote research, development, and innovative activities; disruptive interactions between workers and supervisors; ineffective management; and, of course, a number of other sources. We feel our research clearly indicates that specific causes of decreased productivity are multifaceted and multidimensional, and it is extremely difficult, if not impossible, to rank the specific causal factors objectively in order of importance. Attempts at doing that, in fact, might well have mitigated against a solution. Anyone even superficially following discussions in newspapers, in magazines, and on television during the past three or four years cannot help but be confused. Many are soft on the budget deficit, while others are fastidious budget balancers. Some argue strenuously for tight money, while others feel that this is the time for easy money. Taxes must be increased, some say; others feel tax decreases are in order. And such disagreements go on and on.

Before arriving at conclusions and making recommendations concerning these particular problems in Chapter 6, however, we might speculate about general approaches to the overall problem of decreased productivity. To do this, we must first decide what has brought the economy to such a dismal state. In this connection, the question that entered our minds is whether all the problems that are alleged to be causing the decrease in productivity are really independent problems or are symptoms of a more basic problem. Are they the disease or only the symptoms of a serious disease?

You will recall from the discussion in Chapter 2 that some writers blamed high interest rates, others inflation, some government deficits, others labor unions, some management, others the high cost of energy, as *the* cause (or, at least, the major cause) of productivity declines. A few said that all of these, and other problems as well, were at fault. Certainly the empirical data in Chapter 3 show that many factors are affecting the productivity of businesses unfavorably.

Since we began this writing, the prime interest rate has dropped from a high of 22% to 10½% in mid-July 1983, rising to 12½% in June 1984; the inflation rate has dropped from 14% to between 3 and 4% annually; wages and fringe benefits have dropped in some industrial areas such as automobile and steel production; the cost of energy has dropped somewhat and appears to have stabilized, at least temporarily. Certainly 1983 saw the economy bottom out and turn around. Production, productivity, personal incomes, and consumer confidence are on the rise. The Dow Jones average went above 1,250 at one point. Unemployment has dropped to about 7.5%.

Nevertheless, a number of economists, businessmen, educators, and others have expressed reservations concerning the recovery. Some feel the economy is recovering too rapidly, which might bring a return to high inflation rates. Interest rates are still high, and they have started to rise again, which could seriously dampen the recovery. The increased production is being handled mainly by utilization of excess capacity. Some feel that there is little incentive during this stage to modernize plants or make any substantial advances in technology, which is so critical to sustained long-term growth. Workers are demanding reversals of concessions made during the past few years—many are demanding even more. All such reservations about the recovery lead to the question of whether or not the basic problems really have been solved, or whether we are heading back toward a situation as bad as—perhaps worse than—before.

Our considerations discussed in Chapter 4 and these expressed reservations lead us to believe that there is a basic problem that is much more serious than any of those mentioned: that they are really subproblems, symptoms of a basic disease that must be cured if we are to have prolonged, steady recovery without resurrecting the specter of high inflation and even higher interest rates. What is that basic problem? How did we come to be in such a depressed economic condition?

We did not reach that state because the free market economy has not worked well, as some people contend. We got there because we do not have a free market economy, as described in Chapter 4, and have not had one for many years. At the very least, the dictates of the free market economy have been eroded or eliminated consistently, and devastatingly, during the past five decades, and the ultimate consequence has been a severe decrease in productivity. Certainly productivity gains were high during the 1950's and 1960's, an apparent contradiction to the previous statement. In fact it is not a contradiction, as the following discussion indicates. A free market economy can withstand a great deal of abuse before it is severely damaged. It cannot be destroyed overnight, but neither can it be restored immediately once severely damaged. The seeds of destruction have been planted since the 1930's, but their cumulative impact on productivity simply was not felt or observed until a decade or so ago. What are those seeds of destruction?

In certain important respects we are not following the dictates of a representative democracy, mainly those related to economic matters. Our failure to follow that basic philosophy has led to inconsistent, illogical, and counterproductive solutions being suggested and followed. We are like a rudderless ship at sea, at the mercy of the winds and tides, moving in whichever direction they are pushing at the moment. And, as indicated in Chapter 4, the systems we have created to aid in carrying on our activities often thwart, even denigrate and eliminate, the possibility of following some of the tenets of the basic philosophy.

The Basics of the Philosophy

The ingredient basic to an economic philosophy that would provide a foundation for solving the specific problems necessary to increase productivity is an acceptance of two facts: (1) that individual freedom is critical in all aspects of life and (2) that resources are scarce and wants are insatiable. Why are these basic?

Individual Freedom

We have stated previously that people in general desire individual freedom—it is human nature to wish to act independently and in one's own best interests, constrained only by those rules and laws absolutely necessary to maintain a viable society. Certainly we believe this to be true of most citizens of the United States, and there is no question that it is true of those we interviewed during the course of our research. Accepting that the American people want a representative democracy, the real question becomes, what can and cannot be done while still preserving and strengthening a representative democracy over the long run?

Remembering the discussions in Chapter 4, freedom of the individual is at the very heart of democracy. As freedom is decreased, *in whatever manner,* a political system moves toward totalitarianism in one form or another. As we stated in that chapter, what some apparently do not recognize, or have forgotten, is that all freedoms are interrelated, interdependent, and equal. A true democracy protects property rights, for example, just as surely as it protects the right of the individual to worship as he or she desires. Independent economic action is protected as surely as the right to vote. Ultimately, either all essential, basic rights and freedoms exist, or none do. An elimination of one is a move toward the ultimate elimination of all, as we have stated.

Of course, certain rules and regulations are necessary when large masses of people live together. Otherwise, anarchy and complete chaos would result. And people, being human, will make mistakes. What we are suggesting is that the inevitable errors should be made on the side of individual freedom when there is any doubt whatsoever regarding the consequences of an action. That often has not been what has happened. Following this guideline has a number of implications.

A Long-Range View Is Needed

First, a long-range view or outlook must be adopted. This, in turn, means we must be willing to accept the short-term economic, political, and sociological consequences of representative democracy. In other words, acceptance of the responsibilities and consequences of a representative democracy is critical if the system is to work. The system must be flexible enough to adjust for the disequilibriums that certainly must arise in complex societies.

In terms of economics, we have been too concerned with the short run at all levels over the past five decades. Government politicians and officials have invested much effort into fine-tuning the economy. We have concentrated in colleges on teaching short-term decision making for managers: how to maximize profits in the short run. Union leadership has sought to maximize wages and benefits in the short run. At all levels, in fact, our attitude has been to get it now and let the future take care of itself.

All these decisions and others might be compared to tactical as opposed to strategic decisions in conducting a war. According to *Webster's,* strategy represents the "science and art of employing the political, economic, psychological, and military forces of a nation . . . to afford the maximum support to adopted policies in peace or war." The same dictionary defines tactics as "the science and art of disposing and maneuvering troops, ships, or aircraft . . . and of employing them in combat." Hence, it is also "the art or skill of employing available forces with an end in view." In solving our problems, we have ignored strategy and concentrated on tactical decisions, ignoring, or forgetting, that without a well-defined strategy, tactical decisions become arbitrary and uncoordinated, and will often work at cross-purposes because there is no overall plan or objective to determine and guide actions. Neither a war nor an economy can be run on such a basis.

The Word "Fair" Must be Reevaluated[1]

Second, we must accept a different meaning for the word "fair" from the one that has apparently been accepted in the past. Everyone

likes to think he is fair, and no one denies that each person ought
to give careful consideration to the concept of fairness in his everyday
dealings with his fellow man. It is the usefulness of the concept as
a basis for establishing rules and regulations that we challenge, not
the importance of the concept itself. Opinions do vary considerably,
and the more complex a subject becomes, the more likely it is that
any uncertainty about the meaning of a word, however slight, will
manifest itself in ambiguity.

> When we come to words of which the logical concept is a complex
> relation, an obscure, intangible attribute, the defects of the popular
> conception and its tendencies to change and confusion are of the
> greatest practical importance. Take such words as "monarchy," "tyr-
> anny," "civil freedom," "freedom of contract," "landlord," "gentlemen,"
> "prig," "culture," "education," "temperance," "generosity." Not merely
> should we find it difficult to give an analytic definition of such words:
> we might be unable to do so, and yet flatter ourselves that we had a
> clear understanding of their meaning. But let two men begin to discuss
> any proposition in which any such word is involved, and it will soon
> be found that they take the word in different senses.[2]

It is a relatively simple task to reproduce a word. It is a much
more difficult thing to reproduce the idea for which it stands. In a
word, "fairness" has no operational context that can be utilized by
a few people in power as a basis for deciding a complex issue dealing
with the citizens of a country. If we look at the groups affected by
such decisions, it becomes abundantly apparent that what is or is
not considered fair depends upon the position of those being affected
by the decision. And, if we consider opposing groups, one group is
very likely to consider a decision fair while the other considers it
grossly unfair. We have no fixed standards by which to gauge
whether or not something is fair. If we empower a few people to
make decisions for all these groups, therefore, those in power are
likely to reap a harvest of wrath from all of them. The only way
such a system can work is for those in power to be dictators.

The Consumer Is King

A free market economy is part of a representative democracy; the
two go hand in hand. As we have stated, in a free market economy
it is the consumer—not management, not capitalists, not credit
granters, not laborers—who is king. The consumer determines what
is produced, and in what quantity, by casting his individual vote in

the marketplace. These decisions, transmitted through the pricing system, also allocate and distribute the resources and determine the rewards for management, capitalists, credit granters, laborers, and others.

In an ideal state, those who work to satisfy consumers are rewarded according to their abilities and contributions. Those who do not are removed from the marketplace. Individuals must be willing to accept the dictates of such a system as being "fair"; otherwise, the system cannot survive. The question, then, is simple: is it better for consumers, en masse, to make such determinations, or for one person or a few people to do so? We maintain that in a representative democracy it must be consumers. Certainly consumers are a special-interest group, in one sense. The critical point is that they are the only special-interest group encompassing all the citizens in a society. Economic power is thereby spread across many people rather than being concentrated in the hands of a few.

As we previously discussed (but it stands repeating), success should depend solely on an individual's honesty, intelligence, innovativeness, aggressiveness, perseverance, hard work, personality, and competence. The only barriers to success in a free market economy should be "natural," i.e., based on the degree to which any of these characteristics do not match up to those of competitors. Within such a system, each person could exercise his capabilities to the fullest, with maximum benefit accruing thereby not only to the successful person, but to society in general. Any rule, regulation, law, attitude, or circumstance that prevents individuals, and hence society, from achieving this ideal state is an artificial barrier; ideally, all such barriers should be removed from the system.

Special-Interest Groups

Good examples of the consequences of this misplaced, erroneous concept of fairness, played to and encouraged by politicians, are certain special-interest groups. Congressmen from those states heavily involved in tobacco growing emphasize how unfair it would be if subsidies weren't given to tobacco farmers; the same thing happens in states heavily involved in dairy, wheat, and corn farming; many politicians argue that workers are not getting their fair share. The list is endless.

In a nutshell, eliminating all the rhetoric, in such instances these people are arguing that rewards shouldn't be determined by a free market economy, but should be established according to whatever that special-interest group feels is its fair share of the gross national product. This is nonsensical, of course, because it is difficult, if not impossible, for any individual or group to decide objectively what is fair for itself. And how can a senator or representative from any state that depends heavily on a given industry, interested in his or her reelection, determine objectively what is a fair reward for that industry? The answer is obvious.

Any number of examples of the costs and inefficiencies brought about by the actions of special-interest groups and politicians acting on their behalf could be presented. We will use farm subsidies here only as an additional example, since we mention a number of others throughout this writing. We emphasize that most, perhaps all, of us fall into one or more categories of special-interest groups—academicians, lawyers, physicians, accountants, managers, etc. The *general* ideas we will express regarding farmers are applicable to *all* special-interest groups that attempt to thwart the dictates of a free market economy. Some do not, of course.

"Farm subsidies this year (1983) will run some $21 billion compared to $3.5 billion in 1980, and this doesn't include the $12 billion cost of the PIK (payment-in-kind) plan recently put into effect."[3] The PIK plan, as was true of plans before it, was thought to be innovative, an approach sure to get the farm economy in high gear, and to remove (or at least reduce) the high farm subsidies.

> ... instead of receiving cash for not growing crops, farmers who agreed to idle cropland would be paid from bulging surpluses of wheat, corn, grain sorghum, rice and cotton.
>
> The surplus crops—held in government warehouses as well as private granaries as collateral against loans to farmers—would be reduced, government farm subsidy payments would decline and market prices would rise, the administration said. More than 60 percent of the 2.4 million farmers in the country signed up, and a record 82 million acres of farmland was taken out of production this year.[4]

Administering such programs effectively is extremely difficult and costly. Farmers learn to play the rules, and the consequences have been the opposite of what was hoped for. Surpluses have become huge, and farm prices, consequently depressed.

> Much of the surplus now being paid out under PIK represents the grain, wheat, cotton and rice which had been in reserve for the past few years because of outstanding loans. Under PIK, farmers actually

get double aid. Not only are the crops given back to farmers to sell, the government writes off the outstanding loans as losses.[5]

In a word, rather than being subjected to the disciplines of a free market economy and making their decisions accordingly as individuals, for farmers the name of the game is maximizing income within the rules of the PIK plan (and, in some cases, outside those rules). Inefficient as well as efficient farmers are being subsidized as they are receiving surplus crops they can sell without incurring the production costs of growing them. Those engaged in farm-related activities—such as sellers of farm equipment, fertilizer, seed, and machinery repair—also are hurt. Another good example is the dairy industry.

> The attractive dairy-support price, now at $13.10 per 100 pounds, has encouraged farmers to keep up steady production and has drawn others into the business, adding to the glut.[6]

The only workable long-range solution is to return to a free market economy for farmers and other special-interest groups operating outside its constraints. Keep in mind that the free market economy is a system basically dependent upon *individual*, not group, not social, actions. These actions, in turn, should be determined only by the consciences, interests, desires, morals, and attitudes of those people acting independently.

Certainly people have the right to form themselves into groups. Within these groups they have the right to listen to discussions of the issues, to consider them, and to make their views known. Beyond this point, however, each individual should act independently in the actions he takes, whether in casting his vote, performing services for his employer or withholding them, or in any other of myriad ways. It is when members of the group coerce other members to take a certain position or to act in a certain way regardless of the beliefs of those members that the dictates of the free market economy are being violated. (We are all aware, for example, of instances when people have been forced to act in certain ways, sometimes under threat of physical harm, by members of a special-interest group.)

Beyond that, when one acts, even of his own free will, as a member of a special-interest group intent on obtaining rewards different from those that would result in a free market economy (which, by the way, could be greater or smaller), the dictates of the free market economy are violated—and other special-interest groups will be created to do the same thing. Each group is trying to control, to dictate, the distribution of wealth, and to seek subsidies to offset the results of their mistakes, such as overproduction. In fact, this system encourages mistakes. In a real sense, each group is seeking totalitarian powers, at least to some degree.

Subsidies of all kinds need to be phased out over some reasonable period of time. (We recognize that dropping all subsidies immediately would not be practical or feasible.) Farmers must be returned to the discipline of the market. It is their problem to remain viable within those dictates. It is foolish to assume that they would not be able to do this and/or that the market will not reward them in the aggregate for the risks they assume, given that food is a basic necessity.

Subsidization results in a misallocation of scarce resources. Resources flow to those subsidized, regardless of whether or to what extent consumers want their products or services. To use an exaggerated example, but one that reflects how illogical subsidies are, with a floor under the price of tobacco, tobacco farmers would still be rewarded for growing tobacco even if all smokers in the world stopped smoking. And to the extent that they were paid for taking acreage out of production, they would be rewarded for producing nothing in order to meet world demand (which would be nonexistent).

When lobbyists first started operating, their prime function was to present politicians with information that would help them to make rational decisions. They were primarily an informational service. Although this remains one function of lobbyists, their prime function now appears to be advocative: to plead the case of the special-interest group they represent in order to obtain legislation favorable to that group, without serious consideration of the impact on other groups or on the economy in general. Although the individual members of special-interest groups must bear some blame, they are not basically at fault, or at least not entirely. This system, built up over the years and supported and encouraged by politicians, is basically at fault. People have come to feel that their interests and desires will be considered only if they join and support one or more special-interest groups.

Nevertheless, regardless of blame, many special-interest groups as presently constituted and utilized are one of the artificial barriers to the free market system. That barrier must be removed. First, we feel that if members of special-interest groups are made aware of the possible consequences of many of their actions, if they are shown that their individual best interests are not served in the long run by certain of their actions, they will react differently. Second, politicians when they see that the dictates of a free market economy are being thwarted, have the responsibility to make decisions that would fall within the dictates of that system. Third, and perhaps basic to the first two, the pressures exerted on politicians by many of these groups through contributions to political campaigns, gifts, provision of additional income through speeches and seminars, and provision of employment or consulting work after the politician leaves office, must be relieved in some fashion.

Although we have a right to expect our politicians to be above reproach, to act objectively and independently, and although they have the responsibility to fulfill these expectations, they often do not. Consequently, as the electorate, we must work actively toward the removal of all incentives for politicians not to be objective and independent. As we stated in Chapter 4, if a representative democracy is to exist, minority groups must be protected against the tyranny of the majority. However, it is just as true that the majority must be protected against the tyranny of a minority of individuals.

Egalitarianism—Unthinkable and Unworkable

Third, we must resist the move toward *egalitarianism*. One of the pervasive artificial barriers that has been promoted in the United States, over the last four or five decades in particular, is egalitarianism: the concept that everyone is equal in all respects. This concept is patently false, of course, biologically, philosophically, and in every other way. I may be older, fatter, less intelligent, and have weaker genes than my next-door neighbor, so I certainly am not his equal in a biological sense. In a more abstract, philosophical sense, few would equate a murderer with Einstein, for example, in terms of their worth to society and contributions to posterity.

Those who promote egalitarianism know these things; so, in terms of economics, they apply the concept mainly to the distribution side of the equation, not to the production side. The concept then becomes: "All individuals are equal in terms of their right to share the wealth, regardless of their abilities and capabilities in producing or generating that wealth." A direct consequence of this attitude is a transfer of individual responsibility to society, meaning that people should be protected from economic hurt by spreading that hurt, in some fashion or another, over all members of society. It is only a small step from this attitude to a welfare state, with all of its ramifications.

Unfortunately, to those having little or no understanding of basic economics or the nature of man, such an approach sounds ideal. It promises cradle-to-grave security, in contrast to the free enterprise system, which promises that you will earn according to your contributions (meaning that there is no guarantee of success; the risk of failure is always present).

The problem with the egalitarian concept is that it cannot work for any extended period of time. It is part of the basic nature of man to want to be free in all ways, as we have stated. Given the knowledge and understanding necessary to make a rational choice, people will generally opt for greater freedom and will accept the responsibilities commensurate with that greater freedom, provided the system is supportive. Certainly this includes the right to choose the manner in which they expend their labor and capital, when the opportunity exists to obtain rewards commensurate with the risks they assume. Without the chance of loss, however, there cannot be the possibilitiy of success. Risks and rewards are inextricably intertwined.

Certainly, from an economic viewpoint, people do not like a system in which the fruits of their labor and capital are automatically allocated to less productive members of society. When this happens, the more productive will reduce their inputs, with a consequent reduction in output—a reduction in wealth generation. And people will react to stimuli provided by the environment (the totality of all the systems). Over the long run, society must suffer a reduced standard of living, certainly on average; and it is likely as well that those at the poverty level will increase in number, as you can't distribute what doesn't exist. Production, not distribution, creates wealth. The following statement by Louis Rukeyser summarizes many of the points we have made.

> Governments cannot make us equal in potential or in achievements. Some are born smarter. Others have more energy. We come short and tall, talented and plodding, coordinated and awkward, stunning and grotesque. The one thing we are not is equal.
>
> When the nation's founders agreed in Philadelphia that we were "created equal," they thought in terms of political rights. In practicial application, this means "one person, one vote." Realistically, it also should mean that it is in society's interest to seek to maximize opportunity. . . .
>
> We make a mockery of the word "fairness' though when we attempt to equate it with redistribution of wealth. That is not the American tradition; it is the tradition of Karl Marx.

. . . The genuine American tradition is not to have government hobble one's more affluent neighbor, but to hope that one's own efforts—or one's children's—will surpass him.

Every country in the world has schemes for wealth redistribution; what few understand is wealth creation. There, governments have no demonstrated ability whatsoever. And ironically, economic policies tilted toward "fairness" invariably result in lower national living standards. Such policies rarely harm the truly rich, those with vast reserves of inherited wealth; but they heavily tax and hamper those trying to get rich, or even those just trying to get by with incomes in the middle range.

The inevitable result, as we have seen in the U.S. in recent years, is a slowdown in productivity growth, nationwide emphasis on tax planning rather than venturesome investment—and a growing feeling of hopelessness among those trying to rise from society's lowest economic rungs. A chained giant may seem "fair" to those who would arrogantly "plan" our economy, but it demonstrably flunks any reasonable test of wealth creation.[7]

Resources Are Scarce and Wants Are Insatiable

Although an oversimplification in some respects, the following statement does reflect the importance of the concept that resources are scarce and wants are insatible (a word we would prefer over "greedy" as used by the author).

. . . the five major economic problems facing the world today—unemployment, inflation, high interest rates, high energy prices and low productivity—can all be traced to scarcity.

Unemployment is due to the scarcity of jobs, inflation is due to the scarcity of goods, high interest rates are due to a scarcity of credit, high energy prices are due to a scarcity of energy and low productivity is due to a scarcity of basic production.

At the heart of every economic problem is the basic economic problem, and that is scarcity. That comes about as the result of a basic observation of human beings—they are basically greedy. We have unlimited wants and limited resources. . . .[8]

Forgetting the basic truism that resources are scarce and wants are insatiable, and compounding that error with unrealistic assumptions and actions—on the part of politicians and labor union leaders in particular—has created serious situations. As we have stated, a free market economy automatically distributes the resources of the economy according to the economic worth of the contributions of members of that society. When a few people or a small group begins substituting its decisions for those of the marketplace, this automatic distribution process is thwarted. Emphasis switches from production to distribution and, unless reasonable assumptions are made about production (which is certainly not always the case), there are often dire consequences. No system, of course, can distribute more than is produced. The free market system keeps distribution and production in line, or nearly so. When a small group of people decides distribution questions and bases these decisions on higher estimates of production than come to fruition, the result is inflation, high interest rates, government deficits, and a misallocation of scarce resources.

Social security payments can be used to prove the point. Over the years, recipients have been led to believe that there is a direct correlation between what they pay in and what they get out of the system. Certainly there is no such correlation in total, and when it happens for any given individual, it is a matter of happenstance. Except for a small burial fee, those who die before reaching retirement age get little or nothing back from the system, regardless of how much they have paid in. Those who live well beyond their life expectancies get back a total amount far in excess of the total they paid in; and, to this extent, social security becomes a form of welfare payment.

However, most recipients (another special-interest group) believe that in essence they get back the dollars they pay in, that there is a separate fund for each person that holds their contributions until such time as they retire and start to withdraw from the fund; in a word, that there is a savings account for each person. As a matter of fact, it is a pay-as-you-go system with current worker contributions used to pay those currently retired. Finally, recipients have been misled into believing that they should rely completely, or nearly so, on social security for their retirement income, rather than as a supplement to retirement income, the purpose for which it was originally established.

Whether their intentions were good or bad, politicians have promoted and helped perpetuate such false hopes and impressions, and have added to them. In the early 1970's, for example, social security payments were indexed so that payments were adjusted for upward changes in the general price level as measured by the consumer price index. At the time, inflation was 3 or 4% a year, so the adjustment did not create any immediate serious problems. During the period of double-digit inflation, due in large measure to indexing, serious reductions in the fund balance took place because of enormous excesses of cash outflows over inflows into the system, in spite of large increases in social security taxes. Also, it should be remembered that inflation adjustments of 3 to 4% per year are compounded and become large adjustments in the future. Further, they increase the base amount received when people retire.

What are the major lessons to be learned? First, no small group of people can hope to make reasonable decisions regarding major and substantial distributions of resources. The system is too complex and variable for any hope of success over the long run without causing serious disequilibriums in the system. It appears that politicians made decisions when indexing was started on the assumption of a 3 to 4% average *real* (inflation-adjusted) growth rate per year, a substantial amount.

If such a growth rate were to persist, perhaps large transfer payments could be tolerated. But when transfer payments are pushed to the limit under such an assumption and then the real growth rate drops substantially, as it has over the past decade, there is no buffer to fall back on. And history teaches us that there are business cycles, that persistently high real growth rates cannot be maintained indefinitely; disequilibriums will manifest themselves and adjustments in the economy must take place to eliminate them. As we have seen over the past two or three years, that adjustment process is much more difficult and traumatic if past excesses have been substantial.

Second, as indicated, more reasonable assumptions must be made as a basis for decisions. A "worst case" basis for decisions must be considered as well as a "best case." Regarding the indexing (adjusting to some degree for changes in the general price level) of social security payments, for example, it appears that those passing the legislation didn't realize (or if they did, chose to ignore) that a 3 or 4% adjustment per year compounded semiannually for, say, 20 years amounts to a sizable adjustment at the end of that time. Using a 4% adjustment factor compounded semiannually, a $100 payment today would increase to $148.60 in 10 years, a sizable 48.6% increase. At 10%, the payment increases to $265.33 in 10 years, a whopping 165⅓%.

Even on a "best case" basis (it certainly would not have been reasonable to assume a zero inflation rate), the increased payments would be substantial. Under a reasonable "worst case" basis, payments would increase to alarming amounts. Add to this that distribution payments are easy to begin but extremely difficult to stop, as we are now seeing, and we conclude that politicians acted incautiously, to say the least. Also, indexing helps to perpetuate inflation, rather than allowing inflation itself to be one of the forces reducing disequilibriums in the economy. Finally, indexing is perpetuated in the system, because base payments to new retirees are increased as a result of indexing, as we stated.

Unless we get transfer payments under control, they will strangle future growth in the United States.

> Transfer payments—defined as outlays for which no goods and services are received in exchange—have grown from $50.6 billion, or 27% of the federal budget in 1969, to $279.3 billion, or 45%, in 1981.
>
> About 90% of these payments go to senior citizens, and as economist Marcy E. Avrin of the National Bureau of Economic Research points out, the number of people over 65 has quadrupled in the past fifty years, while the general U.S. population has doubled. And in the next fifty years, the ranks of the elderly will grow by an astonishing 120%, while the working-age group (18 to 64) will expand by only 6%.
>
> NPA economists predict that if transfer payments keep on growing at a 7%-or-higher rate in real terms, as they have during the last two decades, real Gross National Product will grow only at an average annual rate of 1.2% until 1990—and then will stagnate completely and begin to decline. But if Congress squarely faces the long-range problem and makes the right moves, the NPA forecast estimates that the U.S. will enjoy average real growth of 3.5% from now until the year 2000.[9]

At least we should learn from the experience of other countries.

> Western European governments have awakened from their post-war dreams of creating perfect welfare states.
>
> From Denmark, where some old-age pensions are being cut, to Italy, where subsidies for medicine have been lowered, almost a dozen governments [including Netherlands, Italy, Belgium, West Germany, France, Britain, and Denmark] grappling with recession will try to spend less on social programs this year.
>
> Whether they're socialist or not, the governments are now following the same path. . . . They are all trying to find ways to save money on social security.[10]
>
> The unthinkable is happening. The European welfare states, highly bureaucratized systems that try to shelter their citizens against social risks from the cradle to the grave, are under attack. Only two years

ago, these products of two decades of sustained economic growth were considered morally inviolable and politically unassailable. As Arthur Seldon of the London-based, industry-supported Institute of Economic Affairs explains, they were thought "to enshrine man's humanity to man. Their critics were rejected as unrealistic visionaries, out of sympathy with the moral spirit of the age."

Now, economic and social reality has caught up with even the most free-spending welfare societies. For the first time in decades, social policies are being reassessed and cut back, and the resolution with which Europeans have pursued their welfare programs (which absorb an average 32% of Gross National Product compared to the 16% in Japan and 18% in the United States) has begun to founder.[11]

The critical point is that we draw the same conclusion they have from their experiences.

It is abundantly clear that the real social progress we can achieve is limited by economic means and that methods of achieving social objectives should not be allowed to undermine the economic system that produces the means. . . .[12]

From a conceptual viewpoint, social security provides a good example of a critical point implicit in these quotations. That point is the loss of discipline that follows when people are indirectly, rather than directly involved in the marketplace.

It is natural for decent human beings to have high hopes and wishes. We all wish, for example, that there were no human suffering in the world, that all hunger, pain, and disease were eliminated, that everyone, at minimum, could enjoy the basic necessities of life, and, better yet, that everyone could have a comfortable, good life in every way. But there is a difference between hope and reality. We indicated in Chapter 4 that one important result in a free market economy is that consumers receive *fast* and *direct feedback* from the system. Because they directly influence, and are directly influenced by, the market, reality places an upward boundary on expression of their hopes and desires. When middlemen are thrust into the mechanism, the attempt to realize hopes and desires often is allowed to go beyond reality. We lose sight of the possible, creating serious consequences. In a word, we lose much of the discipline of the market.

For example, when a customer enters a store with $5, he may have a number of choices on how he might spend it, but his choices are limited to some number totaling $5, regardless of his desires and wishes. The same discipline would exist if he had to provide com-

pletely for his own retirement. With social security, a third party
(the federal government) is interjected. All discipline, to the extent
that it exists, becomes indirect. And reaction time becomes much
longer. Since social security taxes are withheld from wages, the employee does not feel increases as quickly. On the other side, politicians
can increase benefits on the basis of hopes and desires for significant
periods of time before the reality of the market reflects the error of
their ways. By then the situation could be traumatic. The lesson,
simply, is to keep middlemen to an irreducible minimum if the discipline of the market is to prevail.

Summary to This Point

Complex societies obviously must have rules and regulations in
order to cause people to act in what are perceived to be acceptable
ways consistent with the political and economic systems of those
societies. Our point is that such rules and regulations should promote
the attainment of the ideal stated above, regarding representative
democracy, as much as possible. At the very least, they should min-
imally thwart attainment of the ideal. Barriers to the attainment
of this ideal can be created and do exist at all levels—the federal
government, business in general, small business in particular, and
even the individual firm level—and we will discuss more of these
barriers in the following pages.

But we should not confuse the legitimate need for some rules and
regulations with the feeling expressed by some that the larger and
more complex society becomes, the greater the need for government
intervention in the marketplace. Nor does such complexity justify
the existence of special-interest groups. In fact, the opposite is true.
Under such complex conditions there are simply too many variables
for one or a few individuals to plan and coordinate the system efficiently and effectively, and many special-interest groups attempt
to manipulate the system to react favorably to what they visualize
as their special needs and circumstances, as we have stated. A system
in harmony with representative democracy, if it is to work efficiently
and effectively, must be flexible and nearly automatic. Most importantly, it must promote and preserve individual freedom and the
responsibilities attendant to maintaining individual freedom. In
terms of economics, a free enterprise system meets those requisites;
other systems do not.

Consequently, the standard is clear. When considering economic issues, the question should always be, which decision will promote and strengthen a free market economy? Perfection is not likely to be attained, of course, but decisions are likely to be more consistent and, in the long run, more beneficial to individuals, and hence to society, if that standard is used and persistently sought.

The question might well be raised here that *if* it is basic to the nature of human beings to desire freedom—and this presumably would cause them to support the free enterprise system—why has the free market economy deteriorated over the past four or five decades? The answer, simply, is that rational decisions cannot be made on the basis of misunderstanding, lack of knowledge, and seriously incomplete or misleading information, particularly when the systems in place support decisions and actions antithetical to a free market economy. Proper education, proper attitude, and reasonable understanding are the keys.

For example, one of the criteria that must be met for a free enterprise system to work is that most events and transactions between individuals be at arm's length or, at least, that the results are the same as though they were. This requires that the buyer be under no particular compulsion to buy and the seller be under no particular compulsion to sell (neither is being coerced), except for the natural compulsion to act in one's own best interests; and both must have a reasonable knowledge of the marketplace.

On a broader plane, the same things are true. Thomas Jefferson once indicated he felt that if the electorate were given factual and complete data and had the right to vote their consciences without coercion, their decision would support democracy with all its ramifications. We agree. A number of factors have made it difficult for the electorate of the United States to act in this fashion, however. First, significant numbers of politicians have forgotten their primary responsibility to their constituents in a representative democracy: to vote in Congress the way the majority of their constituents would vote, assuming they had acceptably complete and factual information on which to base their decisions and were acting freely. The electorate needs to be given the pros and cons of available alternatives and the potential consequences of various courses of action in an understandable, objective, and unbiased fashion. In the main, politicians do not provide this information. They express support for or against tax increases, balanced budgets, and other economic and political issues, but rarely make clear the possible outcomes of each course of action. They often deliberately raise the expectations of the populace far above what it is economically possible to achieve without dire consequences. They rarely discuss sacrifice and responsibility.

In a word, they concentrate on and promote the "insatiable desires" of people without mentioning the "scarcity of resources" side of the equation, giving false hopes and frequently blaming others when their promises do not come to fruition. They appear, in many instances, to be more concerned with reelection than with arriving at conclusions on issues that come as close as possible to the results that would come to pass in a pure democracy. And, for whatever reasons, many politicians seem to have concluded that it is their responsibility to decide what is best for the electorate rather than to be the alter ego of the electorate, as they should be.

Much of this is manifested in the changes in attitudes of the populace during the past 50 years, changes for which they are not primarily responsible. The short-term attitude, the transfer of personal and family responsibilities to government, the change in the work ethic, all lead to reduced productivity and are mainly the result of incorrect stimuli or incentives provided by government through an intricate system of policies, rules, and regulations. If marginal tax rates increase as income increases, a point is reached beyond which people will stop producing. If the government develops programs transferring responsibility for the aged from families, families will no longer accept the responsibility of caring for their elderly members. If consumption is rewarded and saving discouraged, savings will decrease. Numerous other examples could be given, but these are enough to make the point that people will react to stimuli built into the system.

Businesses will continue to evolve along with the environmental factors affecting them, just as all other units of society will. History teaches us that the environment is dynamic, ever changing. New needs and problems will take the place of old needs and problems as those recede. Many of them will reappear in a different setting. It is essential not only that business owners and managers, those concerned with their interests, and, indeed, society in general understand what has happened in the past, but also that they be constantly alert to the changing environment, striving to anticipate the future. Only in this way can we hope to avoid the errors of the past and exert some control over our destiny. Central to all of this is the existence and consensual support of a philosophy that will allow consistent and logical reactions to changes in the environment. We must have a strategy before determining tactical actions to increase productivity. We must have a philosophical foundation as a basis for finding solutions to the specific problems that exist.

Attitudes do not change overnight. Of necessity, therefore, general solutions must be long-range in nature.

A More Demanding and Better Balanced Education

At best, education generally, and economic education, in particular, of the general populace is incomplete; at worst, it has been biased and unbalanced. Education, in a representative democracy, requires that alternative points of view be presented objectively and in an unbiased fashion, so that the learner can make reasonable, rational decisions. It is not the function of a teacher to teach only his own point of view; this is indoctrination, not education. As history so ably teaches, indoctrination is the game of totalitarian regimes, not of representative democracies. It is the obligation of teachers and parents to ensure that their students and children are educated. Without an education, it is easy for the electorate to be misinformed and misled.

An example or two might clarify the point. If you were to ask most people, even college graduates, what "capitalism" means, they would probably answer that it is a system in which individuals own and control the factors of production and distribution. Not a bad answer so far, but if they are pushed further and asked what they mean by "control," most would say the capitalists (owners of wealth used in business) determine what and how much is produced, the prices charged for products and services, and the return to laborers; in a word, that capitalists control the entire economic system and obviously direct it in a coercive way that primarily benefits them. This, of course, is not true. *Webster's* says:

> *Capitalism.* An economic system . . . in which the ownership of land and natural wealth, the production, distribution, and exchange of goods, and the operation of the system itself, are effected by private enterprise and control *under competitive conditions.*[13] [Emphasis added]

Although there may be some minor theoretical distinctions, it is clear in all substantive ways that the terms "capitalism," "free enterprise system," and "free market economy" all have the same meaning and can be used interchangeably. We do so in this writing.

As competition is critical to a free market economy, we need to make clear its necessary meaning. As we described it in another setting:

> An ideal competitor in athletics, for example, is an individual with superior ability who uses challenging competition to upgrade the achievement levels in his sport. He knows he must be superbly conditioned, mentally and physically. He wants all those trying out for his position to be at their very best when he competes with them in order that his achievements can be pushed to the maximum. These things can only be accomplished, however, if he is honest and objective in his evaluation of his capabilities, and sincere in determining what is necessary for improvement. In addition, of course, those evaluating him must have an objective view of the quality of his performance.[14]

Certainly, this means we need to adhere to high moral and ethical standards when competing. It does not reduce our desire to beat our competitors. Quite the contrary. However, it does circumscribe what we ought to do, and the approaches we ought to take in doing it. These approaches do not include lying, cheating, misleading, coercing, or otherwise acting in immoral, illegal, or unethical ways to gain competitive advantage. Such approaches are outside the dictates of a free market system and, when followed, are a reflection on the person following them. They should not, and cannot, be laid at the doorstep of the system.

Another critical point to keep in mind is that we are not arguing for either the liberal or the conservative approach, as those terms are commonly used today. Neither approach consistently favors individual freedom and responsibility. Today, communism is usually placed on the far left of an ordinal scale and fascism on the far right. People to the left of center are considered liberal; those to the right are considered conservative. As we showed in the scale shown in Chapter 4, this is fallacious—economically, politically, and sociologically—from the viewpoint of individual freedom. A movement in the direction of either fascism or communism is a movement away from individual freedom, and to that extent the two belong side by side.

But the problems education is creating regarding productivity extend beyond the lack of sufficient, unbiased approaches to economic education. Many employees lack the basic skills of reading, writing, and arithmetic necessary to perform even the simplest tasks well.

Perhaps more importantly, schools have not taught and required the self-discipline necessary to succeed.

> "When you talk to employers about why they are unhappy with [applicants and employees], they say all the basics are missing." Etzioni [Dr. Amitai Etzioni, professor at George Washington University] says, "Nobody can read, nobody can write, nobody can count. This is quite true, but the most basic thing missing is self-discipline.
>
> "Our schools fail to develop self-discipline, or the organizational skills and other basic character traits necessary for success in the workplace. If you have self-discipline, you can learn to do just about anything else.[15]

Many people seem to be more concerned with placing blame than with seeking improvements.

> College officials tend to blame student shortcomings on the high schools, which undeniably need reform and renewal, but the high schools can blame the elementary schools, the elementary schools the family at home, and everybody blames TV. [University of] Wisconsin's President Robert O'Neil, however, argues that the colleges are "in part to blame." Says he: "Having diluted the requirements and expectations, they indicated that students could succeed in college with less rigorous preparation."[16]

One need not be very observant to realize that some degree of blame resides at all these levels, and an effort needs to be made at all levels if the problem is to be solved.

Schools and homes must begin again to emphasize the work ethic, dedication, self-discipline, and responsibility. Leisure time is something to be earned; it is not an individual right. Perhaps someday we will reach a utopian state in which people can choose to work or not strictly on the basis of enjoyment, and everyone will have everything needed and desired whether they choose to work or not. That state is a long way off, if in fact it can ever be reached. In the meantime, the values of learning, of working hard, and of doing a good job must be emphasized as one step toward increasing productivity.

Perhaps the attitude needed is captured best in the following statement:

> Education thus functioned in the context of a widely agreed-upon moral order and image of man, and there were stable institutional structures . . . primarily responsible for its maintenance. Education emphasized man as both a rational and a moral agent, striving for ex-

cellence within a known cosmos and metaphysic. It was primarily
designed to teach content and reasoning skills within an atmosphere
of discipline, honesty, hard work, and authority.[17]

General Economic Solutions at the Macro Level

Labor Unions and Management

Although labor unions (another special-interest group) could be
helpful in making a free market economy work efficiently and effectively, as they are presently constituted and run, most of their
actions are antithetical to a free market economy—mainly, we believe, because of policies established by their leadership and sold to
their membership. Most unions have work slowdown rules, work
definition rules that allow workers to perform only assigned tasks,
and approaches to keep other workers from being hired when they
are on strike, to keep members of other unions from crossing picket
lines, and to get an ever-increasing slice of the gross national product
pie, regardless of productivity considerations or potential impacts
on others in particular or on the economy in general. They oppose
technological changes, particularly where capital (machinery and
equipment) replaces workers, on the grounds that this causes unemployment. They argue for reduced work weeks—say, 30 hours per
week at the same pay as a 40-hour week—arguing that this will
increase employment as it would now take four people to do the work
that three did before. They increase demands when the economy
improves, claiming that workers are the major, if not exclusive, cause
for productivity increases, while refusing to make concessions when
the economic cycle turns downward, at least not until dire consequences such as firm or plant closings are imminent.

Not only are all these policies and actions unnatural barriers to
a free market economy but, as a consequence, in the long run they
are not in the best interests of the workers. Technological advances
increase aggregate demand for labor; they do not decrease it. The
experience of the 1950's and the 1960's shows this to be true. The
new machinery and equipment must be produced, installed, and serviced, all of which creates a demand for labor. Moreover, labor released from one activity is available to produce new products and
services brought into the market.

Certainly there are some short-term disruptions for specific elements of the labor force, who may be required to learn new skills, move to new locations, and the like, but aggregate demand for labor is likely to increase with increased technology. In addition, if foreign competitors advance technologically more rapidly than United States firms, they will be able to sell their products at a lower price, decreasing aggregate demand for labor and causing unemployment in the United States, a situation all too clear in the automotive and steel industries.

Some labor leaders acknowledge these things, as reflected in this statement by Leonard Woodcock:

> If the market is expanding, then the introduction of labor-displacing machinery has little immediate impact. But if that takes place when the market is contracting, as is true now, then it has a terrible impact. It displaces not only the person who is yet to be hired, but the people actually on the job. Yet technological changes have to be introduced, because without them even more jobs would be lost: the industry here just would not be competitive with Japan.[18]

There is substantial conflict and disagreement within the ranks of certain unions, however.

> Teamsters International President Jackie Presser is pushing a plan which would mean a 31 percent cut in pay for truckers called back from layoff, and dissident members are accusing the new president of a give-away.
>
> He told committee members the rider is needed to "restore union jobs in the face of non-union competition," according to sources at the meeting.
>
> The plan is an apparent move aimed at restoring some health to the trucking industry, which has been an economic basket-case since 1977, and winning back at least some jobs for the estimated 80,000 long-haul union drivers currently laid off.[19]

The same article reported "union membership had decreased by one-third since 1977 and freight hauled by truck has fallen from 925 million tons in 1978 to 717 million tons in 1982."[20] The major point, we believe, is that no matter how strong the influence of a special-interest group is in thwarting the dictates of a free enterprise system—whether unions, management, or others—this influence at best is temporary. Such groups inevitably must follow the dictates of the laws of supply and demand.

High unemployment benefits are not the only "institutional barrier" to a lower level of full employment. The high relative wages of many U.S. workers are a major reason why the nation's economy is not adjusting more rapidly to the threat of foreign competition, according to economist Marvin Kosters of the American Enterprise Institute. "There's nothing wrong with our auto workers that a 30% wage cut wouldn't cure," he says. "That sounds harsh, but it's true." Jason Benderly agrees that, because of the wage differential between U.S. and foreign autoworkers, 400,000 Americans will never again find work making cars.[21]

It is much more logical and productive, however, for all of us to work within the free market system than it is to cause serious aberrations, with the traumatic adjustments that necessarily must follow. We believe, over the long run, that all must benefit much more from the former approach.

And all the other labor union actions and policies mentioned will have the same long-range consequences of decreasing aggregate demand for labor and increasing unemployment. Holding other things constant, as productivity increases, product prices fall, leaving more money in the hands of consumers to save or spend on other products and services. Savings provide the capital for research, development, and technological advances, with the consequences described above. Additional spending increases aggregate demand and results in new jobs. Thus, the more worker productivity increases, the better the long-range interests of labor are served.

Individuals have the right to belong to labor unions and to allow their leadership to negotiate with management for them. And they have the right to strike. We do not deny these things. However, they must be willing to accept the risks in their actions, and the responsibilities associated with them. If they have a right to deny their services to a firm, the management of that firm has the right to replace them if it wishes and is able to do so. Unions have no right to prevent access to the firm. To do so is to deny the rights of other individuals to seek employment at the firm. And it is highly questionable in our minds whether striking individuals should have access to such things as welfare payments and food stamps. To give such access forces all those paying the taxes that support welfare and food stamps to support the strikers.

Ideally, as we have stated, supply and demand factors relating to labor should establish the wage levels. When artificial barriers restrict the supply side and artificial floors are placed on the penalties suffered by those electing to strike, there is little opportunity for a free market economy to operate with respect to labor. Certainly management is not without fault here, an issue that will be discussed in a later section.

Undoubtedly many people in the United States have strong anti-union feelings. Certainly a lot of labor union leaders perceive anti-union attitudes on the part of management. Some even feel that public opinion in general has turned against labor unions. It is difficult to criticize union activities (as well as those of other special-interest groups) constructively without being accused of being anti-union.

We started this section by stating that labor unions could help strengthen and maintain the free market economy. Developing the specific policies and making the necessary decisions will not be easy, of course. The first step must be a change in attitude by labor, management, and the citizenry generally; a belief and acceptance that the long-range interests of labor are best served by a free market economy, as are the best interests of management, capitalists, and consumers. The attitude that it is a zero-sum situation—I win, you lose, we can't both win—must be dropped. Specific policies and actions will follow from this.

Certainly this includes elimination of the adversary relationship between management and labor.

> The Houston business community has "pulled out all the stops" to counterattack the union blitz, according to an AFL-CIO spokesman.
>
> This sort of confrontation worries men like Wayne Horvitz, who believe that a free labor movement and a free-enterprise economy are both essential ingredients for prosperity and social stability. "Again and again, American management has resisted first the existence and second the expansion of unions and of collective bargaining," he says. "This inability to recognize and accept unions as full or even half partners in an enterprise has been a hallmark of our history."
>
> The unfortunate thing about this long-standing adversary relationship, Horvitz adds, is that even the most enlightened attempts by management to set up cooperative work arrangements are often rejected or sabotaged by unions.[22]

Overcoming such long-standing feelings will take effort. A first step is to live by the tenets of a representative democracy, staunchly defending rights for others that we accept for ourselves, and recognizing and accepting the other responsibilities democracy requires of us all.

There is little doubt that in many industries, such as the steel and automotive industries, wage levels in the United States are too high to compete effectively with foreign producers.

> At the start of this year (1982), GM estimated that its average worker now costs the company $19.65 an hour, of which $11.53 is wages, $7.13 fringe benefits, and 99 cents overtime and shift premiums. Detroit generally estimates the Japanese pay package today at between $11 and $12 an hour.[23]

This results in the Japanese being able to place cars on our shores at a cost of $1,200 to $1,500 less than U.S. automakers.[24] Aggregate wages must be decreased if we hope to compete successfully.

But cost differentials aren't the only factor. Japanese cars have improved significantly in quality while the quality of domestic cars has decreased. Japanese cars are much more fuel efficient. Even if costs were comparable, the problem would not be completely solved. And appealing to patriotism to "buy American" is ludicrous, as are import quotas, domestic content laws, and tariffs. Such approaches do not encourage greater efficiency, rapid technological advances, and improved living standards over the long run; on the contrary, such protectionist approaches have the opposite impact.

> Families that indicated an overall preference for products made in this country were asked if they would alter their buying behavior if prices and product quality differed between domestic and foreign-made products. . . . Of the 58 percent that initially favored American products, only half (26 percent) still favored buying American products even if they were higher priced than similar foreign products. Consumers were even more responsive to quality considerations: the initial 58 percent was reduced to just 17 percent which would prefer to buy American-made products regardless of quality differences. Combining price and quality considerations, the initial appeal of American products was reduced from a preference of 58 percent to just 14 percent of all households. Consequently, the majority preference for American-made products only holds when product price and quality are similar. When foreign made products cost less or have better quality, social principle yields to economic self interest.[25]

A protectionist mood has grown throughout the country during the past three or four years, supported by some conservatives, liberals, and organized labor. Their desire for protection from foreign competition is not restricted to automobiles, but includes steel, machine tools, sugar, and other products. Ultimately, the consumer pays for protectionism through increased prices, lower quality, and hence a lower standard of living.

Tariffs, domestic content laws, and import quotas decrease efficiency and productivity in the industries protected, cause prices to rise and quality to decrease, and encourage retaliation by the foreign countries. Often this retaliation is against industries not being protected; in fact, it is usually directed against our industries heavily exporting to the country against which we erect protectionist policies. This reduces income and increases unemployment in those industries. Trade wars help no one in the long run and could lead to a breakdown in international order. Firms, and the industries they are in, are simply going to have to adjust in order to survive.

> Part of the adjustment requires trimming bloated wage rates, wages that help make our products—particularly cars and steel—uncompetitive in the world market. That is precisely why the U.S. trade-union movement, traditionally pro-free trade, has become the vanguard of protectionism.[26]

We must work toward international free trade, with each country producing those products and services in which it has a relative comparative advantage. Certainly we must continue to negotiate firmly with Japan and others on "freer" trade as some of these countries are violating the dictates of a free market system. And international trade is critical for the U.S. economy, as it is for that of other countries.

> In 1960, total trade in goods and services accounted for 10.4 percent of the GNP. Today, it stands at over 22 percent. For every billion dollars of trade, our national economy gains approximately 25,000 new jobs. Between 1977 and 1980, four out of every five new manufacturing jobs were export-related.

> . . . there has been a shift of our nation's economic foundation from manufacturing to services. Today, the service sector—banking, insurance, finance, law, accounting, real estate, and communications, as well as retailing and personal services—generates two-thirds of our gross national product . . . services employ more than 7 out of every 10 Americans; between 1970 and 1980, services generated 14.3 million new jobs; and productivity in services increased at a rate twice that of manufacturing.

> Whether services continue to play this vital role largely depends on how well we respond to the growing threat from nontariff trade barriers that our nation's service businesses face . . . barriers include such things as restrictions on transferring personnel, discriminatory li-

censing procedures and taxation, foreign exchange restrictions, denial of entry into domestic markets, and carefully planned administrative delays. One of the most far-reaching and threatening nontariff barriers to trade is restriction of the free flow of information across national borders.[27]

Management and labor must recognize the importance to increasing productivity of getting workers more involved in the decision-making process.

Throughout every organization there is a small army of "experts" or potential consultants. They are the work force. In any organization, they know a great deal about their operations and often are the only people who can clearly identify the cause of problems and have some excellent ideas on how to correct it. It has been said that practically everyone is the world's leading expert on something.[28]

Workers must be challenged to be inspired. An appeal must be made to their pride, their accomplishments must be recognized, they must be trusted, and they must be motivated.

Granted, employee motivation is affected by a great many factors outside of the work place. Government, family, demographics, and personal, social, and economic status influence a person's motivation. Nevertheless, management must continually support programs that provide an organizational environment and working conditions which foster motivation. The work place must become a place where there are opportunities for recognition, advancement, and challenge.[29]

Certainly unions have a responsibility in this area to see to it that work rules do not interfere with the motivation and initiative of workers.

Our purpose is not to get into narrow, firm-level considerations to improve productivity, as we have stated. Some firms have used "quality circles" as one method to develop personnel and leadership and to improve quality, morale, and productivity. Undoubtedly other techniques could be used. We simply point out the broad nature of the problem and present the attitudes and broad approaches that are needed to solve the problem. Whatever the specific approach, both management and labor must be committed to making it work, and they must be patient. Good results are not likely to be forthcoming immediately.

The human factor in productivity is subtle and often misunderstood. Studies show that more effective management of human resources could add 10% to 25% to productivity growth. In terms of controllable costs, they often exceed 50%. However, it is difficult to estimate, in dollars or percentages, potential improvements related to skill, effort, ideas, imagination, commitment, and other such factors. Measurable factors notwithstanding, the most promising steps toward improving productivity appear to involve the selection, placement, training, appraisal, and compensation of staff.[30]

Supply-Side Versus Demand-Side Economics

As a prelude to the discussion in the next chapter of *specific* recommendations for the solution of macro- and sectoral-level problems affecting productivity, and as a basis for understanding them, we will discuss the important features of what has come since 1981 to be called "supply-side" economics and compare them with the characteristics of "demand-side" economics.

Which of these two—or other possible approaches—is emphasized, and how much emphasis it is given, depends upon a combination of many factors, including those previously discussed: the political, social, and economic beliefs of the people discussing the issue. Because economics is basically "the study of how men and society end up *choosing* . . . to employ *scarce* productive resources which could have alternative uses to produce various commodities and distribute them for consumption, now or in the future, among various people and groups in society,"[31] economics encompasses concepts from political science, anthropology, sociology, and psychology.

Supply-side economics asks one basic question first: How can production or output be increased most efficiently? Increased production (supply) is given paramount importance, and the basic goal is to maximize the output of goods and services with the minimum amount of input factors. Thus, all recommendations regarding fiscal and monetary policies are developed and judged in terms of how they help to reach this objective.

Because the major input factors are labor and capital (and capital formation depends on savings and investment), these broad considerations translate into policies that will increase labor productivity and savings. How to encourage and improve entrepreneurship is also an important consideration.

They generally share the view that for forty years, under the malign spell of Keynesian concentration on demand, economic analysis and policy went wrong by neglecting supply. The most common theme is the sensitivity of work, productivity, saving, investment, and enterprise to after-tax rewards. The more exuberant supply-siders . . . expect cuts of tax rates to generate miracles of production and growth. While the more sober architects of Reagan administration policy do not promise that their tax cuts will pay for themselves in federal revenues, they do predict radical and durable renewal of the vitality of the United States economy.[32]

Income distribution is of secondary importance in the philosophy of supply-side economics:

The best . . . form of social security is a rapid extension of productive employment opportunities to all through the creation of sufficient capital by some. There exists, therefore, a functional justification for inequality of income if this raises production for all and not consumption for a few. The road to eventual equalities may inevitably lie through initial inequalities.[33]

On the basis of these considerations, we can draw the following specific conclusions as to what supply-side economics does and does not mean. First, heavy emphasis is placed on taxation policies. "Aggregate savings [in the United States] dropped from 7.4 percent in 1970 to 4.1 percent in the 3rd quarter of 1979. The British save 13 percent of disposable income, West Germans 15 percent, and the Japanese 25 percent."[34] High tax rates reduce savings available for investment and destroy the work incentive. As observed by economist Edward Browning,

High marginal tax rates (now 50 percent or more for most American families) are inimical to productivity in general, and not just to the amount of time people work. . . . The incentive to undertake job training or get a good education is weakened, since the student will get to keep only part of the higher income that a better education makes possible. Insofar as the return to savings is also subject to tax, the flow of savings, so important to economic growth, can be adversely affected by high marginal tax rates.

Occupational choices can also be influenced: people will be led to take lower paying jobs that do not involve as much risk or responsibility. . . . Although it is convenient to conceptualize the problem by thinking in terms of work incentives, it should not be forgotten that the incentives issue really relates to productivity activity in general.[35]

It follows that tax policies must center on those having a relatively high propensity to save, the "wealthier" members of society; tax cuts must result in increased investments, or capital formation will not take place. In addition, taxes on businesses should be decreased. This will give them a higher return and result in higher *net* cash flows available for reinvestment in the business. The consequent expansion in businesses and the replacement of old machinery and equipment will affect the entire economy, resulting in more jobs, more goods and services, and increased productivity. Poorer citizens will benefit from the greater availability of jobs and from lower prices (or a lower rate of increase in prices) for the products and services they purchase; therefore, they also will be better off economically. This is often referred to as the "trickle-down" theory.

Critics of supply-side economics assert that it is inequitable and unfair to the poorer classes of people, that it results in an even worse distribution of income and wealth, that the rich get richer while the poor get poorer. The supply-siders' counterargument is that because of the trickle-down effects, the poorer classes will end up with a higher average standard of living, and fewer of them will end up below the poverty level. Further, when flat-rate reductions in taxes take place (for example, a 5% cut for everyone), all tax-paying citizens benefit. Supply-siders argue that the 25% reduction in everyone's taxes presently being implemented is fair. The percentage decrease for the wealthy is no larger than that for anyone else. Opponents of the tax cut argue that those in the middle and lower tax brackets should receive larger percentage decreases than wealthier people. Such an approach, the supply-siders counter, would place the money in the hands of those who tend to consume more and save less—thus destroying or seriously damaging the goal of capital formation.

Supply-side economists also feel that the demand side will take care of itself. Consumers have a nearly insatiable desire for goods and services. Given this, and assuming that capital formation results in increasing supplies of goods and services at lower prices (or at least at prices increasing less rapidly than in the past), there will be enough demand for the increased goods and services.

Recommendations regarding government expenditures and monetary policies result from, or trail, these basic considerations. Although some of the tax revenue lost to the government will be made up by a growth in revenue due to the revitalization of business, most feel there will be a net loss to government units. Because it is felt that large, continuing budget deficits are a major contributor to inflation and high interest rates, government expenditures must be cut in order to balance the budget.

Generally, supply-siders agree with a reduction in government spending for two reasons. First, government expenditures remove from the marketplace funds that can be used more productively in the private sector. Second, when high expenditures compete for funds against the private sector, this drives up interest rates, making it difficult and more costly for the private sector to get money and thereby reducing funds available for investment. These factors, particularly in combination with budget deficits, are an important reason for inflation. More specifically, the supply-siders concentrate on reducing those government expenditures they believe to have an inhibiting effect on capital formation and incentives to work. (Removing the inhibiting effect will result in increased productivity.) Welfare and other transfer payments are high on the list, since they reduce the incentive to work and, thus, productivity. Unemployment compensation and the minimum wage also would be decreased for the same reasons.

We can use military expenditures as one example of misconceptions about supply-side economics. Many imply that supply-side economics has as an objective to increase military expenditures. This is not so. Supply-siders, from an economic viewpoint, would decrease military expenditures for the reasons given above (lower taxes, less government spending, and so on). Whether these people support increased or decreased military expenditures is a reflection of their political and social views, which may or may not be consistent with their economic views.

With respect to monetary policies, the supply-side position is not completely clear. No one wants high interest rates, of course, because of their adverse effects on capital formation and productivity, as we have discussed. However, tight monetary policies are particularly effective on the demand-pull causes of inflation (when too many dollars are chasing too few goods), so most supply-siders would agree to high interest rates until inflation is brought down to acceptable levels. They are aware, however, that high interest rates add substantially to government deficits and in this way to inflationary pressures.

F. Thomas Juster summarizes most of the theoretical core of supply-side economics well:

> 1. Entitlement programs have eroded work incentives; cutting back on those programs will restore incentives and reduce the tax burden

on the working and investing population.

2. The tax system is biased against effort, saving, and investment; reducing tax rates, especially marginal rates, will have a substantial effect on labor supply, saving, and investment.

3. Economic progress has been significantly impeded by an antibusiness climate of regulation designed to protect consumer and employee groups against various risks: many of these regulations not only require large and unproductive investments, but have adverse cost/benefit ratios in terms of protection offered versus the costs of obtaining it.

4. The stubbornness of inflation forces is largely due to the expectational climate built up by the demand-side oriented fiscal and monetary policies followed by past administrations: modifying the expectations of decision makers will thus permit a much more rapid reduction in inflation rates, at less social cost, than would be predicted from past history.[36]

Demand-side economists emphasize policies that will influence aggregate demand. When strong inflationary pressures exist, they are more likely to support tax increases. High taxes reduce disposable income. Hence, the total demand for goods and services is decreased and, with it, inflation. If there is unemployment and excess capacity, demand-siders would recommend decreasing taxes. The resulting increase in demand would encourage manufacturers to produce more and, as full capacity was approached, to expand operations. In turn, this would encourage businesses to retain more funds and/or seek funds in the capital markets. Capital formation would result from the increased demand, but is not directly sought as a primary goal.

Demand-siders are also likely to support government policies that directly affect the market. They are likely to support the redistribution of income and wealth on economic grounds, for example, as well as for social reasons. When lower taxes are needed to stimulate demand, they are likely to decrease taxes of the poorer classes the most because that would have a more substantial impact on the economy because of low-income groups' high propensity to consume, and for the social reasons given. When tax increases are needed to dampen inflation, demand-side economists are likely to support larger percentage tax increases for the more affluent than for the less affluent in order to produce a more even distribution of income, even though the less affluent have a higher propensity to consume. They, too, support decreases in government expenditures when necessary to combat high inflation, although they are usually more reluctant to do so. They will support decreases in transfer payments such as welfare only when absolutely necessary, and to a lesser degree. They are more likely to advocate cuts in other parts of the budget, such as military expenditures.

Demand-side economists also dislike high interest rates and tight monetary policies, but primarily because these affect consumers by tightening credit restrictions and increasing the costs of borrowing money to build homes and to purchase goods and services.

Admittedly, these are broad, general descriptions of supply-siders and demand-siders. What is actually happening at present? What are the actions being taken at the macro level to reduce inflation and interest rates and to increase capital formation? What needs to be done?

Supply-siders seem to have won the day, at least for the present. Federal income taxes are being reduced, in the sense that they will be 25% less for individuals after the reduction is fully implemented than they would otherwise have been. Because of inflation and other factors, dollar outlays for taxes will increase during the next three years, but they will increase at a much lower rate. All these decreases were supported by a large majority in the Senate and House, by so-called liberals and conservatives, by supply-siders and demand-siders, mainly because of the mandate given to President Reagan by the voters after his campaign promises to reduce taxes.

Heavy expenditure cuts have also been approved, although again, a more accurate description is that expenditures will increase at a lower rate than they otherwise would have. Actual total dollars expended will increase. There was generally wide support for such cuts because of campaign promises, supported by the electorate, with hopes to balance the budget by 1984 (a hope that did not come to fruition), although some senators and representatives have expressed the view that transfer payments were cut too much and military expenditures not enough.

The question still remains: Are the supply-siders or the demand-siders correct? Which recommendations are correct? On balance, supply-side economics probably is more supportive than demand-side economics of a free market economy, but neither represents a perfect paradigm of what is needed. Again, the basic tenet of a free market economy is dictated by the word "free," as we have discussed that word. The market must be "free" on both the production and distribution sides. This means that government and special-interest groups must limit their activities to those that are essential to keeping a society viable. (And even such limited activities, although necessary, are an unnatural barrier to the free market system.) Beyond, that point, and to the extent such government and special-interest group activities increase, the flexibility of the system decreases until a point is reached at which the viability of society itself, at least in the economic sense, is threatened.

In sum, it really isn't a question of supply-side or demand-side economics; it should be a question of what is necessary to promote and preserve a free market economy. James Tobin synthesizes our views.

> A serious intellectual challenge to the neo-classical–Keynesian synthesis . . . is the . . . view that a competitive market economy . . . is continuously in demand-equals-supply equilibrium. Unemployment and idle capacity then appear not as pathologies but as voluntary choices at prevailing prices and taxes. The remedies, if any are needed, are not Keynesian demand stimuli but improvements of incentives, e.g., less generous unemployment insurance, more take-home pay for workers, businessmen, and investors. Forget about fine tuning, counter-cyclical fiscal and monetary policy. Set up a good stable framework of incentives and price signals and the market, preferably deregulated, will take care of both short-run stabilization and long-run growth. . . . That involves minimizing or countering the distortion that taxes, subsidies, and regulations inject into market choices—work is taxed but leisure is not, income saved is taxed twice but income consumed only once, etc.—and then accepting whatever short- and long-run outcomes occur.[37]

The basic answer depends on changing attitudes in the manner we have already described. This will require additional substantial decreases in government expenditures and, ultimately, the establishment of budgets that balance continuously over short periods of time (say, three to five years), except for national emergencies. Six former cabinet members have suggested the cuts shown in Table 5-1 in order to cut the projected 1985 deficit by $175 billion. These suggestions would reduce the projected deficit to about $75 billion. Without this, they feel the financial and investment situation in the 1980's will be even worse than in the 1970's. We agree with the general thrust of their recommendations, but draw no conclusions here on the specifics.

Summary and Conclusions

From a macro viewpoint, in summation, we must all adopt a free market mentality and judge all actions that affect the economic sys-

Table 5–1.
Proposed Reduction in Federal Deficit[38]

Area	Reduction (Billions)
Entitlements and other nondefense programs	$ 60
Defense	25
Taxes (consumption-based)	60
Lower federal interest costs as a result of these cuts	30
Total reduction in 1985	$175

tem on the basis of what would preserve and strengthen that free market system. Management must do more than give lip service to it. It must live it in developing and carrying out the policies of its firms. If the potential benefits of a free market economy are to be sought, the commensurate risks and responsibilities must be accepted. It is inconsistent with the system, and destructive to it, to support it when things go well and run to the government for help when problems arise. Government regulations have been decreased and there are promises to remove even more; federal government bureaucracy needs to be reduced, and new regulations should have to meet a cost–benefit test, as we discuss more fully in Chapter 6.

The major conclusions and recommendations can be summed up briefly.

1. *All* of us are at fault to some greater or lesser degree for the decreases in productivity. We must acknowledge that fault as a necessary first step. Otherwise, attitudes between labor and management, customers and businesses, and most other special-interest groups will remain adversarial, divisive, and counterproductive.

2. As a result of 1 above, we must come to recognize that it is not a zero-sum contest—we must not feel that we both can't win, so either you or I must lose. We can effect a synergism if we work together, and bring about productivity increases that will mean we all win.

3. The best system for overcoming the productivity problem, which we must develop and promote, is the free enterprise system. Only by following the dictates of that system can we use our scarce

resources most efficiently in satisfying as much as possible the insatiable wants of consumers. To do this:

a. A long-range view must be taken. We must accept the short-run consequences of a free market economy as being fair.

b. The concept of egalitarianism as it is being applied to income redistribution must be abandoned.

c. We must be patient. It took years for us to get into the present situation. There are no short-term fixes that will get us out. In fact, attempts at short-term fixes will make the situation worse; such attempts at manipulating the economy are one reason for our present state.

d. Ideally, special-interest groups working against the dictates of a free market economy should go out of existence. At the minimum, their activities must be substantially constrained.

e. In the long run, workers will be better off if they and their union representatives take an active role in supporting and strengthening the free market economy. In any case, their activities must be constrained when they interfere with the rights of others.

f. Management must support the free enterprise system by deed as well as word.

g. Government intervention in the free enterprise system must be reduced drastically. From an economic viewpoint, the government must redefine its role as being one to do only those things necessary to promote and strengthen a free market economy.

h. Transfer payments need to be reduced drastically. Individuals and their families must be encouraged to accept greater responsibility for their own well-being, including retirement.

i. The budget must be balanced as soon as practically feasible and should remain in balance for some revolving period, such as five years. Deficits created during any year(s) in such a period must be counterbalanced by surpluses during one or more years during that period (except for national emergencies).

j. Education in general economics and business must be improved, most importantly at the junior high and high school levels.

k. All barriers to international trade must be eliminated. We must work continuously toward international free trade, whereby each country produces those products and services in which it has a relative comparative advantage.

Thomas Jefferson was one of the most ardent supporters of individual freedom who has ever lived in the United States. Almost 200 years ago he gave the following sage counsel to the American people:

> I place economy among the first and most important virtues and public debt as the greatest of dangers to pursue our independence. We must not let ourselves load up with perpetual debt. *We must make our choice between economy and liberty, or profusion and servitude.* If we can prevent the government from wasting the labors of the people under the pretense of caring for them, they will be happy. The same prudence which in private life would forbid our paying our money for unexplained projects, forbids it in the use of public money.[39] [Emphasis added]

To paraphrase an overused cliché: A free market economy is not everything; it is the only thing. It not only is good because it works; it works because it is good.

Notes

[1] Much of the discussion related to "fair" was adapted from Harold E. Arnett, "The Concept of Fairness," *The Accounting Review,* Vol. 42, No. 2 (April 1967), pp. 291–297.

[2] William Minto, *Logic, Inductive and Deductive* (1896), p. 86.

[3] Robert Gettlin, "Farmers' Subsidy Program Becomes Embarrassment for Reagan Administration," *The Ann Arbor News,* July, 31, 1983, p. B4.

[4] *Ibid.*

[5] *Ibid.*

[6] Ward Sinclair, "Overproductive Farmers Fatten Their Silos and Federal Deficit," *The Ann Arbor News,* July 31, 1983, p. A15. These quotations are from an article written for the *Washington Post* and are reprinted with permission from that newspaper.

[7] Louis Rukeyser, " 'Fairness' as National Policy Is Unfair," *The Ann Arbor News,* July 10, 1983, p. D14.

[8] Martha Sullivan (quoting Lewis Mandell), "Consumers Must Understand Basic Economic Problem—Scarcity," *The Ann Arbor News,* August 2, 1983, p. A7.

[9] Marilyn Wilson, "The Greatest Threat to Economic Growth," *Dun's Business Month,* August 1982, p. 40.

[10]Henry Gottlieb, "Europe Finds Pot of Trouble at End of Welfare Rainbow," *The Ann Arbor News,* February 2, 1983, p. F1.

[11]David Fairlamb, "Welfare States on the Defensive," *Dun's Business Month,* December 1981, p. 98.

[12]*Ibid.*

[13]*Webster's Third New International Dictionary,* Merriam Co., Springfield, Mass., 1981.

[14]*Harold E. Arnett and Paul Danos, CPA Firm Viability: A Study of Major Environmental Factors Affecting Firms of Various Sizes and Characteristics* (Ann Arbor, Mich.: The Paton Accounting Center and Division of Research, Graduate School of Business Administration, The University of Michigan, 1979), p. 13.

[15]Marsha Taylor, "Lack of Self-Discipline Blamed for Dwindling Employee Productivity," quoting from *An Immodest Agenda* by Professor Amitai Elzioni, *The Ann Arbor News,* August 26, 1982, p. D4.

[16]"Five Ways to Wisdom," *Time,* September 27, 1982, p. 66.

[17]John B. Muller, "Educational Bankruptcy and the Hillsdale Vision," *Imprimis,* Vol. 11, No. 11 (November 1982), p. 2.

[18]Doris McLaughlin, "A Conversation with Leonard Woodcock," *Michigan Quarterly Review* (Fall 1982), p. 24.

[19]Stephen Cain and Robert Lewis, "Teamsters Boss Pushes Pay Ct," *The Ann Arbor News,* July 14, 1983, p. A1.

[20]*Ibid.,* p. A4.

[21]Marilyn Wilson, "What Is 'Full Employment'?" *Dun's Business Month,* Vol. 121, No. 2 (February 1983), p. 38.

[22]Marilyn Wilson, "Big Labor Faces Reality," *Dun's Business Month,* Vol. 119, No. 2 (February 1982), p. 43.

[23]"Japan's Automakers: An $8-per-Hour Labor Cost Edge," *Dun's Business Month,* Vol. 119, No. 2 (February 1982), p. 39.

[24]*Ibid.*

[25]Richard T. Curtin, "Unemployment Adds to Interest Rate Distress," *Economic Outlook USA,* Vol. 9, No. 1 (Winter 1982), p. 15.

[26]Rowland Evans and Robert Novack, "Protectionism—A Call to Chaos," *Reader's Digest,* Vol. 123, No. 736 (August 1983), p. 102.

[27]Thomas L. Holton, "Trade in Services Vital to Economic Growth, Peat Marwick Chairman Stresses," *Executive Newsletter,* Vol. 9, No. 7 (July 25, 1983), p. 1. These quotations are from a speech given by Mr. Holton, reprinted in the *Executive Newsletter,* and used by permission of its editor, Edward McEnerney.

[28]Robert Shaw, "Tapping the Riches of Creativity Among Working People," *Management Focus,* Vol. 28, No. 5 (September–October 1981), p. 25.

[29]*Ibid.,* p. 26.

[30]George Drakey, "How to Help People Be Productive," *Management Focus,* Vol. 28, No. 4 (July–August 1981), p. 18.

[31]Paul A. Samuelson, *Economics,* 8th edition (New York: McGraw-Hill Book Company, 1970), pp. 4–5.

[32]James Tobin, "Supply-side Economics: What Is It? Will It Work?" *Economic Outlook USA,* Vol. 8, No. 3 (Summer 1981), p. 51.

[33]Kenneth P. Jameson, "Supply Side Economics: Growth versus Income Distribution," *Challenge,* Vol. 23, No. 5 (November–December 1980), p. 27.

[34]*Discussion and Comments on the Major Issues Facing Small Business.* A Report of the Select Committee on Small Business, United States Senate, to the Delegates of the White House Conference on Small Business, 96th Congress, 1st Session, December 4, 1979 (Washington, D.C.: U.S. Government Printing Office, 1979), p. 28.

[35]Edward K. Browning, "How Much More Equality Can We Afford," *The Public Interest* (Spring 1976), p. 95.

[36]F. Thomas Juster, "The Economics and Politics of the Supply-side View," *Economic Outlook USA,* Vol. 8, No. 4 (Autumn 1981), p. 81.

[37]James Tobin, p. 51.

[38]Deloitte Haskins & Sells, "Former Cabinet Members Urge Deeper Cuts in Federal Deficit," *The Week in Review,* January 28, 1983, p. 1.

[39]Thomas Jefferson, as quoted by Herbert V. Prochnow, *The Complete Toastmaster* (Englewood Cliffs, N.J.: Prentice-Hall, 1960), p. 36.

Chapter 6

Applying the Philosophical Foundation to Solving Macro Problems

The possible solutions to specific problems at the macro level of decreased productivity growth are as varied and complex as the problems themselves—perhaps more so. This is not surprising. If the causes of the problems cannot be agreed upon, if a reasonable consensus cannot be reached, agreement on solution is bound to be even more elusive. In this chapter we present and analyze solutions recommended by various individuals, committees, and organizations concerned with improving productivity. We then draw conclusions regarding the merits of these suggestions and present alternative possibilities based on our research.

Overview of Small Businesses

Because of the special needs of small businesses, additional recommendations to increase their productivity have been made. Certainly the recommendations we will make at the macro level, if acted upon, would benefit small businesses generally, but many writers and small business owners and managers, as well as various organizations representing their interests, feel that more is needed. Although primary emphasis in this chapter will be placed on the macro level, we will also consider some recommendations specifically for the sectoral (small business) level.

We emphasize again that we use data on small businesses primarily as a stepping-stone for understanding the problems and suggesting solutions at the macro level. In addition to the other reasons given in Chapter 1 for this approach, we must take cognizance of the fact that small businesses constitute a substantial portion of total business activity in the United States, although there is disagreement on precisely how substantial this portion is. Estimates range along the following lines.

Small businesses with fewer than 1,000 employees produce 24 times as many innovations per dollar spent on research and development as do large companies with 10,000 or more employees. . . . Over most of the past decade, when employment in the *Fortune* 1000 largest companies grew by only 3.9 percent (about half of one percent each year), employment in the rest of the private sector grew by 65 percent, or 9 percent per year.[1]

"Small businesses" play a significant role in the U.S. economy. They account for 44% of private productivity, 47% of employment, 46% of payroll and 43% of gross sales. Over 99% of American businesses have fewer than 500 employees and almost 49% have fewer than 100 employees. . . .[Small businesses] are particularly vital to the creation of new jobs. Between 1969 and 1976, more than 86% of new jobs were provided by small businesses. Economic opportunity for minorities and women are also greatest in small businesses, especially in those industries affording easy entry, such as retail trade, construction and services.[2]

Others feel that the impact of small business on the economy has been overstated, mainly because small divisions, branches, and subsidiaries of large companies have been considered and analyzed as part of the small business sector.

From 1978 to 1980, private sector employment increased 7.4%. About 78% of this increase occurred in establishments with fewer than 100 employees, yet these establishments employ only 49% of the private sector labor force.

On an establishment basis, therefore, small businesses employ about half the nation's work force but generate nearly 8 of every 10 new jobs. These figures indeed support the conventional wisdom that small businesses create most new jobs.

But a significant portion of these growing small establishments are branches or subsidiaries of large firms. In fact, nearly half the establishments with 20 to 99 employees are owned or controlled by larger firms. And a sharply different picture of the role of small business in the job-creation process emerges when employment growth is measured by the size of the firm rather than the size of the individual establishment.

If a small business is defined as any "firm" with fewer than 100 employees, then small businesses employ 33% of the labor force and generate just 37% of net new jobs.[3]

Although the estimates vary widely, all agree that the influence of small businesses is substantial. Consequently, anything adversely affecting the productivity of small businesses has a substantial impact on all businesses and on total productivity.

Inflation, Capital Formation, and Interest Costs

To regain our position as a high-investment economy, we need to exert efforts in the areas of tax policy (discussed later), keep inflation under control, and reduce the government deficit in order to bring down interest rates.

> . . .quite clearly the major direct efforts have to be in the area of tax policy. . . .There's no question but what the combination of the intellectually arthritic conventional accounting procedures together with the inflation that we've had in the last decade or so have had an absolutely lethal effect on the rate of economic progress in this country.[4]

Inflation has been at unacceptable levels in the United States for about a decade, running well into double-digit figures during a number of those years, although by mid-1984 it had dropped to an annual rate of 3 to 4%. Nearly everyone agrees that something needs to be done when inflation is high, but there is a great deal of disagreement on exactly what that "something" is. And even when substantial agreement exists as to which approach or approaches should be taken, people still disagree on how far these approaches should go. In a word, each approach has its costs, and there is no consensus about the point at which costs and benefits equal out. Low capital formation and high interest rates also have had an adverse impact on productivity, and the solutions to these problems also generate controversy.

Interestingly, the Dow Jones average fluctuated from a high of about 1,250 to a low of 790 between June 1981 and May 1984, staying mainly in the low 800s until late 1982. Although high interest rates were partly to blame, many feel the basic reason was the difficulty in making the additional cuts necessary to balance the budget by 1984. Because of decreased tax collections and increased transfer payments (welfare, unemployment compensation) brought about primarily by the recession, it appears the federal deficit will exceed $200 billion in 1984. Many feel that unless the budget is balanced, inflation will be difficult to control and interest rates will remain high. Thus, the market is expressing doubt, not about the tax cuts, but about the likelihood that the budget will be balanced. The administration has promised additional cuts.

High Long-Term Interest Rates

Even though the prime rate decreased from a high of 22% to a mid-1984 12 1/2% and the inflation rate dropped substantially during this period, long-term interest rates have refused to decline significantly. In fact, the differential between inflation and interest rates, sometimes called *real* interest rates, has actually been increasing for certain items, such as home mortgages. And short-term interest rates have not dropped as much as many expected. Many industries, such as housing, automobiles, consumer durables, and business capital goods, have been affected negatively as a consequence.

Investors are simply unwilling to commit at fixed rates far into the future. Long-term funds—the 25- and 30-year fixed-rate bonds—are no longer available, except at excessively high rates. Without such capital, companies are not making the kinds of investments needed to expand facilities, modernize plants and equipment, and increase productivity, all steps essential to ensure our future ability to produce competitive goods and services for Americans and for the world market.

Since the ability to finance on a long-term basis has all but vanished—perhaps forever—and rates have been too high to encourage extensive intermediate financing, companies are simply refusing to participate at all in capital markets. This means that basic industries have decided not to raise capital, not to expand, not to modernize, not to produce new products, not to provide new jobs.[5]

One of the basic reasons that interest rates, particularly long-term rates, have remained high is because the expectation persists that inflation rates will remain high well into the future. And a primary reason for this expectation is the expectation that government deficits will remain high. The other edge of the high deficit sword impacting interest rates, if we assume that present restrictive monetary policies will stay in effect, is that the government competes with private enterprise in the capital markets for funds, keeping interest rates high. Many economists still feel that the inflation rate in the 1980's might run from as high as 10% to as low as 4%, with a median rate of about 6 1/2%; and many feel that deficits will remain at significant levels during the 1980's.[6]

The upshot is that a substantial number of experienced business economists continue to see a perfectly plausible economic scenario for the 1980s as one consisting of double-digit inflation rates, fueled by deficits that are out of control. In short, a lot of people in the business community think that the administration will not be able to solve its economic policy problems in a way which is consistent with the outcomes of lower inflation rates and higher real growth rates, and they continue to be concerned that current economic policy contains considerable potential for the worst kind of economic performance. Those concerns about the potential path of the system during the 1980s may well underlie the stubborness of long-term interest rates in holding at near record levels.[7]

Certainly the present low inflation rate is likely to reduce somewhat the expectations of high future inflation rates; but until the belief becomes widespread that the continuation of low inflation rates is plausible, high interest rates are likely to prevail. And no one will believe that inflation will moderate until the budget deficit shows large reductions on a continuing basis.

It seems to us, therefore, that immediate action must be taken to reduce the deficit significantly. In our opinion, moreover, such efforts must persist until the budget is balanced. We recognize that this cannot happen overnight; we simply recommend perseverance until the budget is balanced. Such perseverance will itself alter expectations and therefore have a favorable impact on interest rates. Furthermore, the restraint on money and credit growth should be maintained to keep inflation under control. To finance the deficit through a rapid growth in the money supply would mean a return to high inflation and an elimination of the advances made to this point.

Government Safety Nets—Not the Answer

Some have gone so far as to recommend government efforts along the following lines:

I think we must face up to the fact that a crisis demands extraordinary measures. As reluctant as U.S. corporate leadership is to have government intrude in the workings of the free market—and I share this reluctance—I think we must acknowledge the need for Washington to assist in the resuscitation of our basic industries. Unless there appears some magical substitute for the nonexistent long-term financing market—and it better show up fast—do we have any choice but to give serious consideration to some sort of temporary government-supported safety net for long-term bonds for basic industries? We have today many safety nets for small business, for farmers, for international trade, among other economic areas. A bailout is not what I have in mind. The mechanisms should reward competent management and investors willing to make long-term commitments. I cannot offer precise details of how this would work, but in the absence of recognition of the problem, let alone answers that would command widespread support, I suggest it as an almost desperate solution.[8]

Such an approach is wrong in our view. Government intervention breeds more government intervention and control, with all of the bad consequences we have previously discussed. We have and will argue against the so-called safety nets for small business, farmers, and others mentioned by the author. We argue as strongly against them for big businesses. Moreover, some crisis or another is always lurking around the corner, and one serious error we have made over and over in the past is to yell for government help when crises arise. We are not saying that people do not have the right to yell for help; we only point out that when they do, they are yelling for something other than a representative democracy and the free enterprise system—they are yelling for a move toward socialism. That movement, once started, is hard to stop and even harder to reverse, and has consequences reaching far beyond the economic system that it would foster.

Small Businesses and High Interest Rates

Some are suggesting the adoption of a two-tier interest policy that would allow a discounted rate—three or four points below the prevailing prime interest rate—for small business borrowing. To encourage banks to loan at this rate, the Federal Reserve System (FRS) would grant them relief by lowering FRS rates for funds loaned to small businesses. Perhaps small businesses are hurt more than large businesses by high interest rates, but the question is why? If they are hurt more because of the natural differences between large and small, one conclusion might be reached. If, instead, it is because of an arbitrary, man-made rule that is biased against small business, a different conclusion is warranted.

But certain industries, such as construction and automobiles, and small businesses in general suffer disproportionately. Large corporations raise capital through long-term issues of debt with fixed interest rates and through the equity market. Small businesses raise their initial capital from friends and relatives and seasonal and expansion capital through short-term borrowing from banks, with interest rates that move up and down with the prime rate. Thus, periods of high interest rates affect small businesses immediately but affect large businesses only when they go to the money market.

One response to high interest rates is, of course, to avoid borrowing. But most small companies don't borrow to spend; they borrow to "roll over" their short-term debt. The only way small companies can avoid borrowing is to convert debt to equity or to contract (by selling or liquidating operations earning an inadequate inflation-adjusted return on the market value of assets). While these may be attractive options, they are not always feasible.[9]

Thus, it seems to us that the differential in impacts of high interest rates, to the extent that they do exist, result from intrinsic differences between small and large businesses. Certainly, businesses, large and small, are in difficulty partly because of high interest rates, as Chapters 2 and 3 clearly demonstrate. High interest rates are the villain, and actions must be taken to get them under control. We do not feel that special consideration with respect to interest rates should be given to any segment of the economy, for a number of reasons. First, subsidization of lower interest rates for small businesses, or any other segment, means even greater government intrusion into the economic system, damaging the free market economy even more, as we have said. It is illogical to argue for decreased government influence in some areas and increased influence in other areas.

Second, special consideration for one group introduces still another artificial barrier into the economy. Although many small businesses unquestionably are hurt by high interest rates, as our empirical research in Chapter 3 demonstrated, so are many large firms, such as those in the automotive, steel, and construction industries. Many individuals also have suffered. It is impossible, objectively, to say who is hurting the most. Preferential rates for one group reduce funds available to others. The free market economy guarantees neither equal rewards nor equal difficulties for business firms.

Of course, one might argue that huge government deficits are a major factor causing the high interest rates, and that this has caused some elements of the economy to be hurt more than others. Some reach the conclusion that the government should help overcome the problem it helped to create by subsidizing interest rates, particularly for those who are hurt the most. This is not correct for several reasons. In the first place, it is an example of circular reasoning, as previously indicated. You don't increase government influence to help decrease government influence. (When you allow the donkey out of the corral, as the saying goes, you can't control which way he wanders.) In the second place, such an approach treats the symptoms, not the disease. Extremely high interest rates are an indication of disequilibriums in the economy—insufficient savings, excessive government deficits, and the like. Actions should be taken to cure the disease.

Third, some individuals and firms are helped by high interest rates. Those who enter an era of high interest rates in a highly liquid position and are able to save benefit from the high interest rates, as our research has shown. Savings—one requisite for decreasing the interest rates—are encouraged. In other words, assuming a free market economy, high interest rates are not only a reflection of disequilibriums, but will themselves hasten the recovery—if they are allowed to do so—by encouraging savings, discouraging government expenditures, and discouraging borrowing in general. Preferential rates, subsidized by the government, reduce the flexibility, the automatic adjustment features, in the free enterprise system.

Regulations

As shown in Chapters 2 and 3, it is certain that regulations have had a very detrimental effect on productivity in business firms. And we applaud the present efforts to provide relief. But the effort is not well coordinated and certainly is not sufficient.

So the problem of regulatory reform doesn't lie in inactivity but, according to Marvin Kosters, director of the American Enterprise Institute's Center for the Study of Government Regulation, in a flurry of activity that's unfocused. "The Administration is not building a strategy for changing deregulation. It's providing [scattered] relief from burdensome requirements, which is useful for business but fails to tackle the reform essential for regulatory goals."[10]

Changing Basic Attitudes and Approaches

The basic requirement for bringing about regulatory reform is a change in basic attitudes. We must adopt the attitude that the only justification for business regulations is to preserve, promote, and strengthen a free market economy. If a proposed regulation does not satisfy this criterion, it should not be put into effect. Even then it should meet a cost/benefit analysis. And those presently in effect that are not fulfilling that objective should be eliminated.

We recognize that reasonable people may not see eye to eye in applying that standard. We also realize that it will take time to implement. But that standard, agreed to and adhered to in developing and implementing regulations, is much more likely to get us nearer the ideal state than the illogical and inconsistent policies we presently follow. One economist, Lester Thurow, a liberal Democrat, even argues for abolition of the antitrust laws:

> . . .because they are a waste of time, a waste of money and a waste of government effort. While there is supposedly an environment for deregulation in Washington, no Administration has enough political capital to deregulate more than a few things.[11]

Professor Thurow went on to say:

> In any case, these antitrust battles divert scarce resources from the real problem, which is productivity. After all, IBM has spent untold millions to defend itself in an antitrust case that has lasted twelve years and is still a long way from being resolved. That money would be better spent in research and development and new plant and equipment, instead of on lawyers and economists who have spent years in court testifying that the company is not a monopoly. There are many other examples of how the antitrust laws inhibit both the nation's productivity and its foreign trade.[12]

Whether or not antitrust laws were ever necessary to preserve a free market economy by ensuring competition in the domestic markets, it is pretty certain that they are no longer needed in this era of worldwide competition. This indicates another serious problem with regulations, particularly in large, complex societies such as ours. Once put into place, they are likely to remain even when the business environment has altered to the point where they are no longer necessary, perhaps even harmful. Once promulgated, they usually last until specifically cancelled or superseded.

At the minimum, all existing regulations should have a "sunset" rule of five years (regulations would automatically terminate unless new decisions are made to continue them); a cost/benefit analysis and justification should be required of all new regulations; and government agencies should be subject to close, persistent oversight. Although some of these things are being done—as evidenced, for example, by the Task Force on Regulatory Relief chaired by Vice-President George Bush—more effort is needed. Again, however, a change in basic attitude must come about if success is to be obtained.

No Special Consideration for Small Businesses

Many feel that the special position of small businesses requires special consideration. The major recommendation is for the development of a two-tier system in which regulations are tailored to the size and nature of the business. In essence, the argument is that even if a regulation can meet a cost/benefit test on a macro basis, it may not do so on a sectoral or micro basis. As we have pointed out, small businesses pay a proportionately higher amount in order to conform to regulations, and many feel this should be taken into account in the development and enforcement of regulations to achieve the intended economic and social goals. In a word, so the argument goes, all agencies should provide exemptions or require less complex reports from small firms whenever possible. Others have proposed that small businesses be reimbursed by the federal agencies for the costs of filing reports to those agencies. Again, the culprits are excessive regulations and excessive, often duplicative, reporting requirements even when the regulations are justified.

One of the major problems, as we have said, is that little oversight control is exerted over the operations of federal agencies. As a result, they can run amuck, issuing regulations and rules more or less at will—regulations and rules that may not conform to Congress's intent. Thus, we agree with proposals that have been made

> to require each federal agency upon promulgating a rule to publish and submit to Congress: (a) A statement of the need for the rule; (b) a preliminary analysis of its economic impact; and (c) with respect to major rules: (1) An economic impact statement; (2) estimates of related paperwork requirements; (3) estimates of its effects on the operation of Federal Courts; and (4) an index of all other rules pertaining to the same subject matter.[13]

If such proposals were enforced and if existing regulations were reviewed in the same light, we feel that the number and complexity of regulations would be reduced substantially.

Perfection in ensuring that regulations meet a cost/benefit test is not likely to be reached, of course. Again, however, if the attitude that a free market economy is to be supported and strengthened can be developed and maintained and regulations are considered in that light, reductions in their number and complexity are bound to result.

Assuming, for a moment, that perfection were attained, there still probably would be differences between large and small firms in compliance costs. However, there would probably also be differences in costs of compliance between firms in different segments of the economy.

Once it has been determined as well as possible that the benefits of a regulation exceed its cost, no preferential treatment should be given to any firm because of size, the segment of the economy in which it is located, or any other considerations. It should be left to consumers to decide whether or not they are willing to pay the additional regulation-related costs for the products and services they desire. If so, the firm will survive and prosper; if not, it will go out of existence. Any other course of action places an artificial barrier in the free market economy by requiring all citizens to subsidize the consumers of those firms' products and services.

> Government intervention is a barrier to economic re-vitalization, not the solution. Government policies have produced inflation and regulatory uncertainty which have discouraged investment in technological innovation.[14]

Taxes

Taxes overlap many of the other areas of concern, such as capital formation, research, development, and innovation, and were covered generally in the preceding chapters. Recommendations regarding taxes also will be covered more fully in the sections discussing these topics. A few additional general observations are in order here, however.

Basic Criteria for a Good Tax System

Many tax theorists argue that a basic—perhaps *the* basic—criterion of a good taxation system is *neutrality*. This means that income tax regulations should interfere with the decisions of individuals and managements of firms as little as possible. Otherwise, tax regulations become coercive and dictate decisions. At best, tax impacts will have some influence on decisions. Neutrality simply requires that the tax system be designed and operated in such a manner as to minimize its influence on decisions, the standard being the decisions that would be made if there were no taxes.

Another important criterion often suggested as a requisite for a good tax system is *certainty*. *Certainty* requires that taxpayers know which types of taxes they are paying and the amounts of each they pay. Without such certainty it is impossible for them to make knowledgeable decisions regarding taxation and expenditures.

Over the years, these two criteria for a good tax system—neutrality and certainty—have become so obscured that they are now nearly nonexistent. Certainly many taxes are not neutral. And even though most taxpayers know something about the total direct taxes they pay—such as state, federal, and city income taxes, payroll taxes, and state and city sales taxes—many, perhaps most, know little if anything about the total indirect taxes they pay as a part of the price of goods and services they buy. For many families these indirect taxes may be considerably higher than the direct taxes. In fact, no one knows exactly what the marginal tax rate is for the average family, although, as indicated in a prior section, some estimate the rate at 50% or higher. In any case, high taxes reduce the ability of households to save and consume, thereby reducing resources available to the private sector.

Perhaps more importantly, evidence we previously presented indicates that the marginal rate for just the direct taxes is high enough to reduce the amount of time people work, as well as their desire to save, to get better educations, or to accept positions involving greater risk and responsibility. All of these things reduce productivity.

Even though it will take time, of course, the solution to these problems is to make a concerted, conscientious, and continuous effort to revamp and rewrite the various tax laws using the standards of neutrality and certainty as guidelines. We cannot discuss all the ramifications here. However, let us go into a few broad considerations of direct concern to the productivity question.

Phasing Out Business Taxation

First, taxation of business firms should be phased out. This means that not only would corporations not be taxed, but partners and sole proprietors would be taxed only on what they took out of the business. Business taxes have a substantial impact on when and how much capital investment is undertaken, the degree of internal and external financing by the firm, when the firm will enter the external financing market, the pricing of products and services, where plants will be located, and a number of other factors. All of these effects are coercive, as we are using that term, and often cause decisions to be made differently from the way they would without taxes. They are artificial barriers to the free enterprise system and certainly have a depressing impact on productivity.

Business taxes provide the possibility for politicians and others to mislead the public, accidentally or deliberately. How often have we heard the statement, for example, that businesses do not pay their fair share of the taxes; that if business taxes were increased, individuals would have to pay less? Of course, such statements are not accurate. Businesses are brick and mortar; they cannot bear the burden of taxation. Taxes may be collected from businesses; business firms can act as a conduit (a collection agency) between those who bear the taxes and the government; but, ultimately, only people can bear the weight of taxes.

One or a combination of three groups ultimately bears the weight of business taxes: consumers, the labor force, and owners. Which group or groups ultimately pay the tax and the proportion each pays depend on many factors—the elasticity of demand for the good or service produced by the firm, the competitiveness of the environment in which the firm operates, and the strength of the labor force, among others. Although no one knows for certain, as a general rule it appears that business taxes fall primarily on consumers and owners. Some have estimated that 60 to 70% of the final consumer price of many products and services consists of the accumulation of taxes along the line from raw material to final product. This represents a significant transfer of resources—much of it hidden—from the private to the government sector, and consequently reduces the ability of people to save or spend on other goods and services, as well as placing large amounts of resources in the hands of politicians. To the extent that taxes are borne by the owners, the risk and uncertainty of investments are increased, causing investors to alter investment decisions.

Taxation of People

Second, taxation of people needs to be more neutral and certain. Many recommendations have been made for tax reform, running all the way from simple reforms of the present system, to replacing the income tax with a consumption tax (such as the value-added tax), to a flat rate tax. We cannot settle here the issue of the best approach in taxation policy to ensure that the standards of neutrality and certainty are met. At the minimum, however, a sincere, concerted effort should be made to simplify the present structure drastically.

On balance, on the basis of limited analysis and consideration, we favor a flat-rate tax applied to gross income less reasonable expenditures necessary to generate that gross income. This system would simplify the tax structure and release the billions of dollars spent each year on filing tax returns to more productive use.

> It would also remove most of the bracket creep which inflation causes in conjunction with progressive taxation. In addition, it would very likely increase the incentive to work, to save rather than borrow, and to invest. Also, some of the estimated $95 billion lost to unreported underground income would end up in taxable income, as well as much of that lost through loopholes. Most importantly, perhaps, by expanding the base, it would reduce the role of governmental agencies, Congress, and special interest groups in the decisionmaking process and leave those decisions to the free market economy.[15]

For instance, the tax code is biased toward borrowers, home owners, and contributors to designated organizations, in that interest, taxes, and contributions are deductible in the calculation of taxable income. A "true" flat-rate tax would eliminate such deductions and thereby, we feel, be more equitable.

In any case, however it can be accomplished, the total taxation system should be altered to become as nearly as possible a vehicle for collection of taxes for government use in the most neutral, certain way possible. Over the years, the taxation system has been altered to satisfy the demands of certain special-interest groups, to redistribute the wealth of the country, and to fine-tune the economic system. All of these objectives represent coercive, unnatural barriers to the freedom of individuals and, consequently, to the free enterprise system. Even if those goals are considered desirable—and we have made clear that we do not so consider them—at least in the form and to the extent they are presently being implemented, they should be approached in some manner other than through the tax system.

Increase Taxes to Reduce the Deficit?

An important question remains: namely, should taxes be increased in the face of large deficits? A great deal of disagreement exists regarding the answer to this question. On balance we feel taxes should not be increased. We agree with those who feel that marginal tax rates are already too high. Increased taxes will damage incentive even more, reduce savings, and further decrease investment. More importantly, perhaps, we feel politicians will be inclined not to reduce expenditures and will use the increased taxes as an excuse, preventing the reduction in government activities we feel is necessary. History clearly indicates the likelihood of this scenario.

Even though we disagree with indexing on the expenditure side, we agree with the plan to index the tax system (assuming that the present progressive system stays in place) that is slated to go into effect in 1985 in an effort to stop bracket creep brought on by inflation in a progressive system. Bracket creep is largely responsible for the estimated increase in personal tax revenues of 176% between 1970 and 1980. Such "hidden taxes" are unlegislated, thereby allowing politicians to avoid responsibility for them. At the same time, the increased tax revenues can be used to maintain or increase expenditures or, at least, as an excuse to avoid decreasing them. As a case in point, it is estimated that during the same period, 1970 through 1980, government expenditures increased 194%—significantly faster than the tax increases.

Capital Formation and Retention—Small Businesses

Regarding the acquisition of capital, we have already discussed the suggestion to loan money to small businesses at three to four points below the prime rate. Recommendations have also been made to authorize the Small Business Administration to guarantee loans to firms that are financing growth through employee stock ownership plans and to employees wishing to buy out small firms to prevent those businesses from liquidating or relocating. In addition, it has been proposed that tax credits be allowed for investment in original stock issuances of small firms. It has also been suggested that Congress reduce the paperwork required for small firms to sell securities to large investors.

Because of the independent nature of small business ownership, many observers feel equity capital is not the way to increase productivity. Arthur Andersen & Co., an international CPA firm, has proposed a new hybrid security called a "small business participating debenture" for companies with less than $25 million in annual sales. This would be a fixed-term, participating debenture, having debt status, and issued at a stated interest rate. Investors would be able to participate or share in the earnings of a firm only during the time the debentures were outstanding.[16]

Proposals for Small Businesses

A number of other tax proposals have been made to promote capital mobility and encourage savings on investment, and thereby benefit small businesses:[17]

1. Eliminate the capital gains tax, or severely limit it.
2. Allow corporations to deduct dividends as expenses on their tax returns, or at least allow investors a tax credit equal to the corporate taxes paid on their dividends.
3. Defer taxation on capital gains on the sale of stock if the gains are reinvested.
4. If capital gains are to be taxed, have a sliding-scale adjustment for inflation that reduces the portion of the gain subject to taxation in proportion to the length of time the asset has been held.

The logic behind these proposals is summarized in the words of a corporation vice-president:

> We believe that the evidence is overwhelming that increases in capital gains taxes are counter-productive. The higher the capital gains tax, the less incentive there is to invest in high-risk enterprises. . .a roll back in capital gains rates would improve the average rate of growth of real gross national product, reduce the unemployment rate, and reduce the federal budget deficit.[18]

To keep existing businesses going, recommendations have been made to limit severely or completely eliminate estate taxes upon the death of the owner if the business is continued by family members; these taxes would be postponed until the family sells the business. Suggestions also have been made to postpone capital gains taxes on the sale of one business if the proceeds are reinvested in another small business.

The Small Business Administration made similar recommendations in 1981:

- To repeal federal estate taxes or to raise the $175,000 net worth exemption to $2 million. [President Reagan's recommendation passed recently by Congress is to raise the limit to $600,000 and to eliminate estate and gift tax on all gifts and bequests between spouses.]
- To raise annual gift tax exemptions from $3,000 to $20,000. [The recently passed bill raises the gift exclusion to $10,000.]
- To assess no capital gains tax in cases where small business owners who sell one firm reinvest the money in another small business.
- To change corporate income tax rates so the highest percentage rate would apply to firms earning more than $500,000 a year instead of the current $100,000. [Legislation passed recently instead reduces the tax rate in the bottom two brackets by one percentage point in 1982 and an additional point in 1983 and subsequent years.][19]

In addition to those mentioned above, other items have been placed in the Revenue Code to aid small businesses.

To avoid the forced sale of a closely held business, the estates of certain decedents can now choose to stretch out payment of the estate tax on the business for as long as 15 years. This provision provides relief where the decedent's interest in the business constitutes at least 35% of his adjusted gross estate.[20]

A unique provision of the tax law. . .allows an original investor in a "small business corporation" to claim any loss (within specified limits) sustained on the sale, exchange, or worthlessness of his stock investment as a fully deductible ordinary loss rather than as a partially deductible capital loss. At the same time, if the business prospers, any gains realized by the investor on the disposition of his stock will be treated as capital gains. The purpose. . .is to remove a possible tax disadvantage to incorporating a new small business venture and, thereby, allow investors to choose the form the enterprise will take on the basis of non-tax, business considerations.[21]

Conclusions Regarding Proposals for Small Businesses

If our recommendations regarding taxation were followed, many of the proposals related to capital gains and allowing corporations to deduct dividends as expenses would not be necessary. Assuming the present system stays in existence, again we generally feel that no special consideration should be given to small businesses or any other segment of the economy. Such approaches are attempts to control and direct the economy, rather than reactions to its dictates under a free market system. They are attempts to spread the risk of investment in small businesses over the tax-paying public. Sharing such risk is not their responsibility. Consumers of the firms' products and services must be willing to pay a high enough price to give owners a rate of return commensurate with the risks they assume, or capital will flow to those segments of the economy where this does occur. Subsidization of risk thwarts, or at least interferes with, the allocation mechanism.

Having said these things, we must also say that we do see some justification for treating small businesses differently from large businesses for certain aspects of taxation. Because tax policies and provisions are established by people, "unnatural" barriers can and do creep in. For example, many small businesses are sole proprietorships and partnerships, as opposed to being corporations. Many are labor-intensive. Thus, we agree that unless radical changes in the system are implemented, something needs to be done to make business continuation easier, to make it easier to liquidate one business and start a new one, and to offset the other unnatural barriers created by the taxation system. However, we feel that due care needs to be exercised in determining what is unnatural.

And we all need to cry "wolf" a little less, and acknowledge a bit more the things we do gain. "Of the 14.5 million or 15 million small businesses in the United States, maybe 13 million are not incorporated and pay taxes at individual rates—so a 25 percent tax cut favorably impacts on them."[22]

Venture Capitalists on the Increase

Venture capital organizations are being created to bring managers and owners of small businesses together with capitalists willing to assume the risk. Such attempts are to be encouraged. In this regard, we should point out that individuals with innovative ideas and concepts in high technology areas are finding it relatively easy to attract venture capital. In a number of states networks of consultants, lawyers, bankers, accounting firms, chambers of commerce, and others are being formed to bring together fledgling entrepreneurs and venture capitalists. In southeastern Michigan alone, six venture capital firms have been created and five more were being formed as of late 1982. There were only two two years before that. And the numbers are increasing rapidly.

The new venture capital boom was initially fueled by the slash in the top capital gains tax rate from 49% to 28% in 1978, a move that sharply enhanced the potential rewards of getting in on a profitable venture. Two years later, the federal government sweetened the pot further by allowing pension funds to invest a portion of their money in venture deals.

Thus, scores of new venture capital groups were formed, including many by banks, insurance companies and large corporations. According to *Venture Capital Journal*, the industry's leading publication, there are now nearly 150 private venture capital firms, 300 Small Business Administration-backed investment companies and an uncounted number of bank and corporate groups in the business.

According to Jane Morris, managing editor of *Venture Capital Journal*, entrepreneurs who couldn't raise a dime in a lean year like 1975 even with the best new-product idea can now choose from among as many as ten venture capital sources to get the most advantageous deal for themselves. Thus, while they could hope for no more than a 25%-to-35% stake in forming a new company in the mid-1970s, they now ask for and often get as much as 50%-to-60%.[23]

Pension funds are now being used to invest in new or young companies, because the rate of return is often two or three times the 5 or 6% usually earned.

Long married to either fixed-income investments or blue chip stocks, many of the nation's major pension funds are now putting their retirees' money into venture capital projects. Since 1979, when the U.S. Labor Department clarified the Employee Retirement and Income Security Act to permit such investments, pension funds have committed $730 million to new entrepreneurial companies. More than $40 million of this money was invested in 1981, making corporate and public employee pension funds the largest single source of venture capital funds.

At least ninety major corporate pension funds have become actively involved in backing the fortunes of new or young companies.[24]

These funds are usually placed with venture capital partnerships that then disburse them to new or young companies. And the future looks bright for an expansion of the use of these funds as a source of venture capital.

And more large funds plan to get in on the action. Indeed, the outlook for greater pension fund participation appears robust. A recent survey by Greenwich Research Associates revealed that another sixty-to-seventy funds definitely plan to enter the venture business over the next two years. Like many other investors, they have been captivated by descriptions of the coming decade as the "Era of the Entrepreneur" and hope to cash in on the dramatic growth new companies occasionally achieve. With the great size of their assets, the pension funds will continue to be the dominant force in the business for the forseeable future. . . .[25]

The point, simply, is that the free market economy will adjust to the needs of small businesses if allowed to do so.

> . . .a recent issue of *The New York Times* reported that new businesses are starting up at double the pace of even seven years ago, and the number of self-employed Americans is around 6.8 million. Many of these were created by persons laid off in other industries who decided to start their own businesses.[26]

Government Involvement

In our view, not only should government not become more involved than at present, it should become less involved. Too often the government becomes the problem rather than the solution.

> Government needs to establish broad incentives for savings and investment and should not target individual industries for special encouragement. To do that implies that there is somebody in government smart enough to pick the winners. . . .[27]

> And rather than help the disadvantaged, the Small Business Administration program often inadvertently sets up the conditions for failure of the businesses it is designed to establish or save. . . .Lax policies and sloppy procedures in the SBA's direct business loan program cost the federal Treasury $571 million from 1970 to 1978, according to an investigation by the St. Louis Globe-Democrat. That figure could reach $900 million if losses in 1979 are consistent with previous years.[28]

Amberg and Montgomery go on to say that:

> There is no respect for money in the agency; it is peddled like soap at low interest rates to many who have no management ability in the types of business activity they are entering. Money is borrowed to pay off creditors and taxes with none left over to keep the business running, so the business fails and the SBA loses. A myriad of other equally bad practices prevail.[29]

Elimination of Estate Taxation

We feel estate taxes should be eliminated completely, and not just when a small business is to be continued by family members after the death of the owner. Estate taxes are based on the idea that people should get only what they have earned by the sweat of their brow—that receiving tax free wealth is somehow unfair to those who aren't recipients of estates. We reject the idea, as previously discussed, that some relatively small group of individuals is entitled to make the judgments on what is or is not fair. More importantly, generally the income giving rise to the wealth in the estate has already been taxed, so estate taxation is a form of double taxation—to say nothing of the fact that it is a tax on wealth, which removes resources from the private sector. Such taxation obviously reduces the incentive to accumulate wealth, and thus reduces the productivity of individuals. In addition, it reduces resources available for saving and investment.

Research, Development, and Innovation

Our previous recommendations regarding taxation policy and approaches to bring down interest rates would have a positive impact on research and development expenditures. More is needed, however.

Consortia of Companies

Many of the recommendations in the preceding section on capital formation and retention apply here as well. In addition, the federal government should establish policies that allow consortia of companies to cooperate in research and development. We now operate in the world market, and many of the old laws put on the books to promote domestic competition are no longer relevant. In fact, they are counterproductive in terms of worldwide competition. Moreover, the costs of certain types of research and development in this complex technological age are too high for most companies to incur alone—the risk is too great. Allowing consortia of companies would spread the risk while putting the choice of objectives into the private sector.

Encouraging Small Research and Development Firms

A number of other suggestions have been made to encourage *small* research and development firms in particular:

1. Allow small businesses to obtain exclusive patent rights on inventions developed with funds provided by the federal government if they pay back the research funds.
2. Allow small research and development firms to carry operating losses forward for at least ten years, and allow immediate tax write-offs for specialized research and development equipment.
3. Reduce capital gains taxes on the sale of these firms' securities by 50% if stockholders have held them for more than five years.
4. Give the Patent and Trademark Office authority to arbitrate patent disputes. This would reduce costs from an estimated average of $250,000 per case to $1,000.
5. Require federal agencies, such as the National Aeronautics and Space Administration and the Department of Defense, to promote greater use of small businesses in their research activities. (As a step in this direction, Congress established by statute that a minimum percentage of the research funds of the National Science Foundation be committed to small businesses.)

Patent laws promote the incentive to research and develop new technology, and these laws are therefore essential to a free market economy. Although we believe funds for most such research and development expenditures should and would come from the private sector in a free enterprise setting, we believe that if the government is to advance funds, the first recommendation above is necessary to provide the incentive for small businesses to seek out the funds for research and development.

Recommendations 2 and 3 would not be necessary if our recommendations regarding the taxation system were adopted.

Recommendation 4 is sound. Such huge expenditures are unproductive and unnecessary.

Regarding recommendation 5, again we feel that funds for most research should come from the private sector, except in such areas as space exploration and military research. If government is to make such funds available, they should be distributed solely on the merits of research proposals and plans. Certainly small businesses must be considered in this light and not discriminated against, but they should not be given special consideration simply because they are small.

Workers and Supervisors

Reasons for Difficulties

There is probably more disagreement about what should and can be done to improve the productivity of workers and supervisors than about any other area of the business world. Labor union officials argue that management first needs to be more amenable to the collective bargaining process. Without this, an adversary relationship exists that is inimical to the atmosphere necessary for progress. Workers have the necessary know-how and knowledge, learned through experience at the work site, to make a substantial contribution toward improving productivity. Allowing them to contribute will make them feel a part of the overall undertaking, and will therefore improve their mental attitude toward their work and increase productivity, so the arguments go.

Those who feel that the general deterioration of the work ethic in the country is one of the basic causes for productivity decreases also feel that solutions can be found only over the longer term. Solutions will be found only when the basic attitudes—the national values—of the people change. Enthusiasm for hard work and sacrifice and pride in doing a job well must be rekindled. Such attitudinal changes must start early, at home and in the schools. These things will take time, as previously stated.

Others feel that the work ethic has not altered substantially, but that the incentive to work hard and well has been reduced by outside stimuli such as the high marginal tax rates mentioned earlier. If these are reduced, people will work harder because they will be able to retain more of the fruits of their labor. We must search for other innovative ways to stimulate employees to do a better job, such as improving the quality of work life on the plant floor.

Radical economists [neo-Marxist interpretation] are inclined to associate diminishing productivity growth with worker alienation and discontent. Workers' dissatisfaction in turn, they say, is rooted in the systematic stratification of labor processes and markets that has accompanied the maturation of capitalism.[30]

For some who feel this way the solution is labor domination, if not complete takeover—in a word, the overthrow of the capitalistic system. Of course, we do not agree.

As is usually true, there are elements of truth and fiction in many of these positions. And what is needed to increase worker productivity varies among firms, because research has clearly disclosed that there is no uniform set of factors consistently present in every firm. The managers of each firm must discover what factors influence worker productivity in their firm and take appropriate action if productivity is to increase.

Freedom of the Individual

Nevertheless, there is one basic, critical factor that goes back to our conclusions in Chapter 4—freedom of the individual. Workers need to feel that they are not slaves to the system, "things" to be manipulated for the good of the firm. Instead, they must be made to feel an important part of the system whose views and ideas are listened to and acted on, where appropriate, to make the system work most efficiently and effectively. They must feel that owners and managers have a sincere interest in their welfare and happiness.

We are not saying that workers should set the objectives and goals for a firm. Generally they have no desire to do so and, in any case, these are the prerogatives of the managers and owners. In fact, there is some merit in the view that one reason for productivity declines is that the strong, individualistic leadership that once characterized many firms and organizations no longer exists; that we no longer have strong people in positions of leadership who can make the hard decisions necessary for successful operations. Too many decisions are made by committees, with the result that we have designed too many camels while striving for race horses.

But workers can help in attaining the goals and objectives of a firm, if allowed to do so. Many managers of successful firms indicated that the suggestions of workers, because of their years of experience and expertise in their particular jobs, have resulted in substantial cost savings and increased quality of output. Frequently, workers are able to develop new approaches and techniques to make a product because of their knowledge and experience in the functions they perform. As we have previously stated, a long-range outlook is necessary, and thus patience is essential.

Jac Fitz-Enz quotes Jeff Scanlen, editor of *Productivity*, who summarized his experience with attempts at productivity improvement:

> Americans have a tendency these days to look for some magic solution to their problem of sagging productivity, hoping there might be some quick fix and easy cure for a crisis that has been brewing for years. . . .
>
> Organizations which wish to improve [human] productivity must take time to organize all resources in support of the objective. The short term project approach simply does not generate and sustain substantial improvements. Unfortunately, most American firms rely on the faddish style of "here today—gone tomorrow" management. . . .The quick fix simply does not work on a problem which is as deeply ingrained as lagging productivity. The approach that does work can be found by studying the success stories of American industry. The most effective American corporations exhibit a common characteristic. Without exception, all of them have a clearly stated organizational philosophy which, for decades, has served to define and support a corporate culture. This culture, expressed through its methods and systems, totally permeates the organization. It integrates the people, the technology and the processes into a common drive toward well-promulgated objectives.[31]

Management

In Chapter 5 we presented general conclusions and recommendations concerning management. Here we concentrate on specific recommendations for small businesses.

Many people say that opportunities must be provided, mainly through the Small Business Administration (SBA) and local agencies, to (1) improve entrepreneurial education for managers of small businesses; (2) disseminate information to help managers comply with federal, state, and local regulations; and (3) conduct and coordinate research into problems facing small businesses for which there are no ready solutions. Others have made several recommendations regarding small business's need for better information. (1) SBA and state agencies should keep information on various regulations and provide one-to-one counseling for small businesses on how to comply with them. (2) A comprehensive library of current information needed by small businesses should be provided and maintained. (3) A referral system should be set up so that small businesses will be aware of people available in the legal, investment, accounting, and financial communities to help with their needs.

The SBA

In line with previous recommendations, we feel the Small Business Administration should be phased out, because one of its major goals is to satisfy the needs of a special-interest group, and that, as we have stated, is antithetical to a free market economy. As a consequence, some feel that its activities can damage some of those in the group it supposedly is helping and supporting. One manager we interviewed, for example, indicated that the SBA was his strongest competitor, since it loaned money to those wishing to start competing businesses. Also, the SBA represents a further encroachment of government into business affairs.

Entrepreneurial Education

We agree that entrepreneurial educational opportunities are needed, but they can be provided in many ways without greatly increasing government influence. Entrepreneurial education can be made available by increasing and improving business education in public schools, particularly high schools. Local firms, chambers of commerce, and other business organizations must work to convince schools that this kind of education is needed. In addition, they should work with local colleges and universities to increase offerings in the small business area and to develop more seminars geared to the needs of small businesses. If, in fact, the benefits of the increased education exceed the cost of providing it, a college, a private organization, or a group of small businesses will step in to fill the need. To require that it be done by the SBA or some other government agency is an attempt to spread the costs of providing the education over the taxpaying public, rather than allowing it to be borne by small businesses and ultimately their customers.

Information Dissemination

The same points can be made regarding the dissemination of information. Major culprits are the number and complexity of regulations. If these were substantially decreased and simplified, a large part of the need would disappear. Beyond this, if a need truly exists, small businesses, through organizations to which they belong and/

or private organizations, will see that information is collected and disseminated.

Free Market Economy

More basic than these measures is the need for management truly to promote and support a free market economy. Often we have heard business leaders give lip service to the free market economy when it benefited their particular firms and run to the government for help when it didn't. Businessmen must either believe in it or not. There is no middle ground. If they believe in it, they must accept the consequences of the system, the risk of failure and loss. To attempt to have only the "good" by eliminating the downside risk through government interference and intervention must eventually result in destruction of the system. There is no such thing as a free lunch.

Energy

A number of people have recommended increasing the potential for small business involvement in helping to solve the energy crisis. Recommendations include increasing the funds available to the Small Business Administration and others for direct loans and loan guarantees to small businesses in energy fields. One of the proposals places energy-related inventions under the joint oversight of the National Bureau of Standards and the Department of Energy. Funding for this joint effort should be increased and the time period needed for evaluation and approval reduced from the present average of approximately two years, say those who recommend this route.

Again, we would prefer allowing private enterprise to solve the energy crisis, which it will do, given the opportunity. Certainly the decisions of the OPEC cartel in the early 1970's had a severe impact on the world economy, but two important points need to be made. First, in a free market economy, firms need not rely on each other to limit supply and stand by fixed prices; the market determines these things. In a cartel, members must rely on such agreements, which generally do not last for extended periods of time. Member countries will begin to act in what each feels is its own best interests and either increase production, reduce or at least stabilize prices, or both. We have seen this happen with OPEC. The forces inherent in a free market economy are nearly irresistible, as some members of OPEC have demonstrated by their actions.

> The Saudis, now selling their oil at $32 per barrel, broke ranks from the more rapacious OPEC members some time ago, and in Geneva they showed that they are not about to be moved by the demands of such illustrious highwaymen as the Algerians, the Libyans, and the Nigerians.
>
> The reason Sheik Yamani is so adamant about keeping the price of oil in the moderate range of $32 per barrel is that his country is a raft, floating on a sea of the stuff. Its interests differ from those of the price-gougers. The extreme gougers have limited reserves. They want every dime they can grasp before their reserves have dried up.
>
> The Saudis fear that such gouging will drive the world into economic doldrums and away from oil toward alternative energy sources, namely: coal and natural gas. They do not want to be left floating on a sea of oil once the market has worked its magic and pushed the advanced countries toward new technologies.
>
> And so once again we see human nature asserting itself against the delusions of quacks.[32]

Second, by keeping prices unnaturally low for the consumers over the years, firms had little incentive to incur exploration and development costs for finding new oil and gas reserves, so that supplies were kept at an artificially low figure. Nor was there any sense of urgency or economic incentive to develop alternative sources of energy. As is true in other aspects of a free market, gas and oil must be allowed to seek their own levels of stability through the pricing mechanism.

Department of Energy (DOE) regulations must be simplified and made less anticompetitive. Between 1974 and 1979, for example, approximately 30,000 gasoline retail outlets went out of business, in large part due to DOE regulations.[33]

Actions by the Federal Government

The solutions proposed by a numer of people all involve actions the federal government should take to improve the position of small business. For example:

● Government contracts should be subdivided into small pieces so that small businesses can participate, and/or large contractors should subcontract to small businesses.

● Funds should be made available to aid small businesses in developing international markets. Communication networks should be improved so that small businesses are aware of international trade possibilities. Forms and reporting requirements should be simplified.

● A national health and safety program, financed substantially by the federal government, should be developed in order to alleviate the high costs of health and safety insurance. Some feel that government should take a more active role in regulating the health and accident industry (hospitals, insurance companies, lawyers) in order to hold costs down.

● In the area of product liability, some suggest that laws should be changed to limit settlements in litigated cases and to restrict the types of actions that can be initiated against producers and distributors of products and services. Others suggest that lawyers' contingent fees, as well as premiums charged by insurance companies, should be controlled.

We reject all such proposals as antithetical to a free enterprise system.

Cumulative Effects

More devastating than the individual impact of these items are their cumulative effects. Michigan, for example, has lost businesses and had difficulty in attracting new businesses because of the cumulative effects of strike-prone unions, high wages, high unemployment taxes, and the Single Business Tax, which is slanted heavily toward payroll costs and is therefore particularly damaging to labor-intensive firms. The adverse effects of any one of these might be tolerated; the cumulative adverse effects of all of them are one major reason for Michigan's depressed economy.

Summary and Conclusions

General

Assuming that reasonably tight reins are maintained on the supply of money and credit—and we agree that they should be maintained—the most critical action that needs to be taken is to reduce, and ultimately eliminate, the budget deficit. This is critical mainly for two reasons.

1. Unless the deficit is substantially reduced, interest rates will remain high and probably go much higher over the long run. Unless interest rates decrease materially the economic recovery will not be sustained, and long-run growth will not materialize. The deficit should be reduced primarily through additional expenditure cuts and whether we like it or not, one area that needs substantial trimming is that of transfer payments, particularly social security benefits. We feel that taxes should not be increased because of the adverse effects we discussed.

2. A reduction in the budget deficit will have a favorable impact on expectations—those of businessmen, consumers, savers, and investors—regarding inflation and interest rates. These changes in expectations will relieve the pressure of attempting to overcome or beat inflation by indexing wages and salaries, adjusting pricing policies, and altering investment decisions, and allow, instead, concentration on generating real, sustained long-run economic growth.

Business taxation should be phased out and individual taxation policies and systems be changed to ensure certainty and neutrality. Regulations must be reduced further, by substantial amounts. If inflation is kept under control and interest rates fall, these measures will help encourage capital formation and retention, research, development, and innovation, with the result, again, of forming a solid foundation for sustained, long-run growth in the economy.

Small Business in Particular

Small businesses can be proud of their historical tradition of accomplishment. They have satisfied a broad range of the country's needs, in spite of having to cope with an increasingly complex, uncertain environment and the conflicting demands such an environment creates.

More accurately, the *owners and managers* of small businesses have accomplished these things—people get things done, not businesses, and these people tend to be strong, very independent free-enterprisers, able to take advantage of new developments and opportunities quickly. Most owners and managers of small businesses are self-made individuals—competitive, hard-working, highly motivated, and strongly individualistic. As such, they tend to conform to the requirements and dictates of a free market economy.

However, as the result of factors generally not of their own making, incentives in society have caused them, as well as others, to perceive that their best interests are served when they act as a special-interest group and exert pressure for special privileges and considerations—often, we feel, as a basis for self-preservation or because they have come to feel that this is the only way they are going to get a "fair shake" in the existing system. Although we can understand why such feelings have come into existence, in our opinion, the only way out of the morass is to join forces with others who will support the free market economy and use resources to eliminate the influence of certain special-interest groups that do not, to eliminate unnecessary government regulations and to reduce in complexity those that are necessary, to work in their local communities (through high schools, colleges, local organizations) to promote and strengthen the free market economy, and to live, eat, and sleep the philosophy of free enterprise.

> It seems clear that our nation needs more entrepreneurial motivation and spirit. Risk aversion—exacerbated in my view by too much short-sighted MBA training—swept our country years before the recession. Too many managements and investors seemingly won't make a move now unless they can see a documented high quick return with no apparent risk. Hurdle rates seem to be getting higher and remain fixed no matter what economic or political environment prevails.
>
> Admittedly, times are uncertain and will remain so. Almost anything we do involves risk. But all of us should face the question squarely—what will be the cumulative consequences of deepening risk aversion for ourselves as well as the nation? We have an old lesson to relearn from the venture capitalists—nothing ventured, nothing gained.[34]

An Overview of the Monograph to This Point

The following excerpts from Ralph Kinney Bennett summarize much of what we have been discussing up to now:

> . . .the entrepreneur, that dreamer and doer who risks everything, including those most valuable capital resources—brains, work and time—to make things happen in an economy . . . these risktakers, have done more to provide jobs and raise living standards than all the poverty workers and social engineers who ever lived. . . .

Entrepreneurs are the dynamic ingredient that makes a free economy outperform a socialist economy even in the worst of times. . . .Socialism and capitalism are not converging at all in their ability to provide food and shelter and higher living standards for their people. The differences between the two sides come not from natural resources or industrial plant but from ideas and attitudes. . . .

The most serious fraud is committed not by the members of the welfare culture but by the creators of it, who conceal from the poor, both adults and children, the most fundamental realities of their lives: that to live well and escape poverty, they will have to keep their families together at all costs and will have to work harder than the classes above them. . . capitalism has no room for "preferences"—racial, religious, ethnic or otherwise. It prefers, and rewards, work and ideas. . . .

The poor choose leisure not because of moral weakness but because they are paid to do so. And just as our income-redistribution policies keep the poor in subtle slavery, so do regulatory and tax policies destroy the tremendous potential—in jobs, wealth, entrepreneurial opportunity—of unfettered capitalism. As it is now, the poor have little incentive to work, and the rich have little incentive to risk their money in investments that could revitalize the economy.

Thus, we have taxed, regulated and constricted ourselves into a situation where—for both rich and poor—risk is neither encouraged nor rewarded. And yet the secret of economic growth lies in the seemingly "irrational" world of risks. A society ruled by risk and freedom rather than by rational calculus, a society open to the future rather than planning it, can call forth an endless stream of invention, enterprise and art.

. . .the attempt of the welfare state to deny, suppress and plan away the dangers and uncertainties of our lives—to domesticate the inevitable unknown—violates not only the spirit of capitalism but the nature of man.

That nature—that impulse to risk everything—has produced new jobs, new ideas, new wealth in incalculable abundance, proving again and again. . .that the greatest poverty program of all is a free economy.[35]

Notes

[1]Thomas L. Holton, "Agribusiness Cited as Biggest, Most Productive Industry in the United States," *Executive Newsletter*, Vol. 8, No. 1 (January 11, 1982), p.1.

[2]Seidman & Seidman, " 'Small Business' and the American Economy," *Clients Estate Planning Quarterly*, No. 3 (July 1982), p. 1.

[3]Deloitte Haskins & Sells, *The Week in Review* (October 8, 1982), pp. 4–5.

[4]*Ibid.*, p. 3.

[5]Malcolm Hopkins, "A Plea to Prop Up Basic Industries," *Business Week* (October 25, 1982), p. 28.

[6]F. Thomas Juster, "The Interest Rate Puzzle: Some Clues," *Economic Outlook USA,* Vol. 9, No. 3 (Summer 1982), p. 59.

[7]*Ibid.*, p. 60.

[8]Hopkins, p. 30.

[9]Deloitte Haskins & Sells, *The Week in Review* (June 25, 1982), p. 3.

[10]Coopers & Lybrand, "Regulatory Relief, Not Yet Reform," *Executive Alert Newsletter* (October 1982), p. 2.

[11]Gerald R. Rosen, Interview with Lester Thurow, "Abolish the Antitrust Laws," *Dun's Review* (February 1981), p. 72.

[12]*Ibid.*

[13]*Discussion and Comments on the Major Issues Facing Small Business*, A Report of the Select Committee on Small Business, U.S. Senate, to the Delegates of the White House Conference on Small Business, 96th Congress, 1st Session, December 4, 1979 (Washington, D.C.: U.S. Government Printing Office, 1979), p. 58.

[14]Egils Milbergs, "Government Role Is to Butt Out, Official Says," *The Ann Arbor News*, September 21, 1982, p. B5.

[15]For a more complete discussion of these points, see Marilyn Wilson, "Flat Tax Fever," *Dun's Business Month,* Vol. 120, No. 5 (November 1982), pp. 34–35; John R. Raedel and Leonard A. Lipson, "Is America Ready for a Flat Tax?," *World*, No. 3 (1982), pp. 40–41; and Lawrence C. Phillips and Gary John Previts, "Tax Reform—What Are the Issues?" *Journal of Accountancy,* Vol. 155, No. 5 (May 1983), pp. 64–74.

[16]For a full discussion, see Statement of William D. Barth (partner, Arthur Andersen & Co.) at the Hearing before the Select Committee on Small Business, U.S. Senate, Ninety-Fifth Congress, Second Session on Capital Formation, New York, May 15, 1978, in *Capital Formation*, Part 2 (Washington, D.C.: U.S. Government Printing Office, 1978), p. 459.

[17]*Tax Policy, Investment and Economic Growth*, A Comparative Analysis of the Economic Effects of Alternative Tax Proposals Affecting Income, Prepared by Securities Industry Association based on Econometric Studies by Data Resources, Inc., March 1977, pp. 367–381.

[18]Statement of Wallace O. Sellers (vice president of corporate and public affairs, Merrill Lynch & Co.) at the Hearing before the Select Committee on Small Business, U.S. Senate, Ninety-Fifth Congress, Second Session on Capital Formation, May 15, 1978, in *Capital Formation*, Part 2 (Washington, D.C.: U.S. Government Printing Office, 1978), p. 486.

[19]Kathy Williams, "SBA Supports Family Ownership," *Management Accounting* (September 1981), p. 22.

[20]Seidman & Seidman, p. 5.

[21]Deloitte, Haskins & Sells, *The Week in Review* (December 17, 1982), p. 7.

[22]Marsha Taylor, quoting Paul Huard of the National Association of Manufacturers, in "Some Small Businessmen Find Reagon Myopic," *The Ann Arbor News*, August 12, 1981, p. D2.

[23]Thomas J. Murray, "Venture Capital: The Game Gets Riskier," *Dun's Business Month* (April 1982), p. 69.

[24]Thomas J. Murray, "Venturesome Pension Funds," *Dun's Business Month* (January 1983), p. 64.

[25]*Ibid.*, p. 66.

[26]Kathy Williams, "1983—A Good Year for Entrepreneurs?" *Management Accounting,* Vol. 44, No. 7 (January 1983), p. 18.

[27]Milbergs, p. B5.

[28]Thomas L. Amberg and Michael R. Montgomery, "SBA Proving Itself More a Hindrance than a Help," *The Ann Arbor News,* October 4, 1981, p. G4.

[29]*Ibid.*

[30]Campbell R. McConnell, "Why is U.S. Productivity Slowing Down?" *Harvard Business Review,* Vol. 57, No. 2 (March–April 1979), p. 42.

[31]Jac Fitz-Enz, "What Causes People to Be Productive?" A Report of a Study of the Nature and Source of Human Productivity, presented at the Productivity—The American Way Conference, Chicago, Ill., June 1982.

[32]R. Emmett Tyrrell, Jr., "We Have OPEC over a Barrel," *The Ann Arbor News,* July 23, 1981, p. D6.

[33]*Discussion and Comments on the Major Issues Facing Small Business,* p. 18.

[34]Walter E. Hoadley, "The Spirit of Entrepreneurial Capitalism Is Very Much Alive, Despite Recession," *Dun's Business Month* (December 1982), p. 43.

[35]Ralph Kinney Bennett, discussing George Gilder's book, *Wealth and Poverty,* "The Greatest Poverty Program of All," *Reader's Digest,* Vol. 119, No. 713 (September 1981), pp. 137–141.

Chapter 7

Some Thoughts About the Future

What is already passed is not more fixed than the certainty that what is future will grow out of what has already passed, or is now passing.
G.B. Cheever

The best preparation for the future, is the present well seen to, and the last duty done.
G. MacDonald

General Overview

When the economy is stable, predictions of the future are easy and fairly reliable. When the economy is unstable, predictions of the future are difficult and often miss the mark by wide margins. We have seen this often during the past few years. Both the timing and degree of changes predicted—predictions regarding interest rates, inflation, consumer confidence, recovery, the stock market, and many more facets of our economy—have often turned out to be wide of the mark. We should not be too hard on those making such predictions. In complex societies, particularly under volatile or depressed economic conditions, accurate predictions are nearly impossible. And this serves to support a basic theme running throughout this monograph: a free market economy is critical to recovery and sustained growth. If it is impossible, or nearly so, for one person or small group of people to predict with reasonable accuracy what is likely to happen, how could it ever be possible to establish production and distribution schedules for a complex society that have any hope of providing for a strong, sustained period of growth? Such decisions must be left in the hands of individuals, acting in their own best economic interest, in order to ensure the flexibility necessary for adjustment.

Throughout Chapter 6 we discussed the causes for the serious productivity problem we face and made recommendations we feel are necessary to solve the problem. In this chapter we discuss what is likely to happen if those recommendations are not followed, and we also give our impressions on the likelihood that those recommendations will be followed.

Table 7–1.
Annual Rates of Change in Leading Economic Indexes[1]

	Latest, %	Three Months Ago, %	Six Months Ago, %
United States	11	7	−2
Canada	8	3	−4
Japan	0	−1	2
United Kingdom	6	4	2
West Germany	6	4	2
France	10	2	1
Italy	2	1	1

Annual rate based on ratio of current month's index to average index over the preceding 12 months. Among the indicators included for each country, whenever available, are new orders, construction contracts, corporate profits, stock prices, and changes in consumer debt.

Interest rates fell dramatically between mid-1982 and mid-1984 (the prime rate in May 1984, was 12 1/2%). The inflation rate is presently running at between 3 and 4% per year. Consumer income is up, production is up, auto sales are strong, and the leading indexes point to world economic recovery. (See Table 7-1). If we are not careful, these developments might lead us to believe that the basic causes of our difficulties have been overcome and that we are on the verge of sustained economic growth. In our opinion, this is not true.

Certainly, we are pleased to see inflation and interest rates fall. The important question, however, is whether they are falling because the basic problems in the economy have been solved or because of other factors, not basic, that could reverse the rather dramatic beginning of economic recovery during 1983 and the first half of 1984. We believe the latter to be the case. Although a number of good, initial steps have been taken, they are not enough to allow us to claim victory at this time. Concerted, sustained effort over a period of time, demanding a great deal of patience of us all, will be required.

Although, as stated, we have made a beginning, overall the problems that caused substantial and sustained decreases in productivity are still largely with us. Let's consider the specific issues first, keeping in mind that our comments are in the nature of generalizations; certainly there are specific exceptions to all of them.

Labor

To date, little has been accomplished in the way of increasing productivity in any real sense. Some concessions have been made and the possibility of job losses undoubtedly has encouraged the labor force to work harder, but these are relatively insignificant accomplishments compared with what is needed. And there is every indication that as soon as businesses start making any profits at all, laborers and their representatives are going to push for recovery of most or all of the concessions they have made. At present, for example, Chrysler workers in the United States and Canada are demanding reinstatement of what they gave up two years ago to help Chrysler survive. They are also demanding parity with workers at Ford and General Motors, regardless of productivity considerations. In certain industries, plants are still closing down and workers are being laid off. A number of major steps must be taken.

Minimum Wage Law

The minimum wage law needs to be eliminated. We recognize that this cannot be done overnight, but the law could, and should, be phased out gradually over some period of time—say five years. In a perfectly competitive market for labor, there is no minimum wage. Supply and demand factors, as we have previously discussed them, would establish the price for labor. We are not suggesting that the market for labor in a complex society such as ours is, or can be, perfectly competitive; we are suggesting that we should strive continuously to come as close to that ideal as possible.

Whatever the historical rationale for a minimum wage, it has created a number of problems. The total number of jobs is reduced. Jobs that are worth doing at, say, $2.00 per hour are forgone if they cost more than that. This is one reason for high unemployment among teenagers. Furthermore, a minimum wage tends to push other wages—and, consequently, the average labor cost—higher than they would be without it. This is one reason the United States is not competitive in many of the world markets. Finally, the minimum wage has added to cost-push inflation in the United States.

Although it is perhaps a somewhat extreme example, what has happened in the commonwealth of Puerto Rico reflects the effects a minimum wage can have. Until a few years ago, Puerto Rico had thriving tobacco and sugar cane industries. Today the tobacco industry is nearly nonexistent and the sugar cane industry is faltering significantly. Although much of the land is fertile, it is estimated that some 75% of the arable land is either underutilized or not utilized at all. Unemployment is at a high level, and a large percentage of the people in Puerto Rico live on welfare in the form of food stamps provided by the United States. Poverty is widespread. Many young people do not know what it means to work because they have never had jobs.

The major reason for this dramatic turnaround is the minimum wage law the United States put into effect in Puerto Rico a number of years ago. Tobacco and sugar cane growers can no longer compete with growers in other countries in the Caribbean and Central America, with the devastating results indicated above.

Conclusion: We do not believe that the minimum wage law will be eliminated; we do not even foresee that the minimum wage will be lowered.

High Average Cost of Labor

There is little doubt in our minds that the cost of labor in the United States, on average, is higher than the productivity of labor would demand in a free labor market. Most of the productivity gains of the 1950's and 1960's were due to innovation and rapid technological advances—not, generally, to employees working harder and longer hours. During this period, in fact, work slowdown rules, featherbedding, and paid holidays were expanded, the "30 years and out" rules came into existence in a number of industries, and fringe benefits expanded explosively, all contributing to a decline in worker productivity. The idea was created and accepted that a worker's real income ought to increase continuously, even when he stayed in a particular job, performing the same tasks, year after year.

As indicated earlier, these policies were established, supported, and brought into being mainly by labor unions although, admittedly, many others were happy to jump on the bandwagon. Their direct effects on industries such as the automotive and steel industries have been severe, but the indirect effects may have been even more substantial. When the economy was operating at near capacity and unemployment was fairly low, for example, nonunionized firms had to match the wages and benefits of unionized workers in order to compete for labor. Furthermore, the wages and benefits of many white-collar workers were tied to agreements that had been established in union contracts.

Not only do such things push average labor costs higher over extended periods of time than they would go in a free market economy but, perhaps more importantly, the results cannot be reversed easily when the economy becomes depressed. Once "won," they become "rights" not easily reversed or removed and have the effects of fueling cost-push inflation, pushing the economy deeper into recession, and causing unemployment to rise. Little has been done to date about any of these problems, and adjustments must be made if we are to achieve sustained growth without reverting to high inflation. At worst, labor costs per unit of output must stabilize; at best they must decrease if we are to have a stable price level. Also important in this connection are technological advances, which we will discuss later.

If the unnatural barriers to which we have alluded were removed, the labor returns of many businesses in the small-business sector essentially would be determined in a free market setting. Many businesses are small enough and competition is such that wages could and would be set by market conditions. And keep in mind that small businesses are a significant portion of the total business community, as we have stated.

For many large firms in certain industries, such as the steel, automotive, and construction industries, the return to labor is not determined in a free market setting. But we believe that laborers, as well as customers and owners, will be better off over the long run if wages and salaries are set as nearly as possible in terms of what a free market economy would dictate. At the minimum, those attitudes and approaches antithetical to a free market economy should be removed.

First, the attitude must be dropped that a worker performing the same task year after year automatically is entitled to yearly raises. Many tasks are such that a worker does not become more efficient and his productivity does not increase as time passes. Holding other things constant, whatever that task is worth, that amount should be fixed; at worst it should vary only within narrow bracket limits, unless supply and demand factors in the market clearly dictate otherwise. This is one significant reason for productivity declines, and is also one reason some businesses are "buying out" older employees making a high wage and replacing them with younger workers at a much lower wage who can perform the same tasks just as efficiently—perhaps even more efficiently. In one sense, businesses are correcting past errors by this procedure.

Also, the attitude that workers deserve annual raises at least equal to the inflation rate must be dropped. Cost-of-living allowances should not be included in future contracts. Such attitudes and procedures perpetuate inflation and remove the automatic adjustment inflation helps bring about. And people whose wages are adjusted for inflation get a larger slice of the gross national product than those whose wages are not so adjusted. Because such shares are not determined by the free market, one group is being subsidized at the expense of other groups. Adjusting for inflation amounts to a transfer of funds from those not receiving the automatic adjustments to those who are.

Certainly management must share the responsibility. In many industries, notably the steel and automotive industries, management has negotiated labor settlements apparently with the attitude that the demand for its product was inelastic; that labor costs, regardless of how high, could be passed along to the consumer. It submitted to work rule demands that reduced quality, and otherwise took very short-term positions that, ultimately, threatened the long-run viability of its firms and industry. Now, suddenly, it has awakened to the fact that wage rates in the United States are significantly higher than those in Japan and something must be done. We agree that something must be done. Our question is, why weren't these things observed and actions taken to solve the problems sooner? The answer, unfortunately, is obvious.

With the heavy publicity given to union contract settlements, they become the standard for other settlements, both union and nonunion, for white-collar and blue-collar workers. Many firms have anywhere from 15 to 30 paid holidays per year, in addition to the regular vacation period, for example. This policy costs consumers billions of dollars per year in lost productivity. In metropolitan areas such as New York City, as another example, the normal work week is 35 hours for many in business and professional firms (a five-hour allowance for commuting), which has a significant impact on productivity.

If these things were the result of a free market for labor, fine. But they aren't. In fact, they are the result of forces thwarting the dictates of such a market because the judgment of a few individuals is being substituted for the market and many others simply "go along" or, as we said, climb on the bandwagon.

Conclusion: We do not feel that our suggestions will be adopted in the intermediate future, if at all. In fact, we see management and labor returning to the same old "business as usual."

Social Security

This is a difficult problem, of course, but a few things are clear, although politicians are having trouble facing up to them. First and foremost, the conclusion of many politicians that the bill signed by the president in April 1983 on social security will keep the system solvent well into the twenty-first century is not likely to be valid. That bill was designed to rescue social security by implementing recommendations of the National Commission on Social Security Reform. Without going into a lot of unnecessary detail, we will mention that the bill imposes higher payroll taxes, broadens and maintains the base of the tax by bringing in new workers and employees, and curbs some benefits. More specifically, it provides for an increase in the levy on the self-employed, mandatory coverage for federal government workers hired after 1983, taxing half of the social security benefits of those above a certain level of retirement income, and a six-month delay in the July 1983 cost-of-living increase; and it requires some workers who had withdrawn from the system to be brought back in (for example, employees of certain nonprofit entities, such as hospitals).

Certainly these actions made the social security system more liquid for the short run, but we doubt that they are enough to provide for long-term solvency. Consider the following background data on social security.

Since its birth in 1935, social security has grown in quantum leaps. For example:

● In the late thirties, the most anyone paid into social security was $30 a year. Today the maximum tax for each worker is $2,392.
● In 1940, 16 workers paid social security taxes for each beneficiary; in 1960, the ratio was 5:1; today, it is 3:1; and by 2025, it will probably be 2:1
● In 1950, social security spending represented 1% of the whole federal budget. Today it represents 26%.
● Between 1935 and 1981, social security outgo totaled roughly $1 trillion. The same amount will be spent from the social security trust funds in the next four years (1983–1986).

By far the biggest government social program in world history, the social security system now spends each year more than the combined net investment in plant, equipment, research and development of all the private companies in the United States.

Last year one out of seven Americans received a social security check, and the total bill came to $200 billion.[2]

Probably for the intermediate run, and certainly for the long run, the changes that have been made are cosmetic at best. Social security taxes, already a heavy burden, higher even than federal income taxes on many families, are slated to increase from the present 6.7% on the first $35,700 of wages (matched by employers) to 7.65% in 1990. This will increase the cost of labor even more, and make the United States even less competitive in the world markets. The result could be a substantial loss of jobs.

> From 1949 to 1981, average wages in this country increased 470 percent. Maximum Social Security taxes went up 6,480 percent through 1981; and if you add in 1982, they will have increased more than 7,000 percent.[3]

We feel, first, that the social security system is still in grave danger for the long run, and something must be done. Second, one major reason for the difficulty is the practice of indexing the payments to recipients. Third, payroll taxes for social security are as high or higher than they ought to be. As stated, the social security taxes of many, perhaps most, wage earners in the United States are now higher than their federal income taxes. Moreover, these amounts must be matched by employers, which depletes the funds that could be used for other purposes and increases the average cost of labor.

We feel that to reach an ideal state, the following actions must be taken. (We recognize that these suggestions could not be implemented overnight but would have to be phased in gradually. We present them as objectives; and even if they are never fully implemented, working toward them is likely to benefit us all and ensure the preservation of the system, it if is to be preserved in its present form.)

First, indexing must be discontinued for the same reasons that COLA must be dropped from labor contracts, and wages must not otherwise be adjusted upward simply to offset inflation. Second, initial benefits should be lowered. Third, social security taxes per individual should not be allowed to rise above present levels; or if they are increased temporarily to bolster the liquidity position of the system, they should be rolled back to present levels or below as soon as possible. Worker incentive is being damaged by the high marginal tax rates for total taxes paid, a major portion of which is social security taxes. Third, high taxes on employers contribute to unemployment, both directly by causing employers to discontinue jobs not worth doing at the higher costs, and indirectly by removing capital from businesses that could be used for innovation and capital expansion to create new jobs.

Fourth, the retirement age should be increased to 70 by the year 2000. As the number of elderly persons receiving social security benefits increases relative to the number currently working who must support such payments, these current workers bear a burden and responsibility far in excess of that borne by those now retired; they supported a much smaller proportion of elderly on social security while they were working. This is particularly onerous if one accepts the philosophy that, basically, it is each person's responsibility to provide for his or her retirement. As previous discussions have indicated, this is not the case under the social security system. To say that everyone who pays social security taxes has earned *some* retirement benefits is a truism. To say that everyone who receives social security payments has earned the *total* amount received (as some politicians have said for reelection purposes) is not only misleading, it is erroneous. Many receive less than they have earned while others receive a great deal more than they have earned.

Consider a 65-year-old man who retired on January 1, 1982, who paid Social Security taxes during his entire working career, and who was an average wage earner. He contributed a total of $7,209 in payroll taxes. Using pessimistic estimates of longevity and inflation, he and/ or his nonworking spouse will receive (during the 25 years at least one of them can be expected to live) some *$520,000*, or *72 times* what he contributed (30 times the value of his contributions plus interest).[4]

Finally, Medicare, the fastest growing part of social security, needs to be completely overhauled, now. Until recently, the Medicare system was highly liquid; social security borrowed money from the Medicare trust fund, in fact, in order to pay recipients. However, things no longer appear so rosy.

The problem is obvious. In the last 16 years, the cost to the federal government of providing hospital care to our senior citizens has increased more than tenfold, from $3 billion to $38.5 billion. Some 29 million elderly or disabled U.S. citizens, rich as well as poor, use a system under which they pay $304 for the first day in the hospital. For the next 59 days, Uncle Sam pays all.

In the social pressures generated by the pain of sickness and the economic pressures generated by the cost of treatment, Congress has consistently come down on the side of the patient and let the cost go. It was both humane and politically rewarding. Now the Medicare trust fund, from which the Social Security system was borrowing only last year, is itself facing bankruptcy.[5]

Medicare, the nation's second biggest social program, is running dry.

It will go broke by 1990, experts say, and by 1995 will roll up a $300 billion deficit. The troubles facing Medicare dwarf the recently resolved financial crisis of its bigger sister, Social Security's old-age fund.

To assure Medicare's solvency would take the equivalent of a 50 percent payroll tax hike or a 33 percent benefit cut over the next 25 years, according to the program's trustees.[6]

This is another good example of what happens when people do not deal directly with the market, subjecting themselves to the immediate discipline of the market, but, instead, are "represented" in the market by intermediaries. Doctors order unnecessary tests to reduce the possibility of being sued. Congressmen spend on the basis of hopes and desires, not reality. Hospitals improve capacity utilization by keeping patients longer than necessary. New technologies and treatments expand more rapidly than economic conditions warrant. And the government pays for it all; more accurately, we all pay for it through taxes levied on us.

If our recommendations were accepted, it would mean that social security payments would have to be adjusted *upward and downward* for increases and decreases in total wages and salaries subject to social security taxes as measured by jobs created or lost as the economy expanded or contracted. This solution might not be very palatable to some, but it is necessary if the system is to remain on the current pay-as-you-go basis.

Some would argue that payments need to be stable over reasonable periods of time, while the preceding recommendation would result in variable payments. If constant payments are desired, they must be established at a level that will create enough surpluses in good times to counter deficits in bad times. History indicates that this is difficult for politicians to do. When surpluses appear, many of them argue for immediate expansion of benefits, using up the surplus and creating the basis for difficulties when the economy softens—which history teaches us must surely happen from time to time.

A better solution, to us, is to phase out the social security system as it is presently constituted. It was a bad idea to begin with, as it eliminated or at least reduced individual responsibility, and has survived during the past four decades only because it was never put to the test until the past few years. During most of the last 40 years (except for the last five to ten years) the economy has been expanding, the work force has increased substantially, and the number of retired people has been relatively small compared with the number of people gainfully employed.

The system was bound to work; everything was favorable for its survival. The real test is whether it works, or at least survives, under adverse conditions. As retired people increased in numbers, as new job creation diminished, and as unemployment increased, the system developed serious problems. If, during years when the economy is relatively strong, a system cannot build up enough reserves to survive a few years of adverse conditions and proportional increases in the number of retired people, it seems to us that the system is poorly conceived or administered. Both are true of the social security system, though we feel that the basic problem lies with the system itself, and we conclude that it should be phased out.

Experts would have to determine the particulars, but our general recommendations follow. Ideally, each individual should again become primarily responsible for his or her own retirement. To make this effective, it needs to be made clear that the government will not bail out those who do not provide for their retirement (save for exceptional circumstances). It would be the responsibilities of their families to care for such people.

Recognizing that attitudes change slowly and that people have been conditioned to rely on social security for part or all of their retirement benefits, we offer the following as an acceptable alternative. Over, say, 15 to 20 years the pay-as-you-go system should be phased out and replaced by a retirement plan similar to those in the private sector. (This assumes that indexing is phased out reasonably quickly.) The government could still be the collection agent, the conduit, between the worker and financial insitutions. The money collected from each individual would be deposited to his account in a bank or other appropriate financial institution. These deposits, plus the interest accumulated, would be available at retirement age. Most retireees would be better off under such a system.

In addition, during periods when deposits exceed withdrawals, these funds would be available to loan to the business sector. It might be necessary during the period of changeover to use federal income taxes to help fund the present pay-as-you-go system, but this would be a small price to pay, *provided* the system is changed as indicated. (At the present time social security is partially financed out of the general fund, anyway, because the employer's share is a deductible business expense.) With the high marginal tax rates that presently exist, we feel it is not acceptable to use federal income taxes to finance a continuation of the present system.

Conclusions: Thus, in our opinion, not enough has been done, and we don't visualize any substantial steps being taken toward the ideal state we have described. Politicians are afraid that such changes would cause them to be defeated, so they are likely to continue to make only whatever cosmetic changes are necessary to keep the system at a survival level, at least until the situation deteriorates to the point where there is no choice. By then, it may well be too late.

> A few members of Congress are sticking their necks out over an issue that their most influential colleagues say is political suicide: cutting the annual inflation increases in Social Security and other federal benefit programs.
>
> The proposal is taking several forms, but most versions would trim the annual cost-of-living increases, now pegged to the Consumer Price Index, to the amount of increase in the CPI minus 2 or 3 percent.
>
> Rep. Barber Conable, R-N.Y., ranking minority member of the House Ways and Means Committee . . . [called] the effort "a waste of time and a phony promotion".
>
> "We are not going to revisit Social Security," Conable says. "If these people think that in the middle of a presidential campaign we're going to cut Social Security, then they aren't living in a real political world."[7]

To us, this is a typical political "copout." If the electorate were told the truth, consistently and persistently, we feel, they would accept some, perhaps most, of the major recommendations we have made. However, that would require a substantial increase in the responsibleness and intellectual integrity of many politicians, and at least in the short run, we cannot visualize that coming about.

This position is also shortsighted, even politically, because it ignores the impact of high social security taxes on the attitudes of young workers in the United States.

> Put bluntly, the old have come to insist that the young not only hold them harmless for their past profligacy, but sacrifice their own prosperity to pay for it.
>
> If there ever was a generation that had reason to take to the streets, it is mine. So far the young have eschewed the streets as well as the voting booths and the halls of Congress. As the government's generosity becomes further limited, the elderly promise to become more militant in advancing their claims of generational privilege. Unless

the young join in this grubby competition for equity, they will find their birthright mortgaged even more.[8]

Whether or not one agrees that younger workers are being treated "unfairly" is not the only problem, and perhaps not the essential one. Younger workers' perception of the system as unfair is creating yet another special-interest group, which is likely to result in increased divisiveness and confrontation, as we have described.

Research, Development, Innovation, and Capital Formation

From a position of preeminence in technological advances from World War II through the early to mid-1960's, the United States has fallen dramatically in terms of research, innovation, and capital formation as compared with many other nations, such as Japan and West Germany. This has been particularly true in basic industries, such as steel. As we have indicated, an important reason for this is the short-term attitude most of us have taken—management, labor, government, and society in general—to maximize wages and salaries, short-term profits, and government expenditures, and to finance these excesses through increases in the money supply, all contributing to inflation and high interest rates.

Theoretically, individual firms, industries, and even countries produce according to their relative comparative advantages, one important aspect of which is substituting labor for capital or capital for labor, depending on the relative cost of each. Over the long run, however, if productivity is to increase at reasonable levels, technological advances must be the foundation for such increases, and capital must be substituted for labor in every industry, whether one is considering restaurants, hotels, steel, or automobiles. As previously discussed, at least for the foreseeable future, such substitutions would be likely to increase rather than decrease total demand for labor, although the demographics of the labor force would certainly change. This is one area in which we feel federal government activity is justified; that is, to retrain workers to perform the tasks such changes will require. Colleges, universities, and high schools should also take an active role in preparing people for such changes.

Many businesses throughout the world are operating at substantially less than full capacity. As of late 1982, for example, the steel industry in the United States was operating at about 35% of capacity.

Conclusions: As the economy recovers in the United States and throughout the world, it will take a considerable period of time for the operations of specific firms and industries to approach full capacity. During this period, such firms are not likely to make mass expenditures for technological advances. (They should, we feel, but they are not likely to do so.) And, as indicated, as firms pass the break-even point, workers are likely not only to demand reinstatement of any wage and benefit packages they might have had before concessions, but also to negotiate for wage increases beyond those levels. This will decrease the ability of the firms to generate enough funds from operations to renovate and modernize plant and equipment. Furthermore, the recession has placed many firms in an illiquid position, and their debt-to-equity ratios have increased significantly. Under such conditions, and even though interest rates did fall, borrowing funds is not feasible until the financial position and operating activities of the firms are strengthened. (In fact, interest rates were on the rise again—by early August 1983.)

Finally, a poll of presidents of small businesses taken in 1981 indicated that 83% felt there would be substantial improvement in the economy during 1982 (which didn't happen, of course). In 1982, only 63% of the presidents of small businesses felt the economy would improve substantially in 1983. (For the first half of 1983, that anticipation was correct.) The owners and managers, in a word, have become even more pessimistic about the future, and consequently are not likely to expand or modernize facilities until this attitude reverses. This, in turn, probably won't happen until there is a sustained increase in demand that appears likely to continue into the foreseeable future. For many firms and industries, such a condition is certainly not evident at present, although autos and home construction have strengthened significantly. In the same poll, the presidents of small businesses also showed a concern about heavy government expenditures and a belief that unless these are reduced further by substantial amounts, interest rates and inflation may again start an upward spiral as the economy recovers.

Certainly some firms, such as automotive companies, have reduced both their costs and their break-even point and have generated significant profits, as we have said.

> The winds of change blowing through the industry are evident in everything from a streamlining of the white-collar work force—the automakers have laid off more than 50,000 salaried employees, most of them permanently—to major improvements in the production pro-

cess: technological advances, dramatic reductions in inventories, an increased commonality of car parts, more efficient purchasing methods, and more.[9]

Lynn Adkins also points out that the break-even point for the industry as a whole dropped from 12.2 million cars in 1979 to 8.9 million cars by late 1982 and that firms are reducing the stifling bureaucracies they had built up, have improved technology substantially, have reduced inventories significantly, are sourcing more work outside, and are developing more cooperative relationships with their suppliers.[10]

Inflation, Interest Rates, and Government Expenditures

Again, some progress has been made, but the basic question is whether such progress reflects significant changes in the basic disequilibriums in the economy that gave rise to the problems in the first place. We think not.

Inflation has dropped significantly, as previously indicated. As we interpret the situation, however, this is not due primarily to significant increases in productivity in most sectors of the economy, one basic prerequisite for keeping the inflation rate down. Inflation has dropped, first, because the worldwide recession has created a glut of oil, causing those prices to fall substantially and stabilize. Second, decreased demand for many products and services has caused producers and sellers to stabilize or reduce their prices to levels that will often not be sustainable over the long run if businesses are to make enough profits to remain viable (unless it is possible to reduce costs commensurately). The decreased demand is due partially to high unemployment and a lack of consumer confidence. Prices have not dropped because increased supplies at lower costs have pushed them downward (increased productivity), except in the case of certain farm products such as wheat and corn.

An important consideration for consumers making consumption expenditures is the relationship of the price of the product or service to their disposable income. The cost of the product or service is the cash price plus the financing cost. Another major reason for the decrease in demand for certain products and services, therefore, is that these costs have become too high. We have tended to blame the decreased demand primarily on high interest rates, but the dramatic increase in the basic price of many items, such as housing, automobiles, and home appliances, has been an important factor also. Consequently, sustained increases in demand will depend not only on lower interest rates, but also on increases in real disposable incomes of consumers and/or stable or decreasing prices for products and services (or at least a faster increase in real disposable income than in prices).

Conclusion: Both decreasing prices and a rise in disposable income depend primarily on sustained productivity increases, which we do not see on the horizon for the reasons given.

> Declines in consumer loan rates will release pent-up demand, but the increase in consumer sales will be constrained by cautious spending plans dictated by concerns with unemployment.

> And Americans won't be buying more goods without a renewed growth in household income as well as sustained declines in consumer loan rates.[11]

And there are other problems that cause some to question whether consumers will bring us out of the recession.

> During this recessionary period, consumers have been forced to change their consumption habits. They have found different things to enjoy. Instead of buying large homes and automobiles, they have used their money for vacations, smaller homes with less furniture and smaller maintenance and upkeep expenditures, reducing debt, and increasing savings. Some feel we may have seen the end to demand (consumption) as a driving force in the economy.[12]

Certainly the tight money policies of the Federal Reserve and the decrease in the rate of increase of government expenditures have helped bring inflation under control. And the recent loosening of the tight money policies is one reason for the drop in interest rates.

> While the consumer price index is now rising at an annual rate below 4 percent, long-term interest rates remain well above that inflation rate, indicating lenders are demanding a high premium to protect their money from the risk of reignited inflation. The interest rate on 30-year Treasury bonds is about 12.5 percent. Lenders are worried about the impact on inflation and interest rates of record federal deficits, and concern that deficits will remain at historically high levels for years to come. Also there has been a surge in the basic money supply— cash in circulation and deposits in checking-type accounts at banking

institutions which grew at an annual rate of 12.8 percent between Dec. 1982 and March 1983, which could contribute to high inflation in late 1984 and early 1985—often there is a two year lag between a swing in growth or decline in money supply and a change in inflation.[13]

But much more needs to be done.

Real government expenditures must be cut. If unemployment suddenly dropped to 6%, the federal budget deficit would be reduced by some $160 billion to $170 billion, as a result of increased tax revenues and reduced unemployment and welfare payments, still leaving a sizable $40 billion to $50 billion deficit for the next fiscal year. Because of the already high marginal tax rates, the shortfall should be eliminated by additional spending cuts, not increased taxes. Whether these cuts are in defense, transfer payments, or some combination is largely a noneconomic decision, but the cuts must be made if inflation is to remain under control during the recovery period. Also, such reductions will relieve pressure in the financial markets, and help to reduce interest rates further—or, at least, to reduce the pressure for interest rates to start climbing upward again during the recovery.

Conclusion: Frankly, given the discussions presently under way in Washington, we doubt that the Senate and House members have the necessary intestinal fortitude to cut government expenditures enough.

A great deal of discussion is taking place regarding a temporary freeze on federal government spending. Although some cut in spending is probably better than none, a temporary freeze could be worse than nothing. First, it is a very short-term approach, which leads further to the idea of a quick fix. After a *temporary* freeze must come the thaw, resulting in the opposite attitude of what is needed. Second, the impact, if any, is likely to be minimal.

Less than 20% of federal spending can actually be frozen under present federal budgeting techniques. Even if Congress froze every conceivable controllable item, the saving would amount to about $16 billion, less than 2% of expected expenditure. And Congress is not likely to do that since it would require freezing the pay of all Federal government employees, cost of living increases for Social Security recipients, grants to states and cities, and a number of other relatively small areas. Most of the large areas of expenditures are relatively immune to freezes, such as interest rates, determined by the market, and interest on the national debt is running at about $100 billion a year, and rising.[14]

Finally, temporary freezes will not affect many other things. Permanent, long-range solutions, of the type previously discussed, must be sought.

Going back for a moment to the necessity for decreasing unemployment in order to balance the budget, we believe it would be an error to expect that unemployment will ever (at least for the foreseeable future) drop below 6 or 6 1/2%. The U.S. economy has been shifting fairly rapidly during the past 10 or 15 years from basic industries such as the steel and automotive industries to service and high-technology activities. We visualize further changes of this kind, requiring alterations in the demographics of the work force. In that workers cannot switch quickly from a particular firm or industry to another requiring entirely different types of knowledge and skills, the unemployment rate is not likely to drop below the 6% level. Also, because of the other considerations mentioned, the drop in unemployment is likely to be gradual, not dramatic and sudden. Consequently, the impact on the budget deficit will be gradual.

Conclusion: Even with substantial cuts in federal expenditures, a budget deficit will probably be with us for a number of years, with the adverse effects we have discussed. Again, we will need patience and perseverance because, as we have stated often in this monograph, when an economic system has been damaged severely over extended periods of time, it cannot be repaired overnight without returning to even larger government deficits, high inflation, and high interest rates. We believe that if the American people were told forthrightly what is necessary to right the situation, they would do what has to be done. Unfortunately, they have not been informed, so we are pessimistic that the hard decisions necessary to lay the foundation for a sustained economic recovery will be made.

Taxes

We made a number of recommendations in Chapters 5 and 6 regarding taxes.

Conclusions: We do not visualize that those recommendations will be followed in the near future, if ever. At present, certain special-interest groups are simply too strong to accept a phasing out of business taxes, elimination of estate taxes, or any drastic changes in the tax system such as establishment of a flat tax rate large enough to make up the shortfall.

We have contended that marginal tax rates (including indirect as well as direct taxes) are too high, with the adverse consequences we have described. President Reagan's tax plan simply amounts to a decrease in what otherwise would have been increases in the rates generated by inflation.

Conclusion: This is a start, but insufficient. Taxes, as measured in *real* dollars, must be reduced, and we don't see that happening in the near future.

In fact, politicians appear to be concerned more with semantics than with real issues. The recent $90 billion tax program is a case in point. Approximately 20%, or $18 billion, resulted from additional taxes on tobacco and alcohol. The other $72 billion will result from tightening reporting, enforcement, and collection procedures for taxes on such things as tips—in a word, collecting taxes that should have been paid all along but weren't because such income often went unreported.

A great debate ensued as to whether the entire $90 billion or only $18 billion was a tax increase—a redundant, meaningless debate that appealed to the emotions of the people and had nothing to do with the basic questions. An additional $90 billion per year will be taken out of the economy, so the average marginal tax rate will increase as a consequence. This is irrefutable, whether or not the $72 billion should have been paid in the past. The $72 billion may have been an "ill-gotten" gain to those who should have been paying it, and from the viewpoint of equity, collecting it can be supported. If equity considerations were the only issue, however, one could argue that the $72 billion should be countered by a $72 billion reduction in income (or other) taxes. This step would leave the money in the private sector while promoting greater equity in the system.

A tax on gasoline of 5 cents per gallon was levied, with the proceeds being used to repair the highway system, thereby, hopefully, creating jobs. Whatever the merits of this plan, billions of dollars in additional taxes will be taken from one segment of the economy and channeled into another.

Conclusion: The point is that taxes, even if they are not increased—and it appears more and more probable that they will be—certainly will not be reduced in real terms to any substantial degree in the foreseeable future.

It should be emphasized that all these factors—inflation, unemployment, high interest rates, and taxes—can work at cross-purposes in terms of their effects on productivity. Although declines in interest rates and inflation tend, generally, to release pent-up demand and to strengthen consumer expectations regarding buying and financial conditions, they can be counterbalanced by high unemployment and its depressing impact on consumer attitudes and outlooks. Also,

> ...if a restrictive monetary policy remains coupled with personal income tax rates indexed for inflation,...interest rates will force Americans to invest their money in "financial assets" rather than consumer investments such as houses and vehicles.[15]

Regulations

Conclusions: Again, some progress has been made; but considering the thousands of rules and regulations that affect business, the surface hardly has been broken. The rate of increase in new regulations appears to have decreased, but many existing regulations are unnecessary or, when necessary, are too long and complex. Years of concerted work will be necessary to bring regulations into reasonable balance.

Special-Interest Groups

Conclusions: We see no diminution in the activities of those special-interest groups promoting approaches antithetical to a free market economy; in fact, the recession appears to have increased their efforts. In the interest of promoting and strengthening the free market economy, we feel that reasonable government regulations are necessary to reduce the influence of such special-interest groups on national, state, and local politicians, but we believe the chances of this happening are remote—mainly because politicians themselves have become a special-interest group.

Workers and Supervisors

Conclusions: We see little or no abatement in the adversary relationship between managers and employees. If anything, the recession appears to have worsened the situation. Because of the long tradition of excesses on both sides, it is very questionable whether management and labor will ever be able to accept the fact that the best interests of both must be served simultaneously, or the best interests of neither will be served over the long run. The establishment of harmonious relationships will take a great deal of concerted effort over a long period of time.

A Wrap-Up

Although we started out by indicating that this chapter would essentially be a pro-forma—"what if"—type of presentation, rather than a prognosis or prediction of what will happen, the temptation to predict is irresistible. The answer to "what if" is clear. Unless we all work diligently together to change the attitudes and procedures that have brought us to this rather dismal state, the future will be bleak—we will slide into a much worse economic condition than the present one. On the prognosis side, we are pessimistic that the hard decisions required for rapid and sustained growth will be made.

In both cases, the overall reason is the same—poor, weak, and/or misinformed leadership at all levels. It is not due, in our judgment, to any serious flaws in the basic nature of man. We feel that given accurate, complete information and a system that supports their desire for liberty to pursue their own best interests within reasonable legal and moral boundaries, people in general will support whatever sacrifices are necessary to reverse the situation.

Those in leadership roles have generally provided incomplete and inaccurate data on which to base decisions. They have created a political, sociological, and economic climate (systems) that is largely antithetical to increased freedom for individuals, by providing incentives that exert excessive control over them and that appeal to their baser instincts rather than their higher values. Perhaps it all goes back to an essential question, debated for thousands of years, on which the various philosophical schools of thought are based: is man essentially good or is he essentially bad? We prefer to believe that he is basically good, while too many of the leaders of industry, labor unions, politics, education, and elsewhere apparently assume that he is basically bad and therefore must be controlled and directed through coercive systems.

Perhaps the most depressing aspect is that we still do not seem to have learned our lesson. Many still concentrate on the short run and search or hope for quick fixes. Although we all wish for improvement, such quick-fix considerations don't touch on the essential question: has a firm foundation been established, or is it being established, for sustained, long-range growth over the next 20 to 50 years? What happens during 1984 is relatively insignificant from that perspective. If we suddenly shot up to near 100% capacity utilization and full employment, however defined, given that the basic causes of disequilibrium have not been removed, we would see a return to inflation and interest rates as high as we had before, perhaps even higher.

We also fear that the public will not be patient long enough, even if some of our recommendations are followed, to give them time to work in the fundamental ways we feel are necessary to long-run, sustained economic growth. Unless unemployment and interest rates are reduced rapidly, pressure will build to loosen the money supply and increase government expenditures further. High inflation would be substituted for high interest rates and take us back in the direction from which we came. For the same reasons, we can visualize greater efforts to restrict free trade and bail out business losers. As stated, we also do not see any substantial efforts at reducing the deficit. Nor do we see management holding the line on wage increases. Concerns over elections predominate over concerns for long-term structural changes in the economy. We don't see big enough reductions in government regulations to place us anywhere near the ideal state.

Perhaps basic to all the necessary changes is the need for a fundamental change in public opinion (attitude) and a citizenry aroused enough to force the leaders in business, government, unions, and other special-interest groups, among others, to take the steps that will promote and strengthen the free market economy. We cannot visualize that fundamental change taking place soon enough to keep us from going backward to a situation that may be even worse than before, perhaps within the intermediate run of five to 15 years. Should that happen, we can see social upheavals that might seriously affect, perhaps destroy, our democratic form of government. Before you write off the suggestion for such a possibility as alarmist, we ask only that you consider it, along with all its ramifications, carefully.

Notes

[1]Deloitte Haskins & Sells, *The Week in Review*, July 1, 1983, p. 4.
[2]Coopers & Lybrand, "Social Security: An Analysis of the Commission's Recommendations," *Executive Alert Newsletter* (March 1983), p. 2.
[3]Russell Palmer, interview with Robert Beck, "How Social Security Can Survive," *Tempo*, Vol. 28, No. 1 (1983), p. 19.

[4]Peter G. Peterson, "Can Social Security Be Saved?" *Reader's Digest*, March 1983, p. 51.

[5]Otis Pike, "Change Proposed for Medicare System," *The Ann Arbor News*, September 6, 1983, p. A11.

[6]D'vera Cohn, "Medicare—The Nation's Second Largest Social Program Is Going Broke," *The Ann Arbor News*, September 13, 1983, p. C1.

[7]"Benefit Cuts Weighed by Some Lawmakers," *The Ann Arbor News*, August 8, 1983, p. C1.

[8]Philip Longman, "Squaring Off on Social Security—Unfair to Young Taxpayers," *Reader's Digest*, Vol. 122, No. 734 (June 1983), pp. 119–120.

[9]Lynn Adkins, "Detroit Gets Lean and Mean," *Dun's Business Month* (January 1983), p. 56.

[10]*Ibid.*, pp. 56–58.

[11]"Fear of Joblessness Counters Lower Interest Rates, Study Says," *The Ann Arbor News*, November 18, 1982, p. 38 (quoting Richard T. Curtin at the 30th Annual Conference on the Economic Outlook).

[12]Marilyn Wilson, "Will Consumers Come Through?" *Dun's Business Month* (April 1982), p. 57.

[13]"Economists Warn of New Inflation," *The Ann Arbor News*, March 7, 1983, p. C1.

[14]"Federal Spending Freeze Won't Take Much of a Bite Out of $200 Billion Deficit," *The Ann Arbor News*, January 12, 1983, p. F1.

[15]"Fear of Joblessness Counters Lower Interest Rates, Study Says," p. 38.

National Association of Accountants
Committee on Research
1983–1984

Donald W. Baker
Chairman
Southwire Company
Carrollton, Georgia

George Bannon
Moravian College
Bethlehem, Pennsylvania

Robert U. Boehman
Jasper Rubber Products
Jasper, Indiana

James Colford
IBM Corporation
White Plains, New York

James L. Crandall
Chicago, Illinois

Willard Cox
Oil City Iron Works
Corsicana, Texas

Dennis C. Daly
University of Minnesota
Minneapolis, Minnesota

Patricia P. Douglas
University of Montana
Missoula, Montana

Margaret Duffy
Arthur Andersen & Co.
New York, New York

James Don Edwards
University of Georgia
Athens, Georgia

Charles L. Grant
Becton Dickinson
   Laboratory System
Parsippany, New Jersey

Wallis W. Grissett
Pensacola, Florida

Robert E. Hampel
Keller-Crescent Co.
Evansville, Indiana

Neil E. Holmes
The Marley Company
Mission, Kansas

John H. Holzapfel
Coopers & Lybrand
Pittsburgh, Pennsylvania

James O. Ingle
Ingle, White & Co.
Atlanta, Georgia

Charles D. Mecimore
University of North Carolina
Greensboro, North Carolina

Larry E. Newman
Ernst & Whinney
Birmingham, Alabama

John A. O'Connor
Fesco Plastics Corp.
Kankakee, Illinois

John B. Pollara
Zieman Manufacturing Co.
Whittier, California

Leroy H. Rogero, Jr.
Touche Ross & Co.
Dayton, Ohio

Mildred B. Stephens
Educational Testing Service
Princeton, New Jersey

Stanley P. Vroman
Prince Gardner
St. Louis, Missouri

Thomas H. Williams
University of Wisconsin
Madison, Wisconsin